AF255173

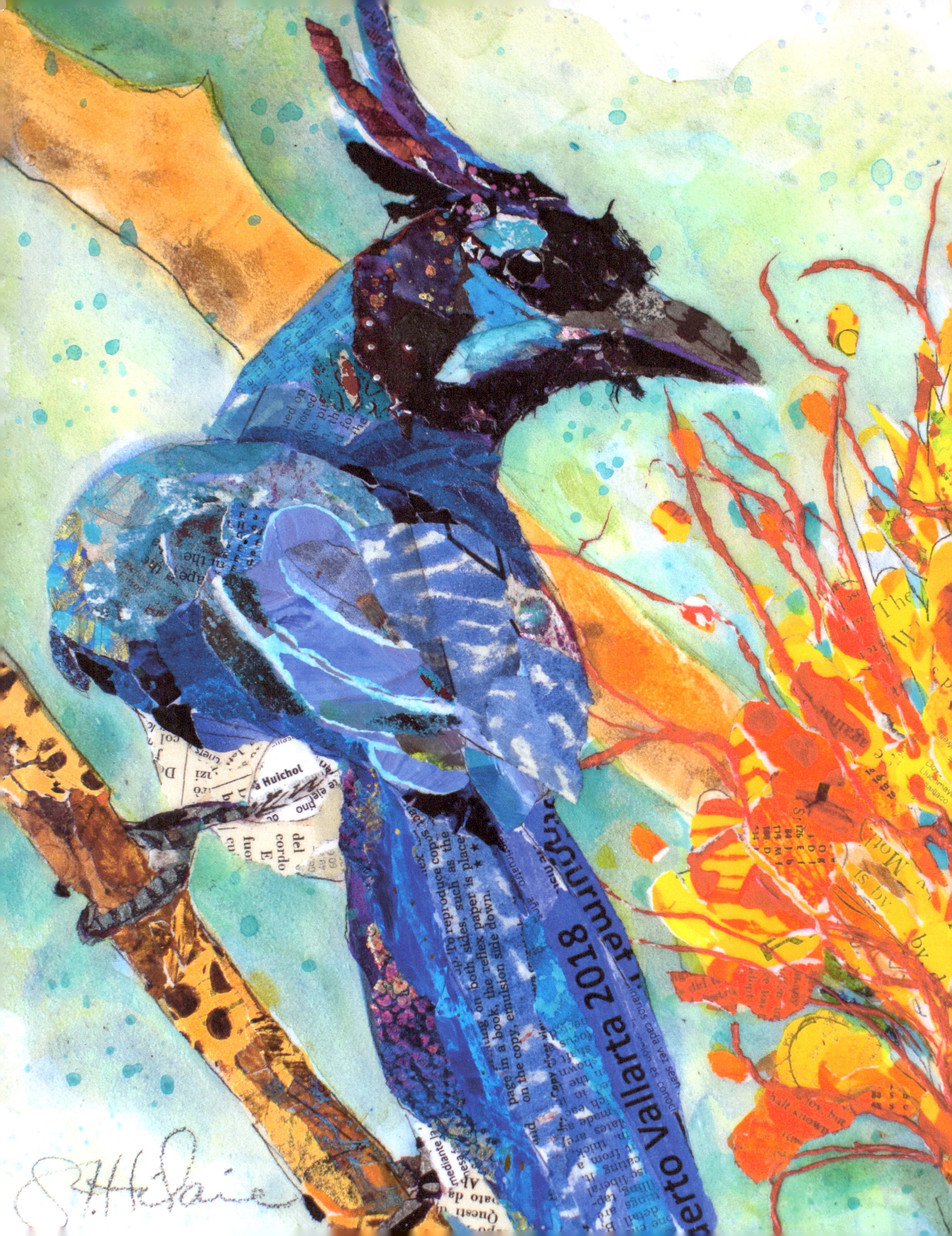

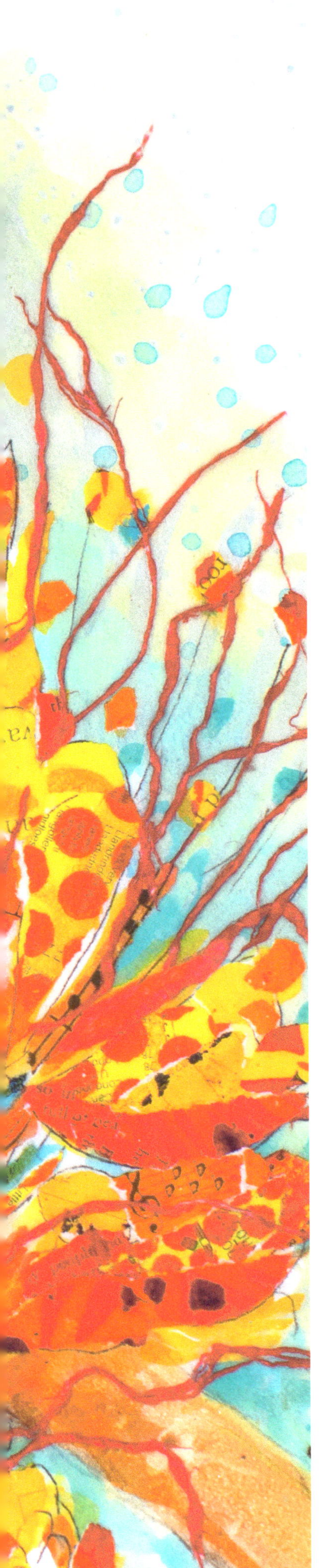

Collage
SONGBIRDS

ELIZABETH ST. HILAIRE

Impressionistic collage paintings, step-by-step

For Emilie and Connor

Thank you for loving me for who I am, for supporting me in what I do, and for understanding both.

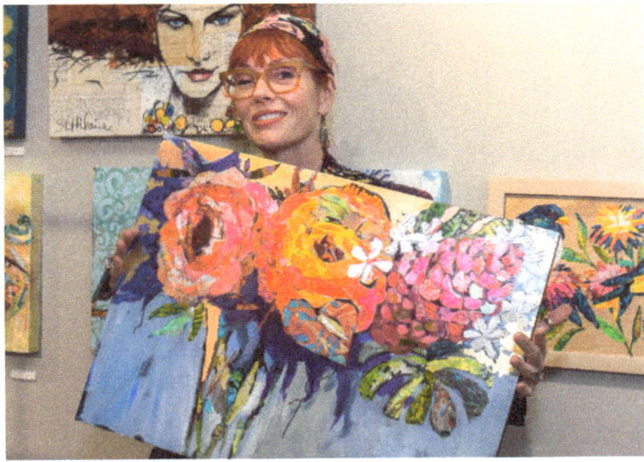

©Johnny White

All photography and artwork ©Elizabeth St. Hilaire unless otherwise noted

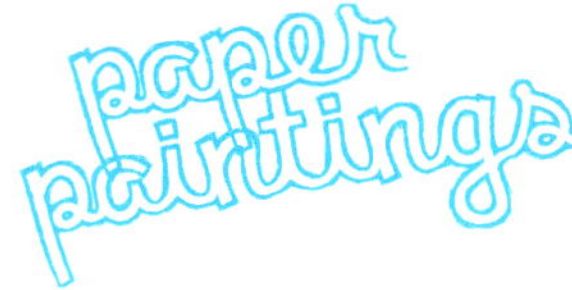

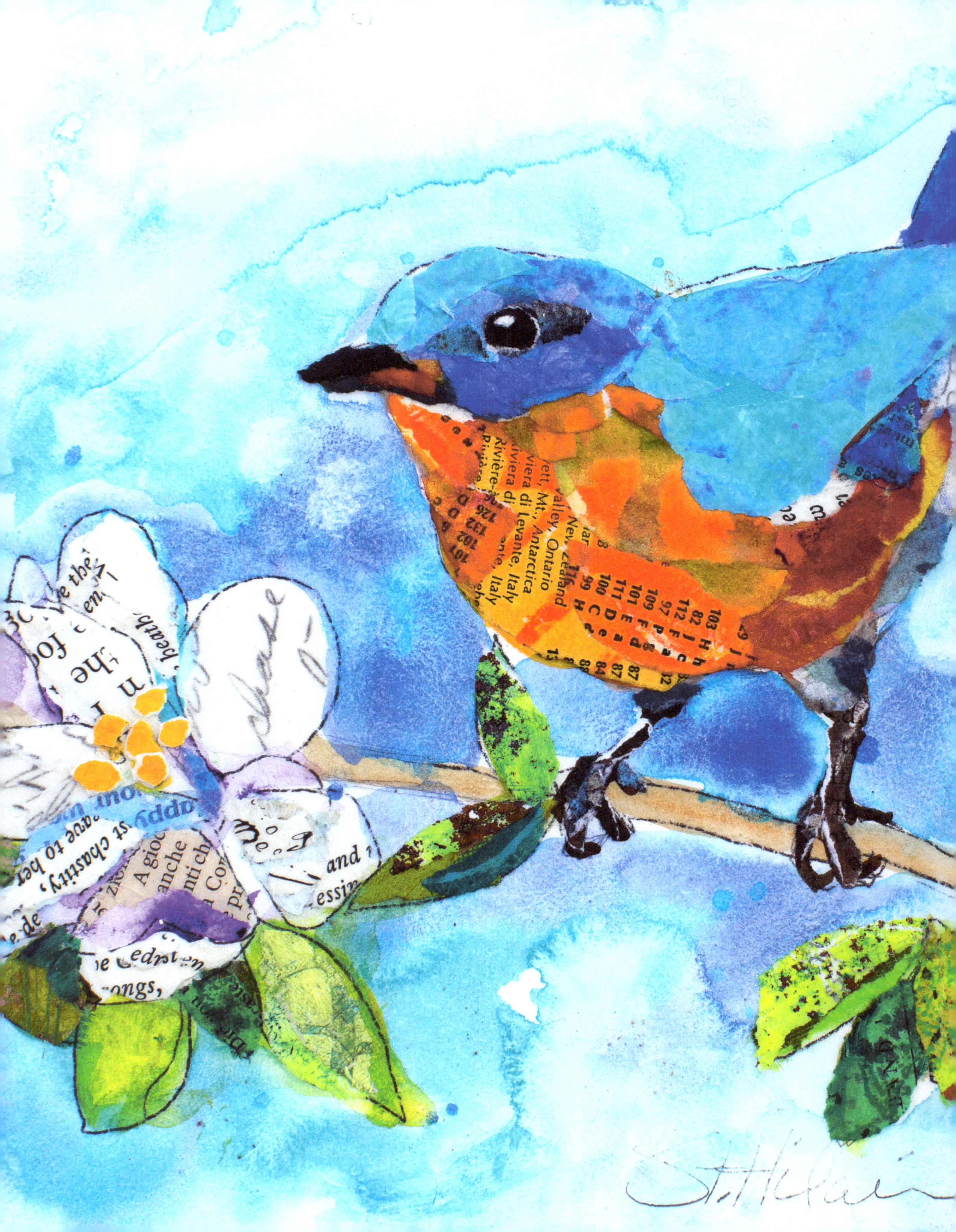

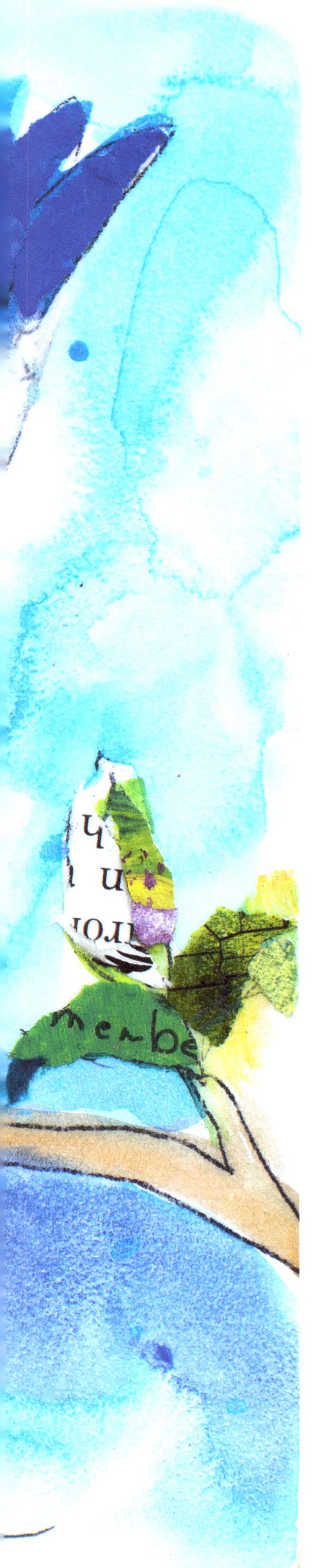

intro

My technique has evolved and changed as a result of experimentation with hand-painted, hand-made, and textured/patterned papers. Layering and weaving, pushing and pulling the colors, patterns, and values makes the collage process like a dance. Undulating, alternating, and overlapping, until the rhythm creates something I love.

In my work I highlight the extraordinary within the ordinary, focusing on intense and vibrant colors combined with a sensibility of design. My collages invite the viewer to look, and having looked, to linger.

what is a paper painting?

A figurative, painterly collage is created by adhering hand-painted, hand-made, and found papers over an acrylic under painting on wood panel.

The overall impressionistic feeling of the work is achieved by treating every bit of torn (not cut) paper like an brush stroke, keeping details loose, and using a variety of texture and shades of paper in every color field.

Creating your own papers for collage offers a custom paper palette with every shade of every color that appeals to you, offering variety and inspiration.

Utilizing the same techniques that apply to painting with acrylic or oil, the success of the work depends on a firm understanding of shading—light, dark, and medium values coupled with "brush marks" that follow the form.

Often times, the viewer will be totally surprised that this artwork is not a painting, but rather a mixed media collage. Even up close, people will still ask, *"You mean it's not a painting?"* This is the a-ha moment that I love.

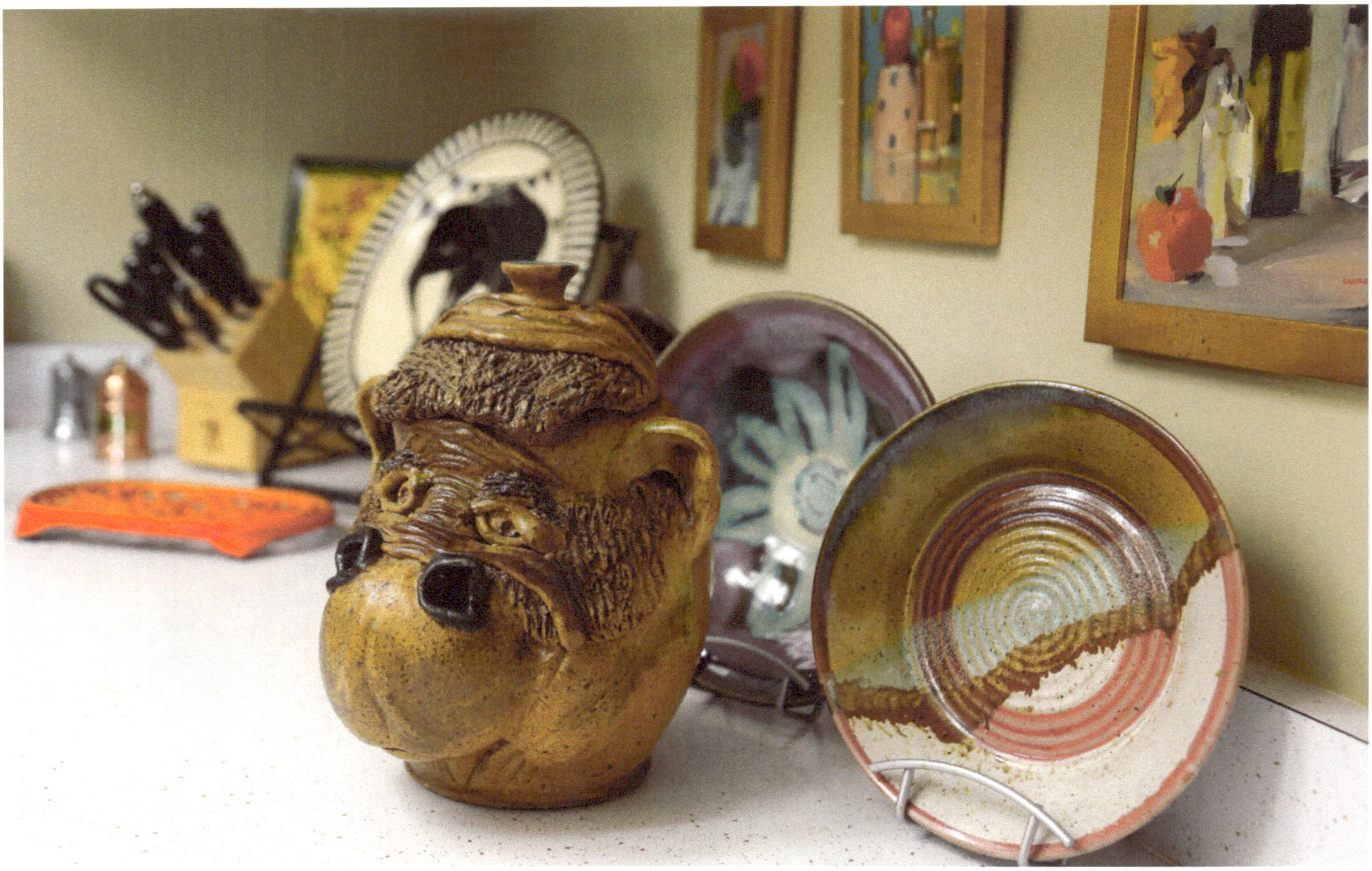

My kitchen is filled with paintings and pottery, I love collecting hand-made items and enveloping myself in color!

inspired living

SURROUND YOURSELF with things that stimulate your creativity and make you happy. As artists, we experience the world in more detail and vibrancy than others. A coffee break on a whimsically decorated patio space can inspire, as you savor the warmth from a hand-made pottery mug in your hands. Art in the kitchen helps to add color to the flavors that we soak up while cooking or baking—enveloping yourself in an artistic space helps spark creativity. We are constantly gathering experiences that influence our work; creating an artistic space filled with rich textures and bold color helps us to process and be inspired by those experiences. Take a moment every now and then to sit and reflect.

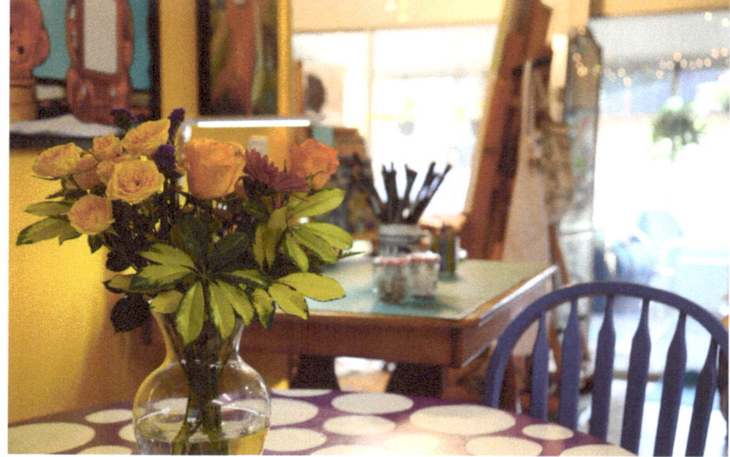

My kitchen is adjacent to my studio, which opens out to a little patio that is adorned with wind chimes, Christmas lights, party decorations, pompoms, retro metal chairs, an artist-made birdhouse, and hanging plants.

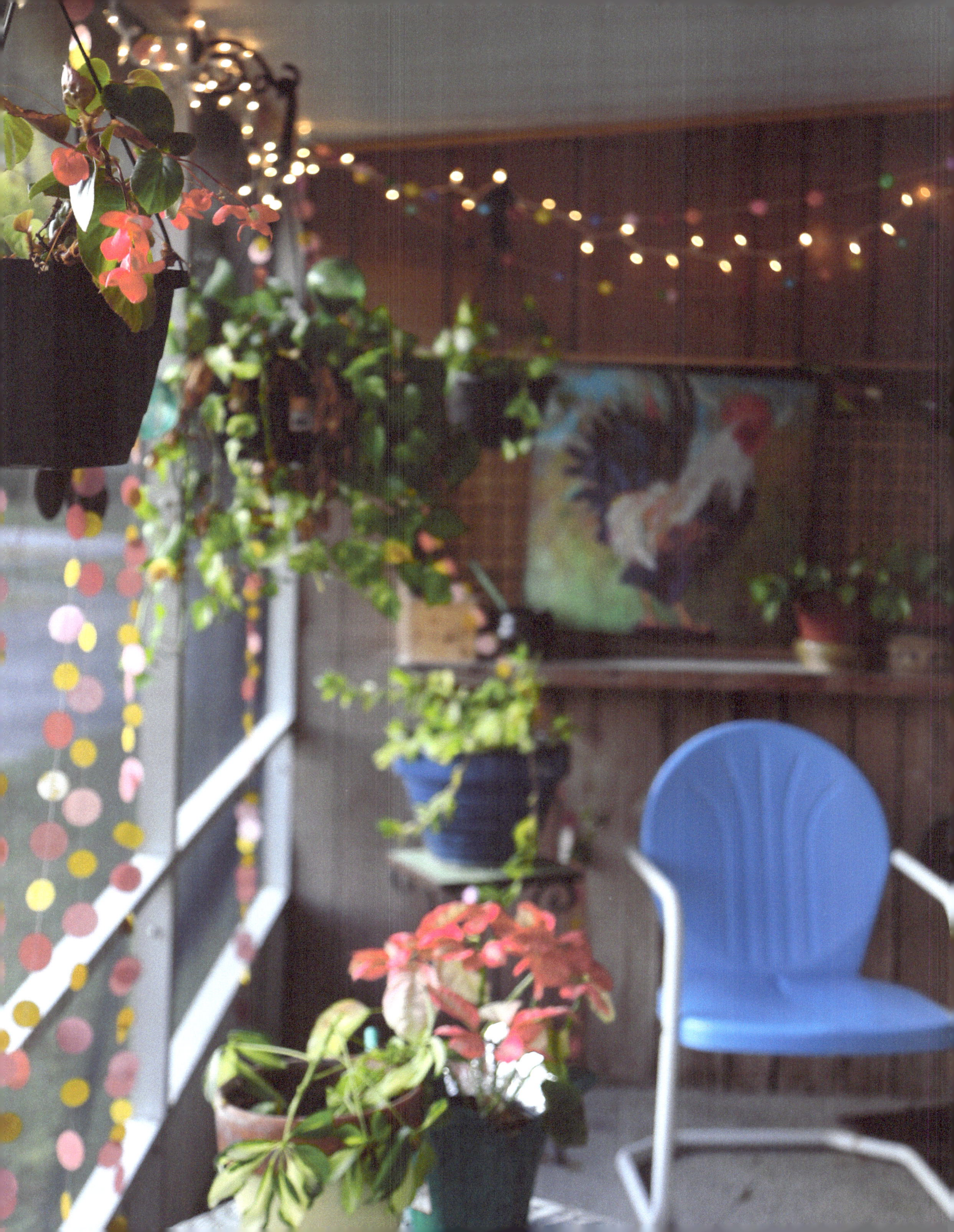

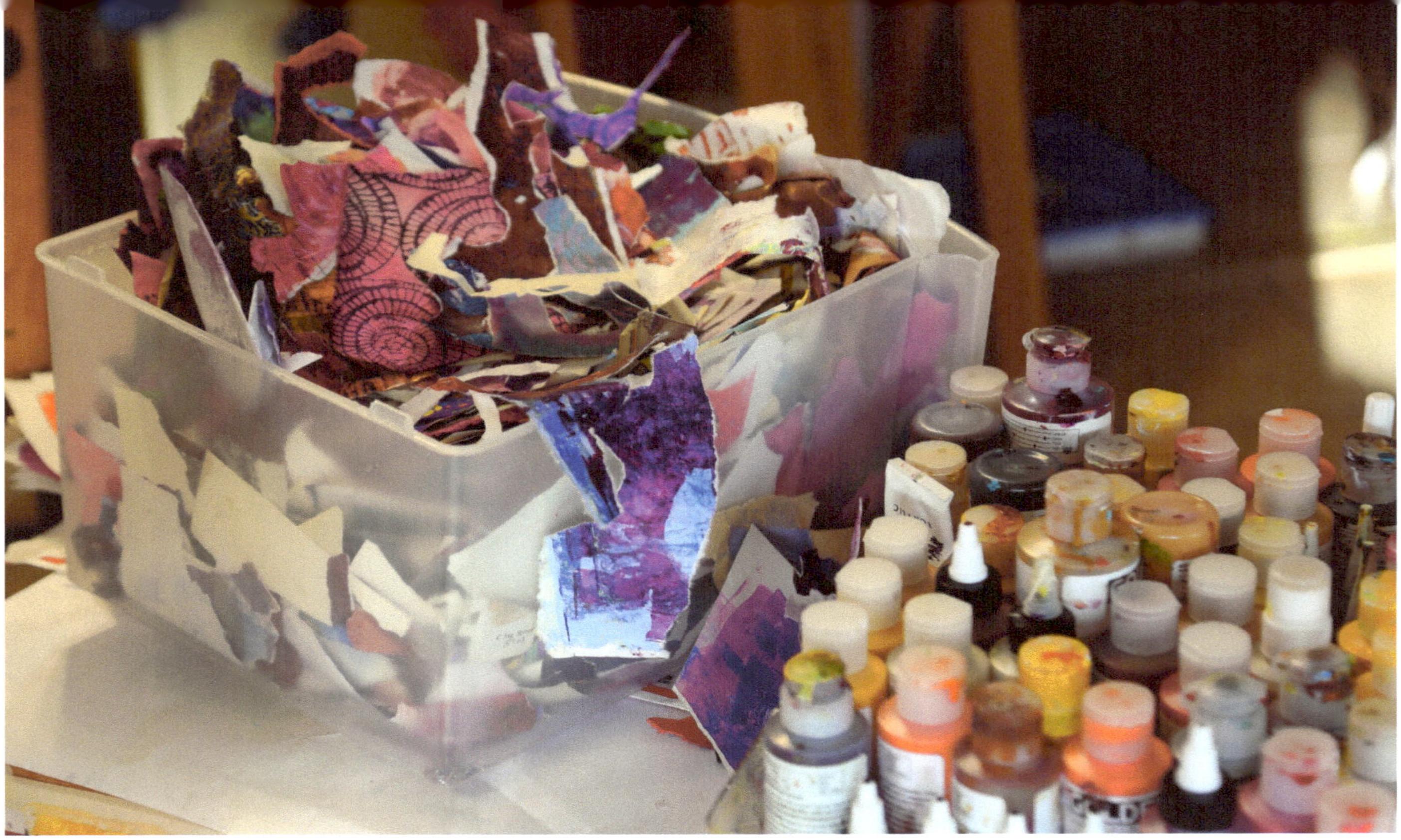

My collage papers and paints are separated by color

work space

PRODUCTIVITY IS KEY and your studio needs to be a dedicated space, if possible. It's very difficult to be productive if you have to clear art supplies off the kitchen table every evening in preparation for dinner.

I have had my studio in many different locations over the years including a separate out-building in the back yard, a commercial retail space, and in my home as it is currently. I find that working from home allows me to be the most productive—I can run a load of laundry, pop a banana bread in the oven, let the dogs out, and check my email all within a few steps. I'll be honest, my art materials and paintings have found their way into the living room and the kitchen, but my easel and main creative space is separate.

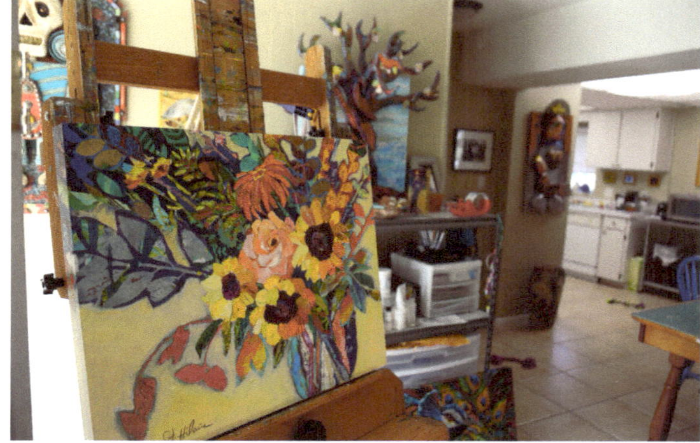

My home based studio space is adjacent to my kitchen

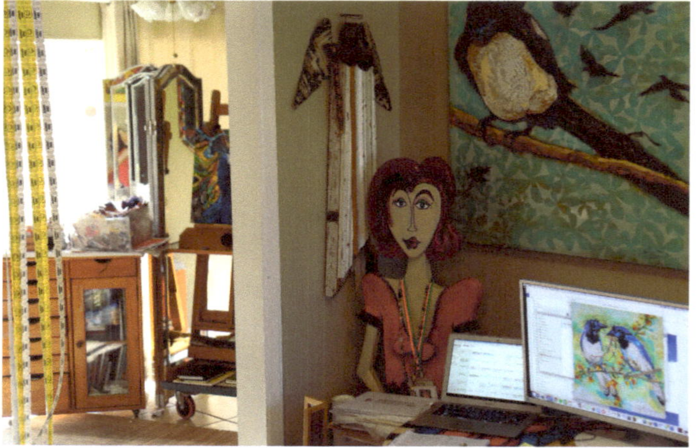

Multitasking, my computer work station is close-by

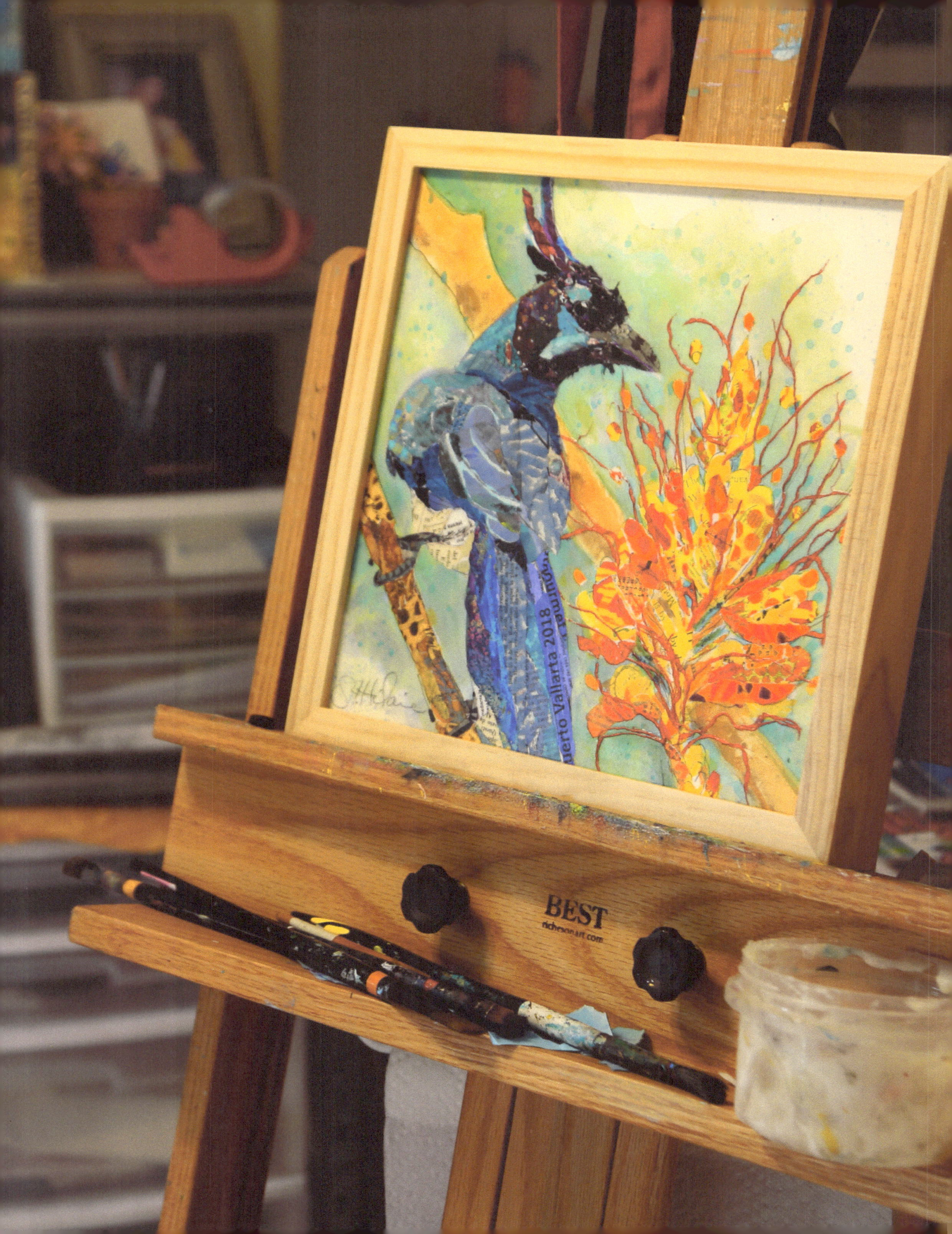
Puerto Vallarta 2018
BEST
richeson-art.com

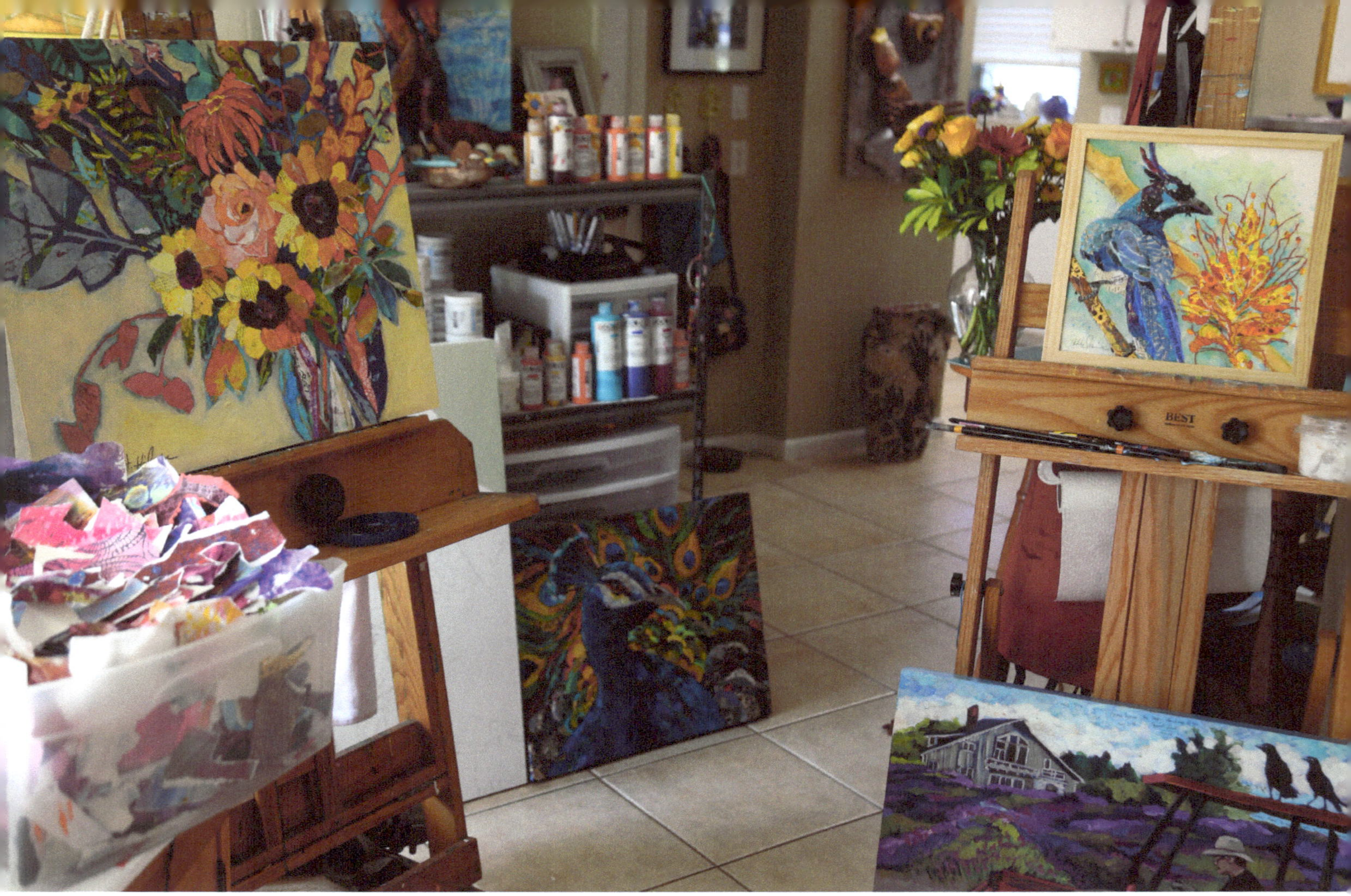

studio space solutions

YOUR PAINTING SPACE should nurture your creative spirit, it's the place where you do the thing you love most, so it should reflect your taste in colors, textures, and artwork.

Good lighting is imperative. Choose overhead or directional fixtures with daylight bulbs and arrange it so that you can see well without any cast shadows. If you can, choose a space with windows that offer natural light in addition to your fixtures, this is optimal.

Your setup should include an easel (or two) and a taboret (side table/cart) that is a good size and height for your paints, water container, collage papers, and glue pot.

Ventilation via an open window or door to the outside is helpful, especially when using some art supplies that might give off an odor or fumes, such as varnish.

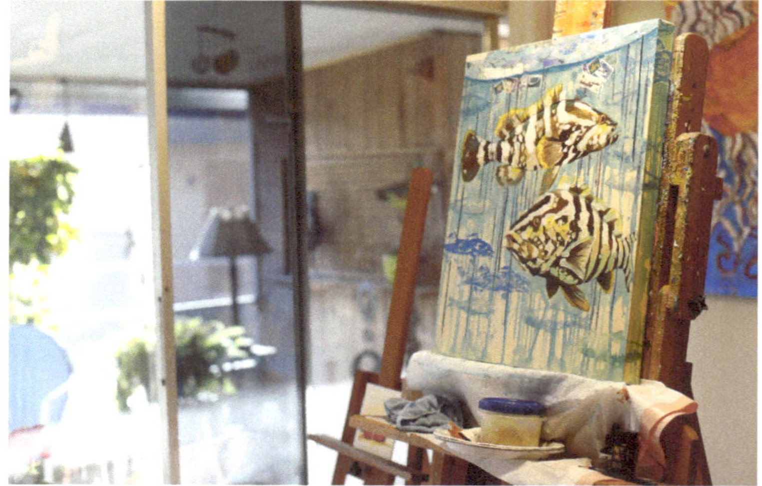

My studio opens to a small patio, this provides ventilation and natural light

Storage for supplies can be easily managed with shelving, bins, baskets, and drawers—I have a combo of all of these in my space—all of my supplies are in sight and within reach.

A worktable is a great place for sketching, painting, priming wood panels, adding hanging wires, and packing up sold artwork.

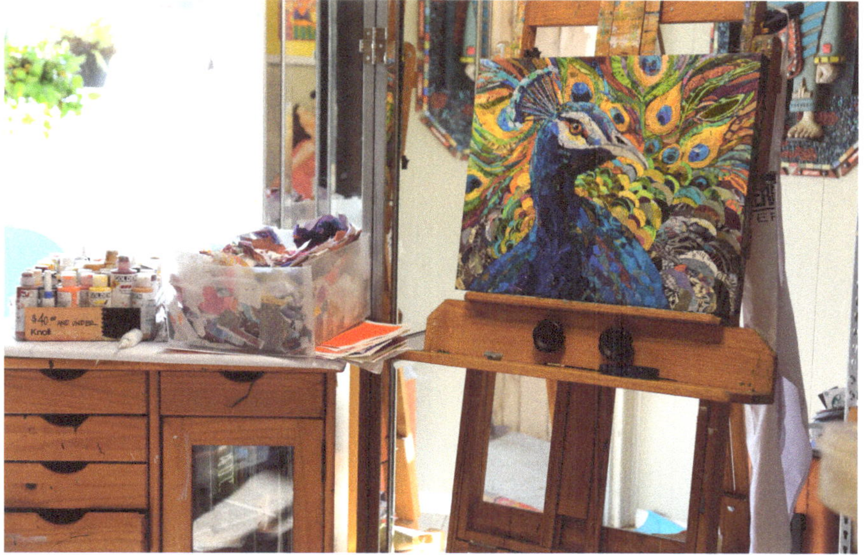

get it together

ORGANIZATION IS KEY for mixed media, if you can't find it you can't use it. My taboret has several shallow drawers where I store the things I use the most. Behind my easel I have an old set of oak card catalog drawers that I scored from an antique store. All of the drawers are labeled as to what is in each one of them, eliminating guess work when I'm looking for vine charcoal, pencils, fine point markers, game tiles, or wooden thread spools.

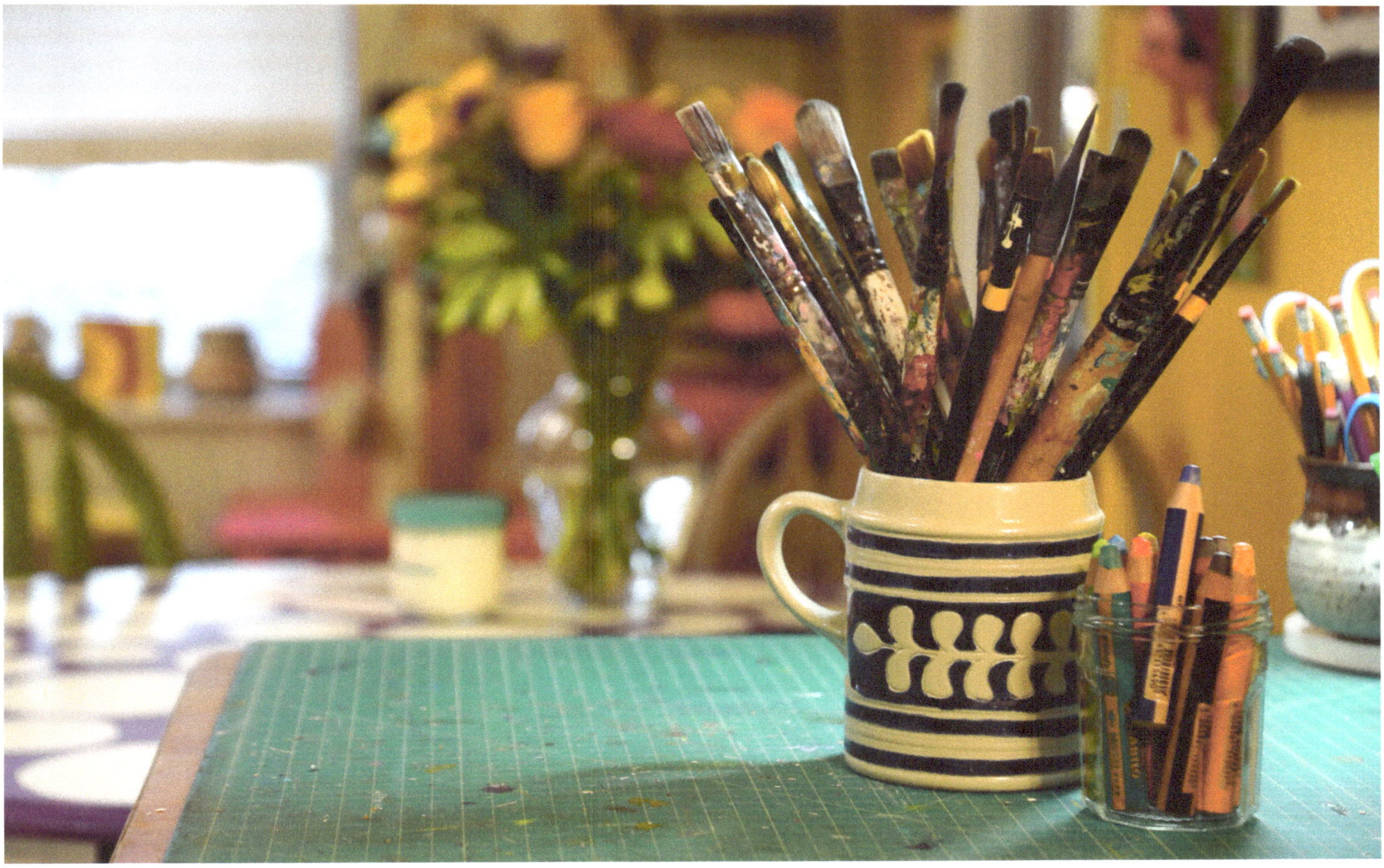

My taboret is the perfect height for standing at the easel

A dedicated worktable covered with a cutting mat helps keep my kitchen table available for dinner!

in motion

Recently I purchased a second easel, so that I could work on more than one project at a time. Both easels and my taboret are on wheels, allowing me to roll them around for the best light, and for cleaning the floor beneath them. I replaced the stock plastic wheels with good quality, swivel locking wheels purchased at the Home Depot on both easels and added them to the bottom of the taboret cart where there were none, what a difference this makes!

art supplies

GATHERING AND COLLECTING art supplies is a source of great joy for every artist. Mixed media collage offers endless possibilities for combinations of supplies. I encourage you to experiment with what you have on hand in addition to what I list below, as you may have already gathered lots of wonderful art tools and goodies that appeal to your personal sense of adventure.

preferred suppplies

- **PENCIL AND ERASER** for sketching your image

- **REFERENCE IMAGE** sized to fit your canvas panel, printed out on basic copy paper, non photo paper

- **GRAPHITE TRANSFER PAPER** to transfer your reference image to the substrate if you struggle with drawing.

- **VARIETY OF FOUND PAPERS**, sheet music, maps, wallpaper, hand written notes, old book pages, hand made papers, deli paper, white tissue – variety of thickness and textures. You can do this totally with found papers.

- **DECORATIVE PAPERS**, papers you purchase at your local art supply store with fiber, embossing, metallic patterning, iridescent patterning. Please purchase in white or natural if possible, this allows for the most color options.

- **NO MAGAZINES** no shiny coated printed papers, no scrapbook papers

- **GEL PRESS MONOPRINTING PLATE AND BRAYER** Gel printing plate and hard rubber brayer

- **GOLDEN FLUID ACRYLIC PAINTS & WHITE GESSO** for under-painting on panel AND hand-painting papers --colors of your choice, keeping in mind the subject matter and your ability to mix color. Small container of gesso for adding white to certain paint colors.

- **CANVAS PANELS** economy surface for support. This is mat board covered with pre-primed canvas, NOT stretched canvas. 12x14 -OR- several 8x8's - your choice on size.

- **PAINT BRUSHES** (various sizes and shapes) for painting your bird image and applying glue. Use what you have on hand. I like Princeton Catalyst short handle #8 filbert specifically for glue application.

- **LIQUITEX GLOSS GEL MEDIUM**, this is the collage glue. Please purchase Liquitex brand in GLOSS

- **WATER CONTAINER & DOLLAR STORE VINYL TABLE CLOTH/SHOWER CURTAIN** for table cover and/or to dry papers on

- **PAPER TOWELS** for cleanup

- **PAPER PLATES** for paint mixing palette

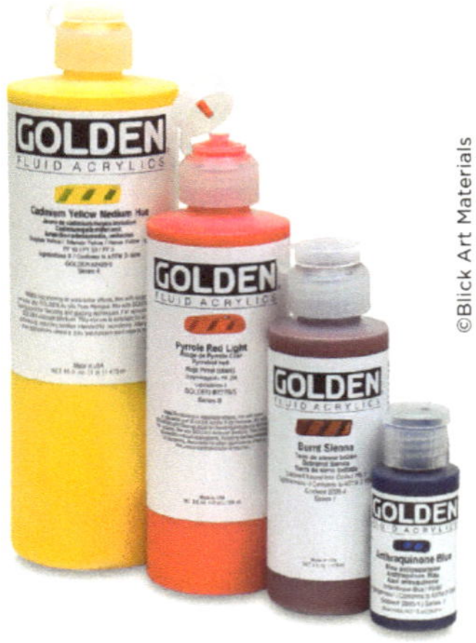

I have been trained by Golden Paints in the use and application of all their products.

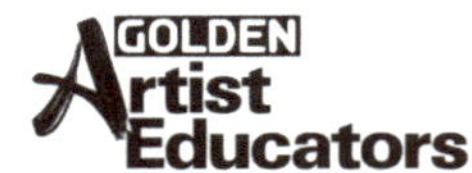

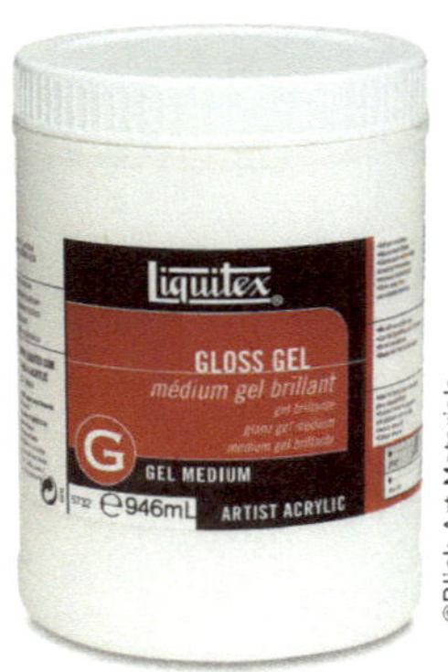

I use Liquitex Gloss Gel Medium as my collage glue, it's thick and stays in place while I work upright at the easel.

Canvas panels are pre-primed and are an economical surface for beginners.

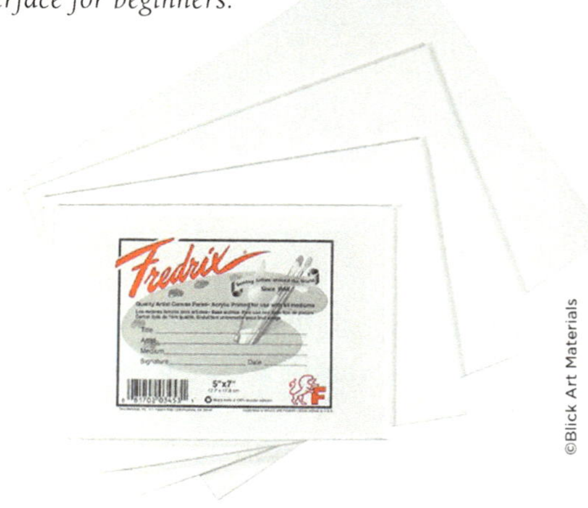

I'm wild about painting rice paper

These acid-free papers are strong and highly absorbent. They are made in the centuries-old Japanese tradition. They are white and natural tones which make an excellent base for creating your own brilliantly colored collage papers. All are available online and most can be found at your local art supply store in the Chinese brush painting section.

Rice paper takes the color all the way through and lays flat when glued because of its' absorbent properties. I purchase rice papers on a roll versus in a pad, this way I can determine how large of a sheet I want to use. Rice paper comes with and without fibers, both have different applications in collage.

Hosho — Hosho is a traditional kozo (mulberry fiber) paper that doesn't shrink or tear easily, making it ideal for woodblock or line printing. Hosho paper is sized.

Kozo — Kozo rice paper is highly absorbent, making it ideal for calligraphy and watercolor painting. Kozo paper is not sized.

Unryu — Unryu rice paper has been used for centuries in Japan for creating Shoji screens and is extremely strong, thanks to molded-in fibers. It's excellent for calligraphy, sumi-e, watercolors. Unryu paper is not sized.

Ricer Paper Sheets — Hanshi Japanese rice paper for brush writing or calligraphy is mouldmade in the centuries-old Japanese tradition makes excellent base for fluid acrylics, available in sheets if you prefer, versus a roll.

Assorted Japanese Sheets — You may purchase a 10-sheet assortment of fine Japanese papers from DickBlick.com. This assortment includes two full sheets of Chiri (sized), Okawara (sized), Unryu (not sized), Kitakata (sized), and Mulberry (not sized). A nice way to experiment and find which papers work best for you.

Thai Unryu — Long, swirling strands of kozo provide contrast and texture in these traditional style unryu papers. Lightweight and translucent, choose from a range of natural tones, perfect for painting your own colors, textures, and patterns.

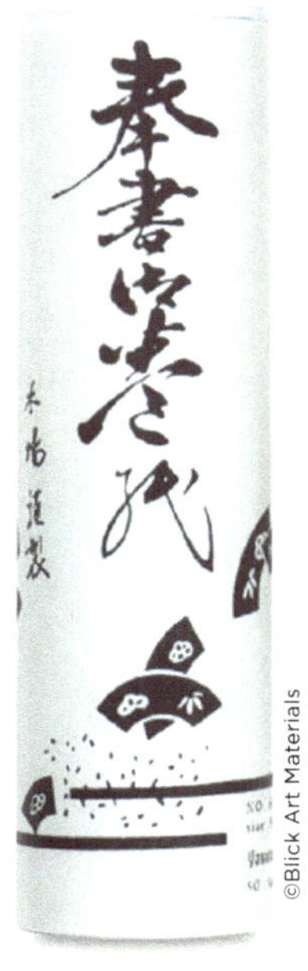

Rice paper comes on a roll in Hosho, Kozo and Unryu

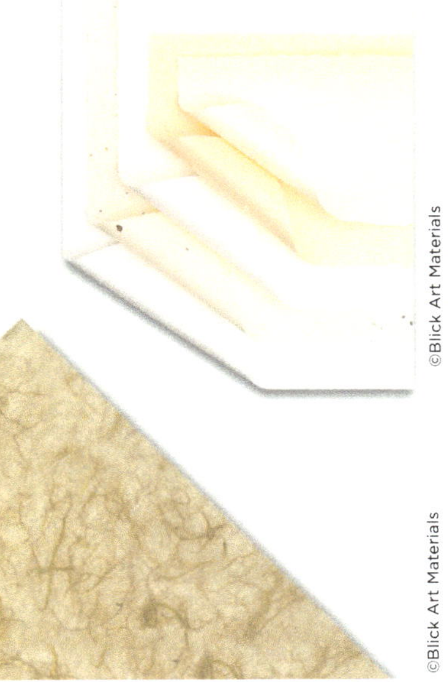

10-sheet assortment of fine Japanese papers

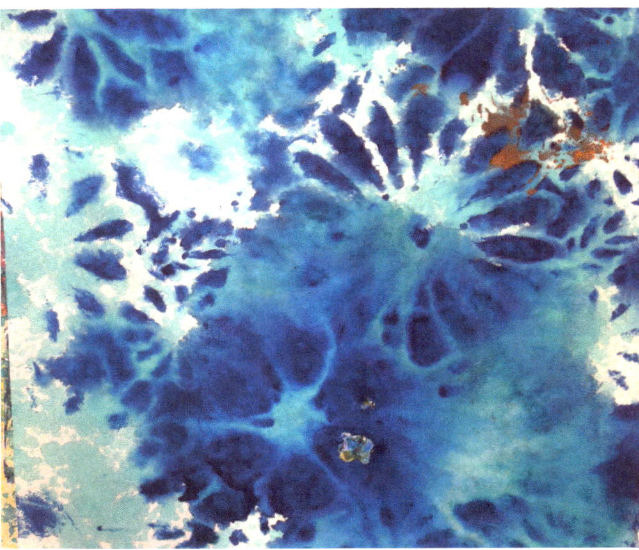

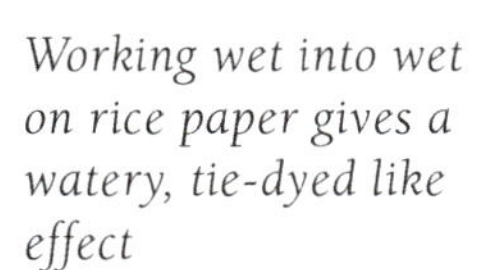

Working wet into wet on rice paper gives a watery, tie-dyed like effect

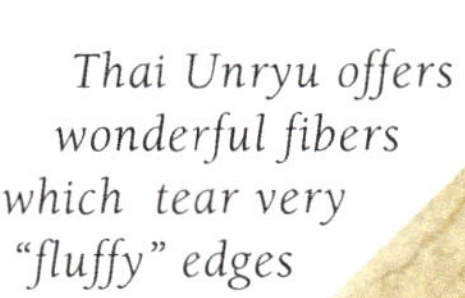

Thai Unryu offers wonderful fibers which tear very "fluffy" edges

painting paper

THERE ARE SO MANY PAPERS THAT ARE GREAT FOR COLLAGE. I paint anything from old maps to printmaking paper to rice paper to my kids homework.

I am also a fan of found papers, so check out your local used book store or library for some old books that you can take the pages out of. This paper is often great quality, the text adds another layer of creativity in the hand painted paper process, and the books are typically inexpensive.

I have learned through experimentation that glossy coated paper stock is not good for collage. This type of paper tends to cockle and that means the viewer's eye knows it's paper, even from afar. Since I want my artwork to appear as a painting, all papers must lay completely flat.

I also enjoy purchasing decorative papers from my local art supply store with fibers, metallic patterning, and textures. I grab these papers in white or natural tones so that I can paint them any color from yellow to black. In painting paper, experimentation is key, and practice makes perfect.

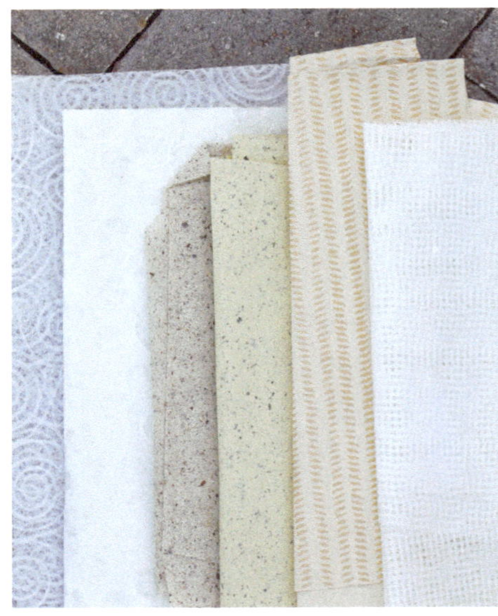

Some samples of my natural toned art store purchased decorative papers. I like the fibers, textures, inclusions, and lace cut patterns.

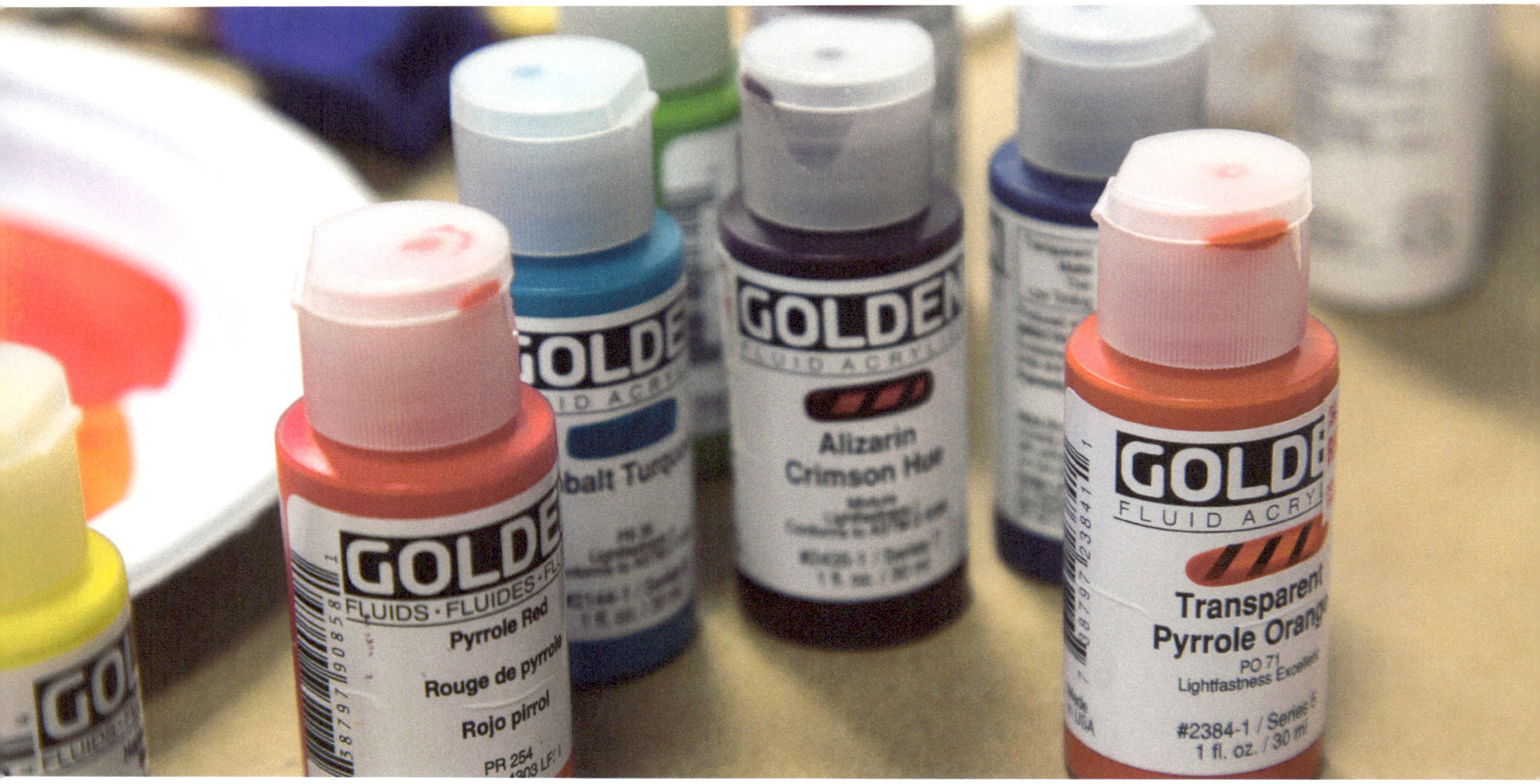

I prefer Golden Fluid Acrylic colors for painting my collage papers and my underpainting. These paints are light-fast, durable, and flexible. They are wonderfully versatile, professional quality acrylic colors with the consistency of heavy cream. Visit them on-line and request a color swatch chart for accurate color representation at *GoldenPaints.com*

Fluid Acrylics are highly pigmented and translucent, this is important. Every layer of paint allows the previous layer to shine through. This is the effect of translucent paints, they multiply and blend as you lay one technique of painting paper over another.

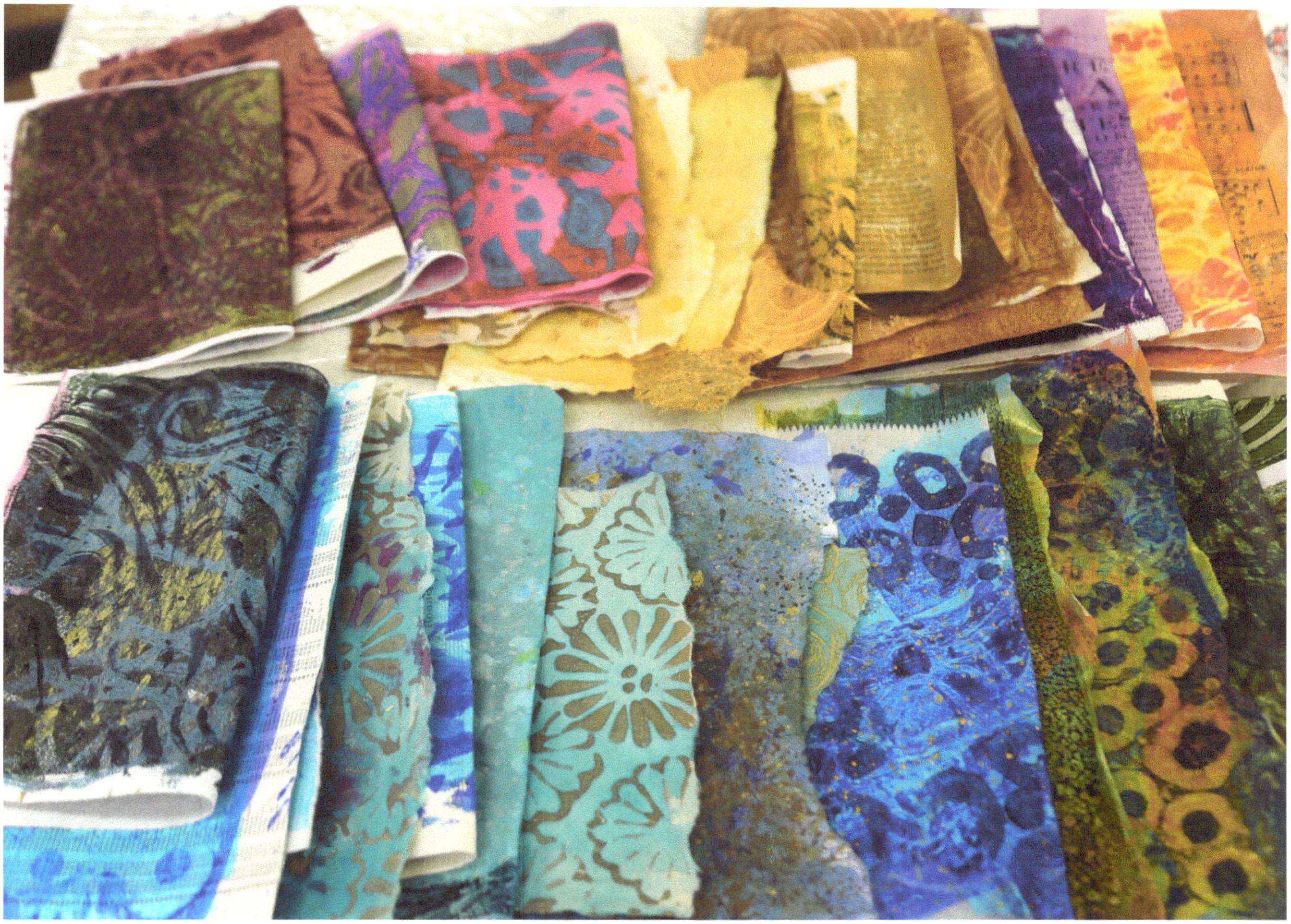

why paint your own paper?

In the beginning, I used pre-colored papers in my collage work. I found the most richly colored, textured, patterned papers in the art store and I collected and coveted them on every trip I took. On a trip to New York City I must have spent over $100 on sheets of luxuriously colored papers at the store Kate's Paper.

What happened next was sad, but true. Most pre-colored papers fade! These papers are possibly colored with dye and not pure pigment (the color that is the base of all fine art paints and pastels). Dye fades over time, depending on its exposure to sunlight. It will break your heart to see a collage fading right in front of you, little by little, as the years go by. At first you might not even notice it, until you look at a photo of the artwork on your computer, and all of a sudden you realize that your original just does not look as vibrant as it used to.

To combat this dilemma, I started painting my own collage papers. I use Golden Artist Colors Fluid Acrylic paints, these are professional grade paints. Painting my own papers offered me a whole new world of possibilities of color, texture, pattern, shading...A perfect *paper palette!*

Fluid Acrylic paints are an excellent choice for painting your own collage papers. You can water them down extensively and they keep the same level of vibrancy, making them excellent for dripping and splattering.

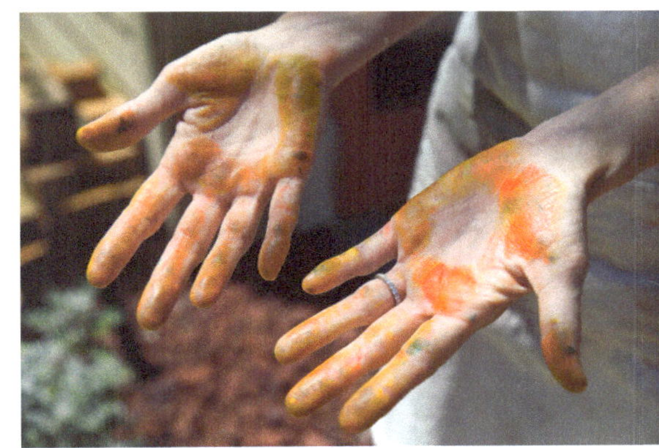

painting with paper

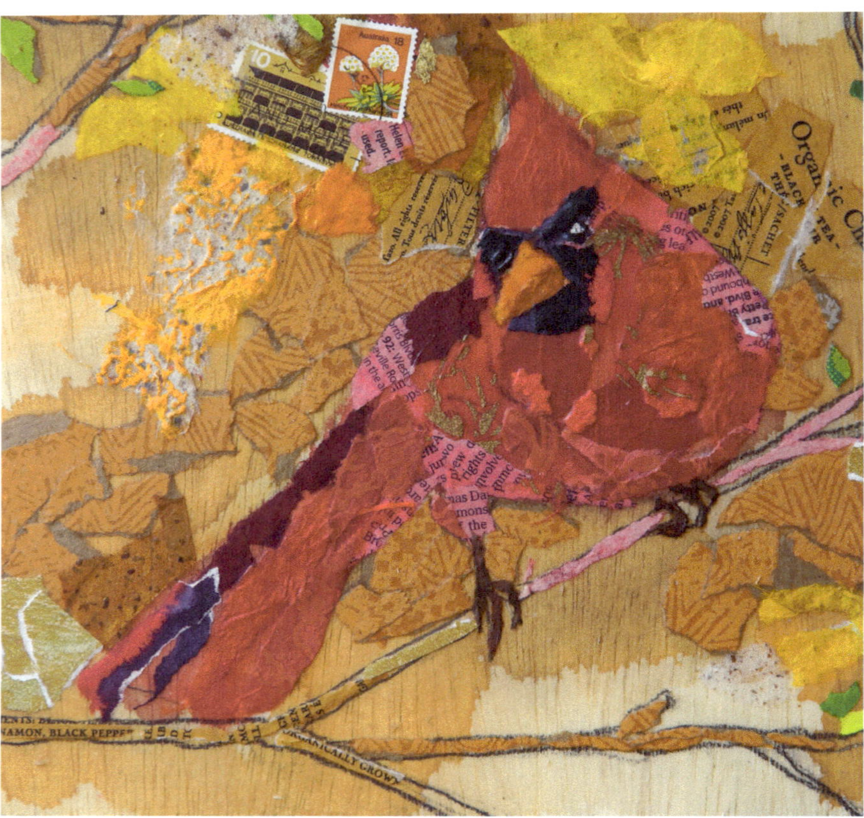

Shades of red are imperative for "Preparing for Flight" 12x12

variety is key

Keep in mind that you'll be painting papers in a full range of values, from the deepest darkest shadow color to the very lightest highlight color and *every* color in between. The cardinal above makes use of the range of red papers to the right, every one of those swatchesv employs a different pattern and layering of techniques.

You can never have enough paper, because each paper brush mark must be different from the one that is glued down next to it. Why is this so? Because if you glue the same paper next to itself, visually the two pieces become one. In order to create a collage that looks like a painting, we must maintain individual paper brush marks–this means within every value of every color there must be many *different* papers.

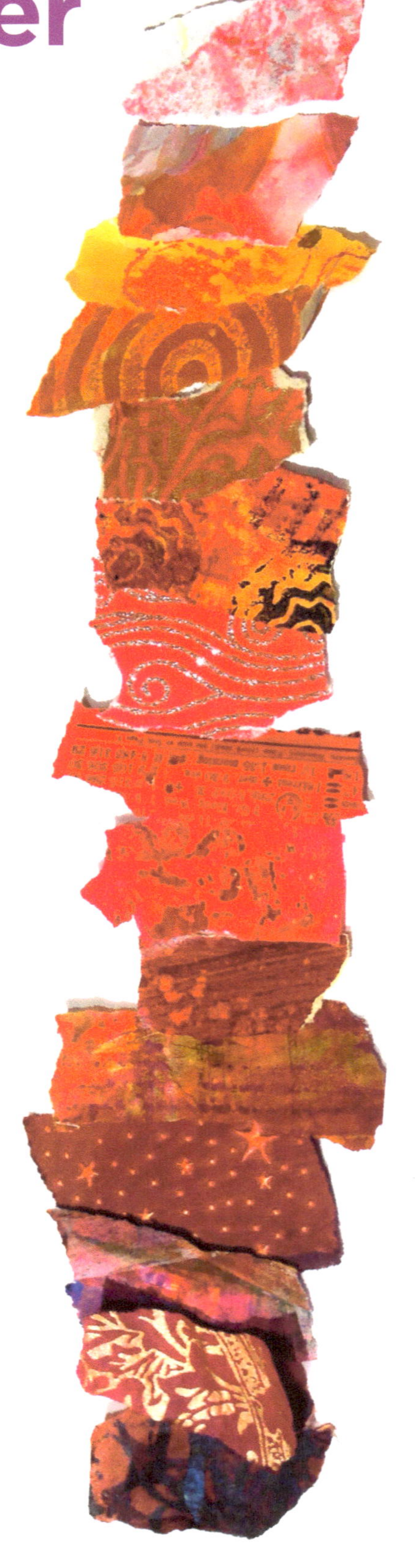

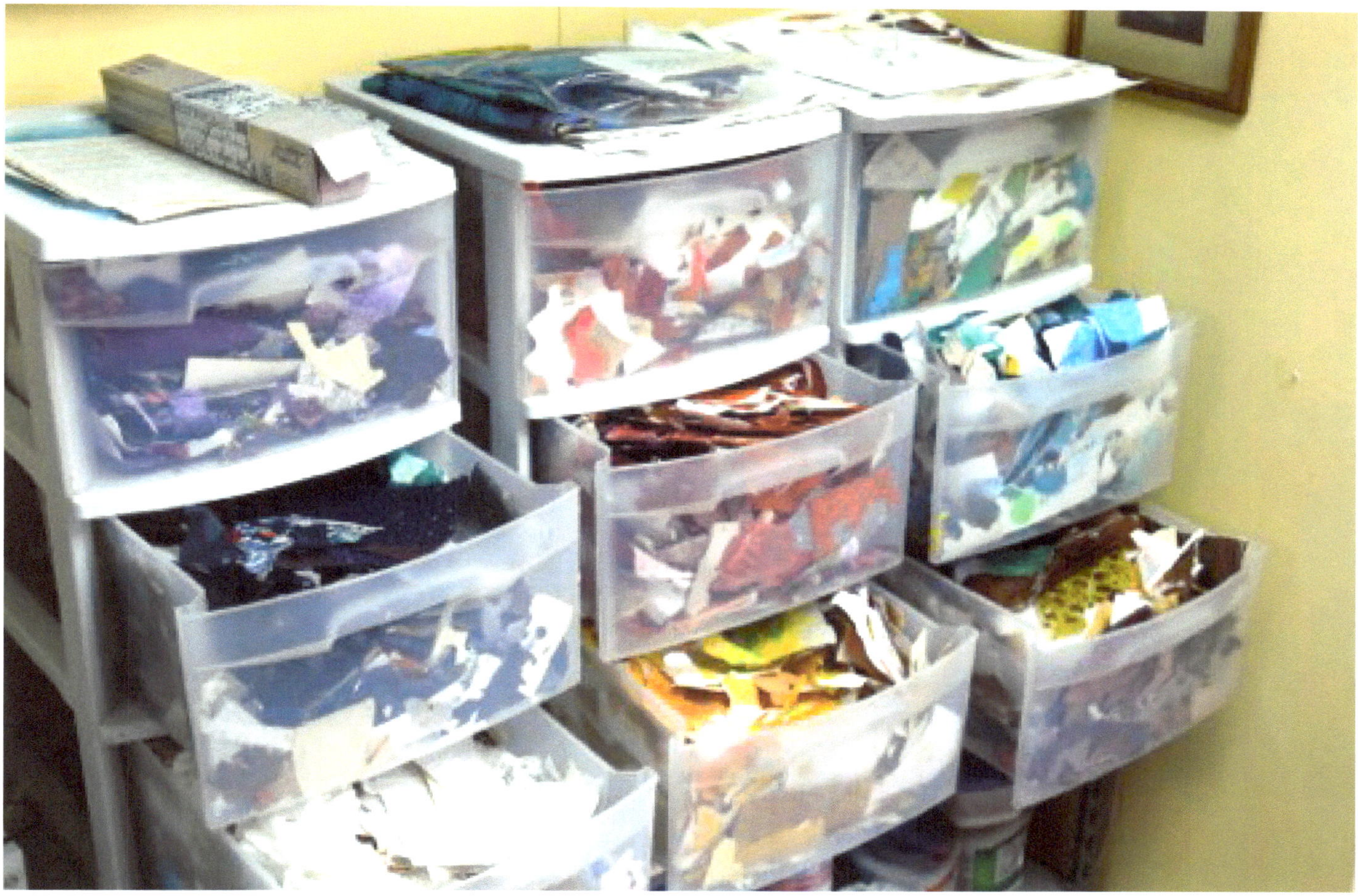

color coordinating

In my studio I divide my papers into nine drawers of color. If a paper includes two different colors, I tear it in half and put it in both drawers.

When you are ready to collage, it's much easier to find the perfect value of green when you have organized your colors so that all of your green is in one place. I use these clear drawers that pull out of the framework easily so that I can set them on my taboret and easily dig through the color I am looking for.

Storage solutions are personal. Although nine drawers work for me, you may need more or less depending on your own organizational process.

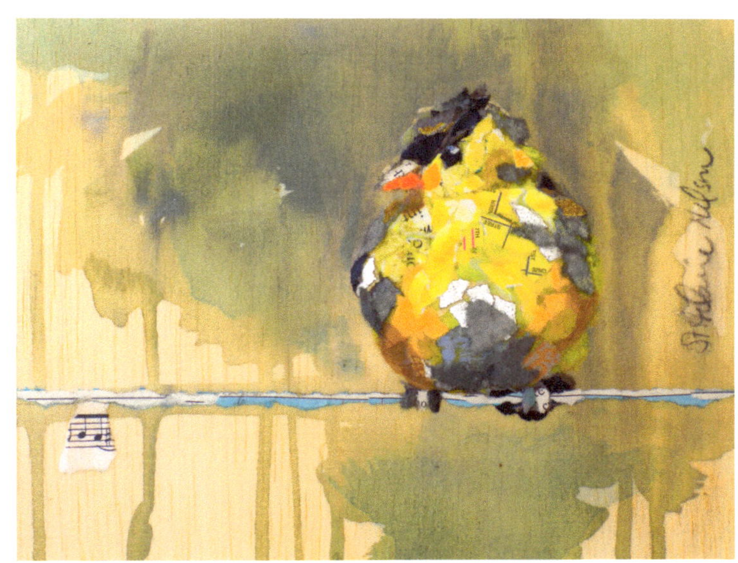

Shades of yellow are imperative for "Small Packages" 10x8

Top: White paper with silver swirls included in it serves as a great base for creating custom colored versions.

Hint: Take your oversized art store sheet and divide it into 4, or even 8 pieces, paint each one a different color. Collage utilizes a variety of bits and pieces of paper, one sheet goes a long way.

Below: Art store decorative papers come with some wonderful printed patterns that you can take advantage of by painting over with diluted fluid acrylics which will allow the patterning to show through. Be sure to paint dark colors over dark papers.

Every couple of months I pull out the paints, the tools, the Gel Plate, the brayer, the brushes, and I make myself a batch of custom colored collage papers.

Beyond just tinting papers with fluid acrylics, I have developed some interesting techniques over the years. To achieve texture and variety of colors, I layer these techniques over and under one another until I achieve highly textured, rich, colorful collage papers in a variety of colors and a full range of values within those colors.

making the most of decorative papers

I gave up using pre-colored decorative papers from the art supply store due to *light-fast* or fading issues. Now I only buy white or natural papers and paint them with Golden Fluid Arylics.

I do like to utilize the printed patterns of decoraitve papers. The papers shown with gold printing below were purchased on a trip to Binder's Art Supply in Atlanta. What's fun about painting these types of papers is that the metallic pattern resists the Fluid Acrylic paint, leaving it to show through multiple layers of techniques.

The paper (below) started out brown. I painted some of the oversized sheet dark brown, some red, some blue and some purple. I stayed with dark colors because the translucensy of the paint does not allow for lightening the base value. Decorative paper that is white or natural the most succesful starting point for any color I want—from the lightest yellow all the way down to deepest black and any color in between.

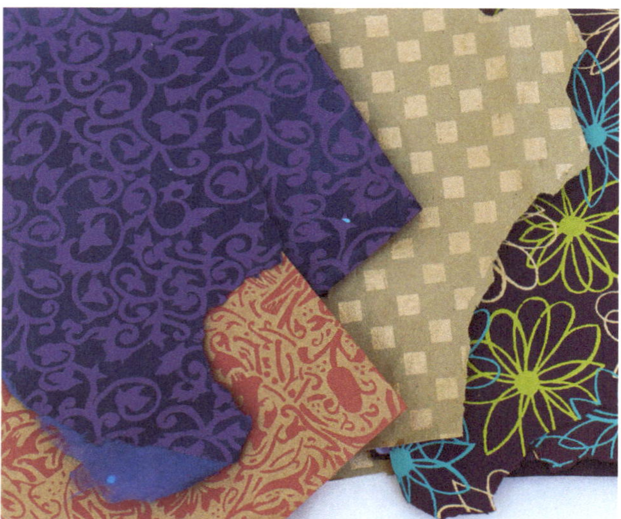

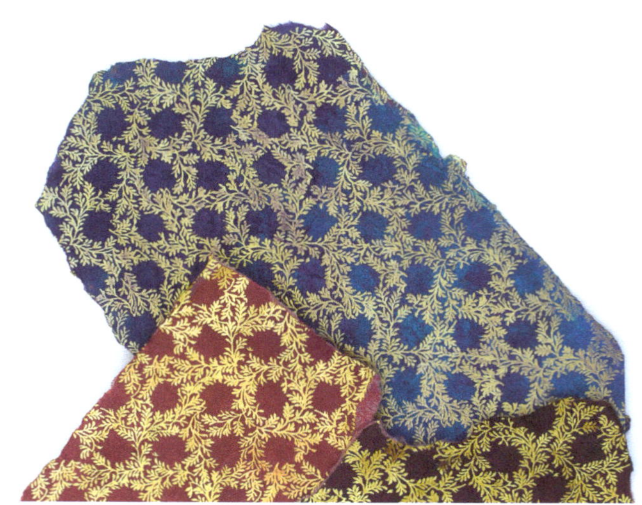

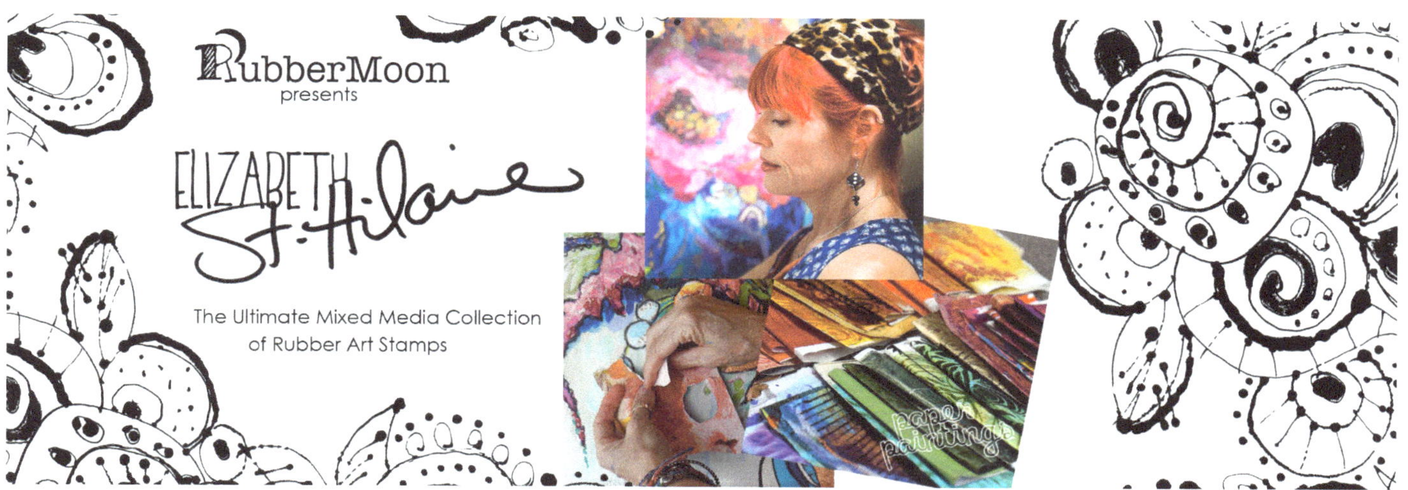

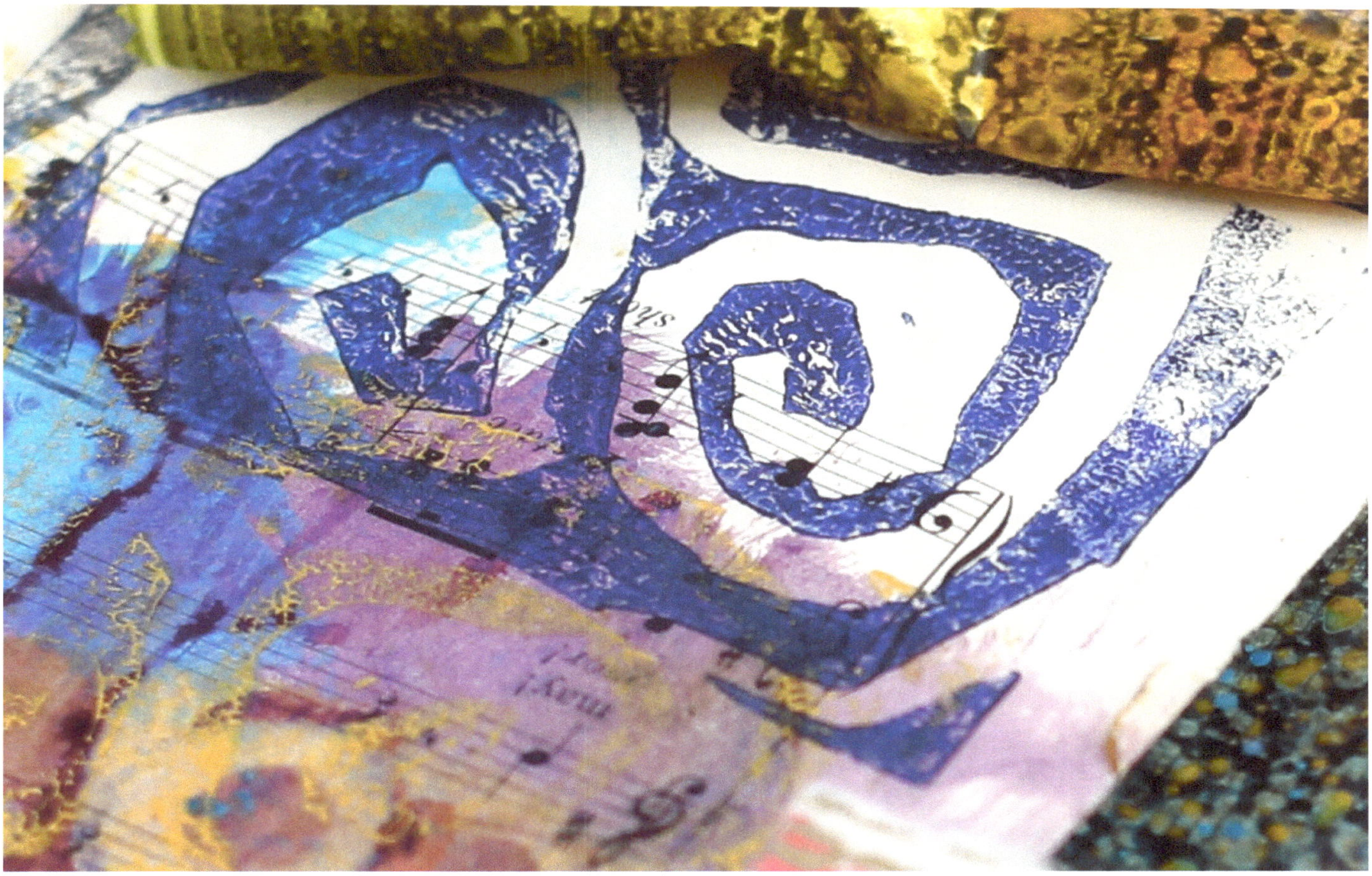

my art stamp designs

Purchasing stamps at your local craft store can offer immediate gratification in terms of adding patterns, textures, and marks to your collage paper.

Recently I have designed a line of art stamps with RubberMoon, an American company based in Missouri. RubberMoon has a full line of Elizabeth St. Hilaire stamps which they sell in sets as well as individuals.

Visit RubberMoon.com and look under the Artists drop down menu for Elizabeth St. Hilaire in order to find my line of art stamps that I use for creating patterns on my hand painted collage papers.

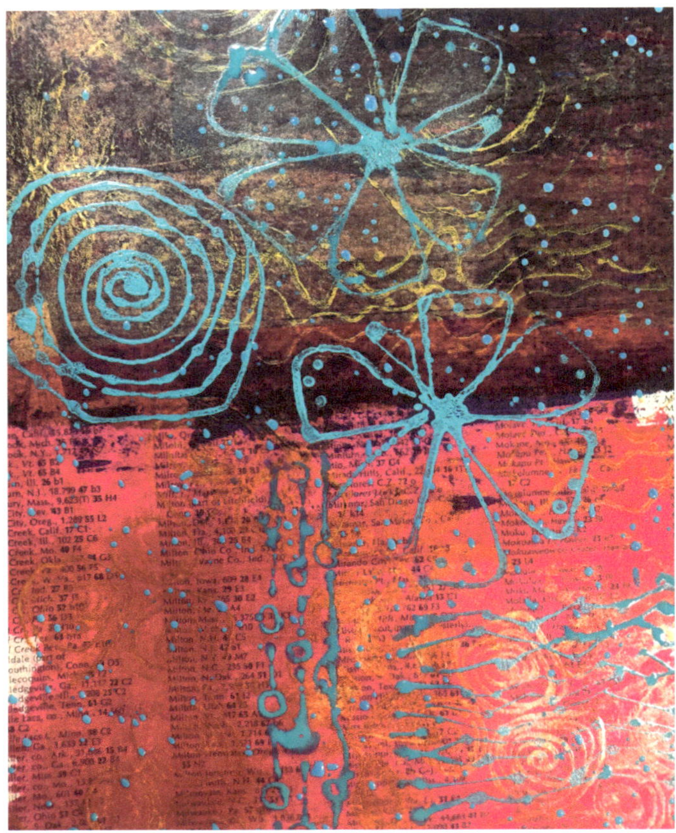

COMBINATIONS: *RubberMoon stamps with splatter over an old atlas page*

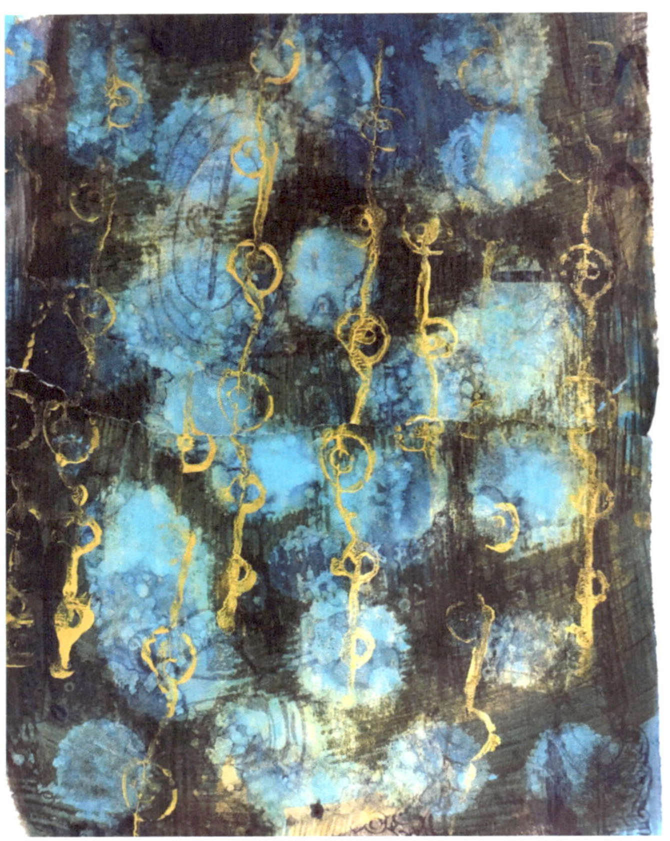

COMBINATIONS: *RubberMoon stamps with metallic gold over blotted alcohol resist on an old book page*

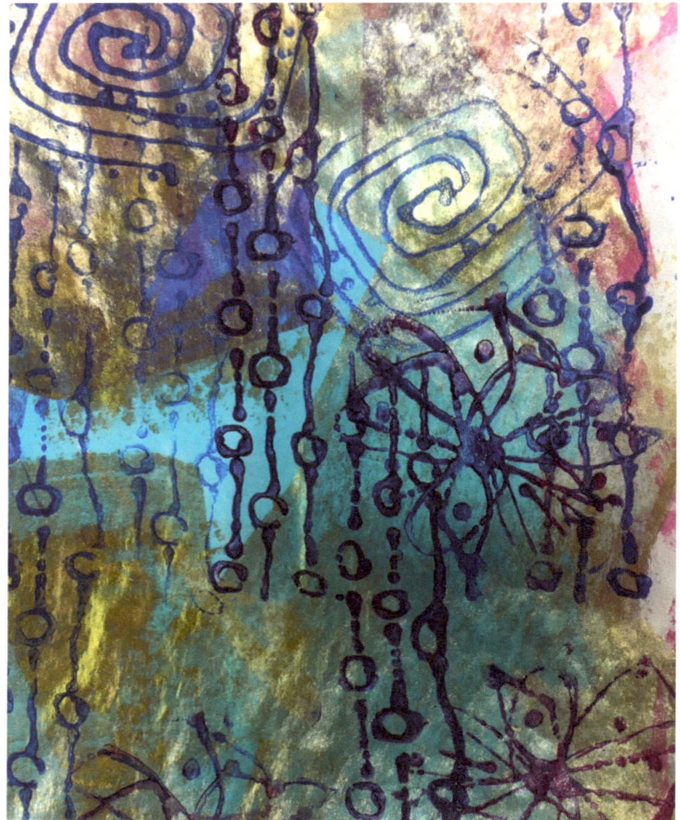

COMBINATIONS: *RubberMoon stamps overlapping with metallic paint over credit card scraping on deli paper*

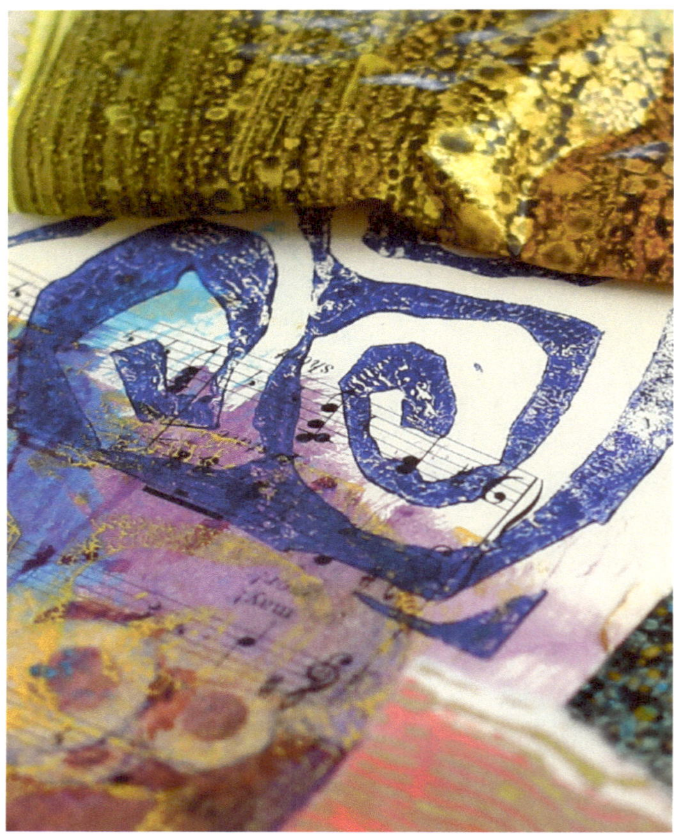

COMBINATIONS: *RubberMoon stamps overlapping with alcohol resist and plastic card scraping on sheet music paper*

painting paper

Stamping
Materials:

- Art stamps from RubberMoon.com
- Paint Brush and/or brayer
- Fluid Arylic Paint or permanent, archival ink pad

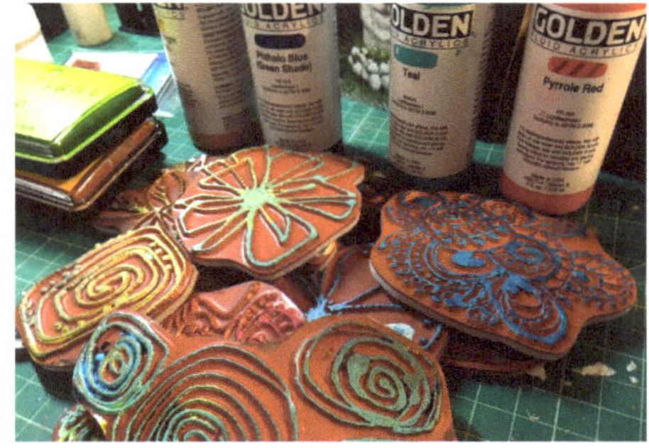

My designed stamps with RubberMoon

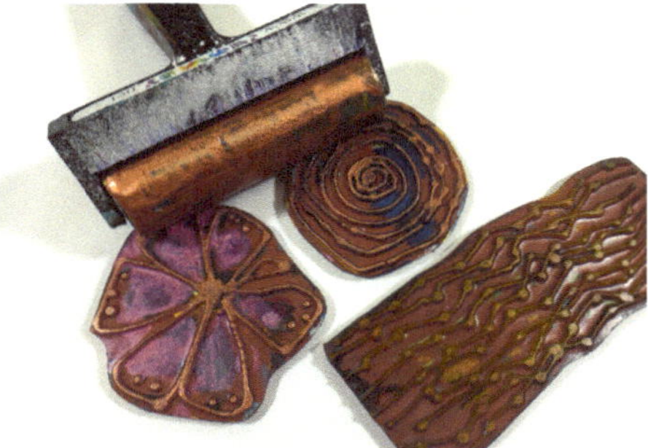

Add paint to stamps

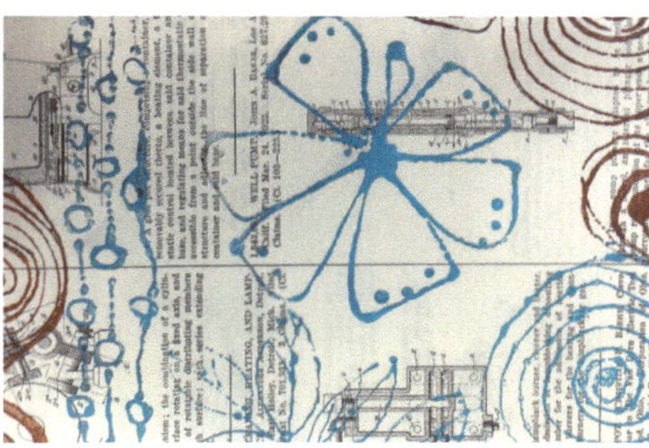

Press stamps onto paper

I typically use my brayer to spread Golden Fluid Acrylic paints directly onto art stamps of my own design with RubberMoon. I use the brayer so that the paint stays on the patterned area of the stamp and does not fill into the negative spaces. You can clean your stamps with baby wipes immediately after spreading paint on them, you can also use a toothbrush with The Masters Brush Cleaner to get dried paint off them. It is not recommended that you soak them in water. I typically print my stamp multiple times in order to remove as much paint as possible before wiping them down.

Companies such as Ranger offer stamp pads that are permanent and fade proof. You can use these for your paper painting or you can use acrylic paint, the effects are different and the choice is yours.

Stamping is just one of the techniques you will use in creating hand-painted papers. The idea is to take one sheet of paper through multiple techniques, adding layer upon layer of texture and pattern. This multi pass process is what makes your papers rich and painterly.

Using your archival ink pad or painting your stamp with acrylic paint, make impressions in multiple colors,

overlapping the images over the surface of a white sheet of rice paper or a paper that you have already layered with other techniques. Once the stamped impressions dry, try adding a wash of color over them to tone down any white areas of the base paper. Colors next to each other (analogous) on the color wheel offer harmonious effects, and colors more close to opposite on the wheel offer more intense and color vibrating effects, both are effective in different applications.

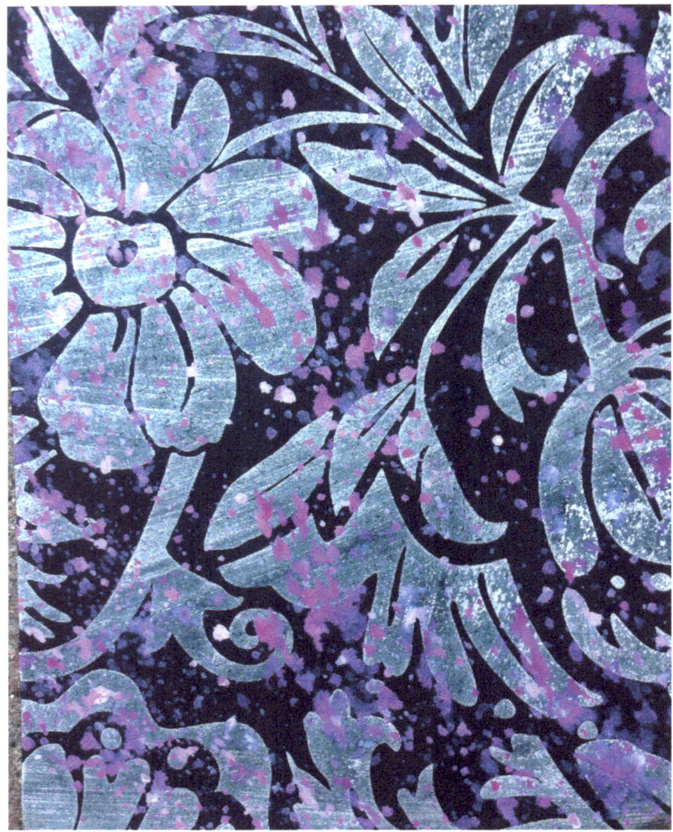

COMBINATIONS: Corrugated cardboard stamping combined with crayon resist & washes of color over an old book page

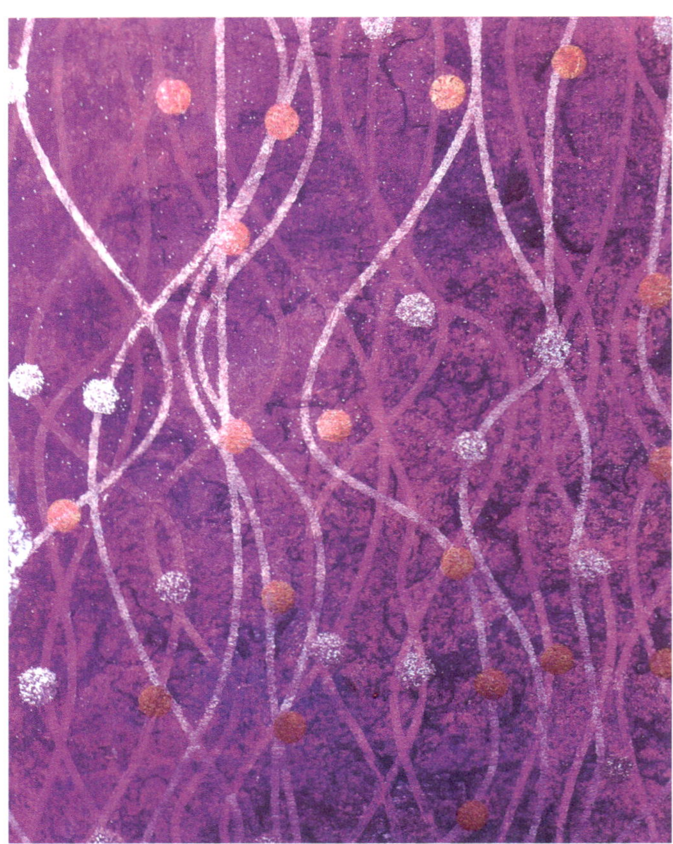

COMBINATIONS: Corrugated cardboard stamping over subtle sink liner stamping with commercial rubber stamping

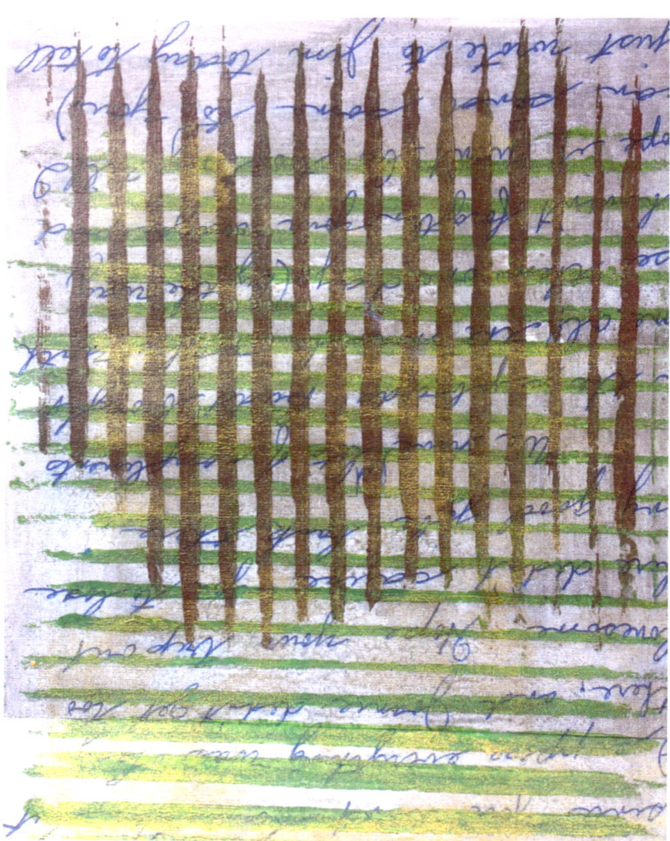

COMBINATIONS: Corrugated cardboard stamping with metallic paints over old hand written letter and pale wash

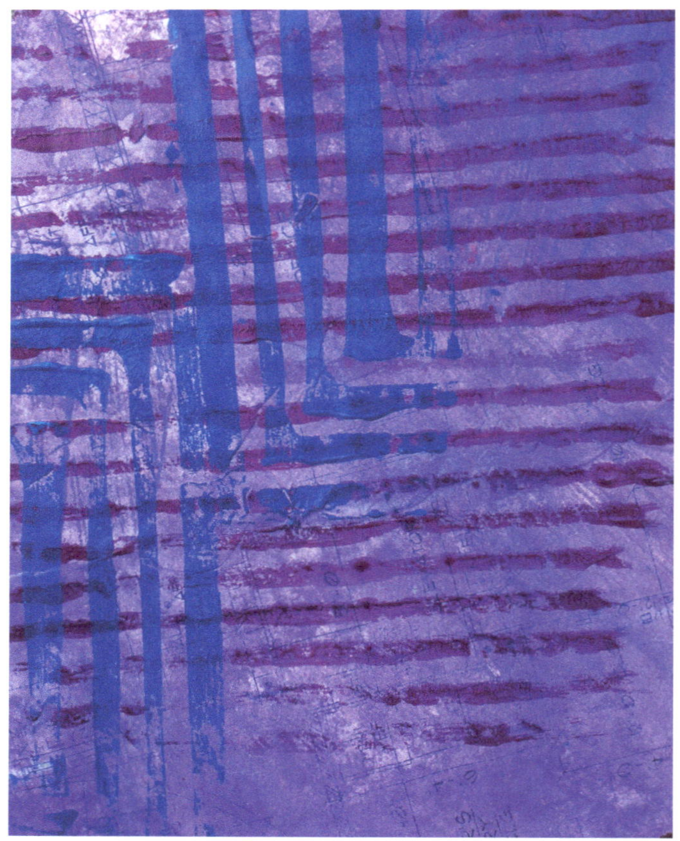

COMBINATIONS: Corrugated cardboard stamping with hand-carved stamp in opposite direction

songbirds in collage

painting paper

Corrugated Cardboard

Materials:

- Corrugated cardboard box material
- Gesso
- Acrylic paint
- Paint brush

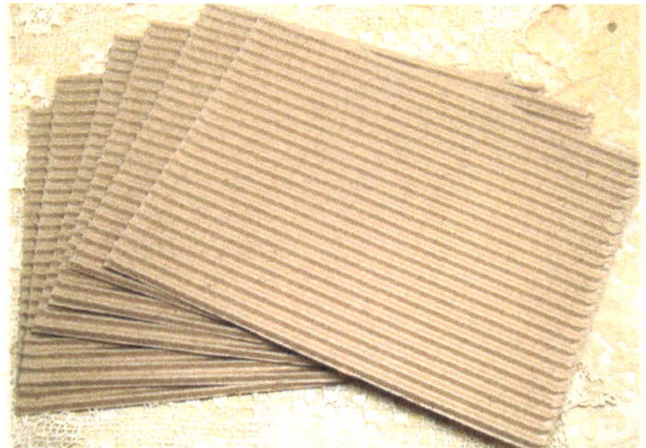

Corrugated cardboard box material

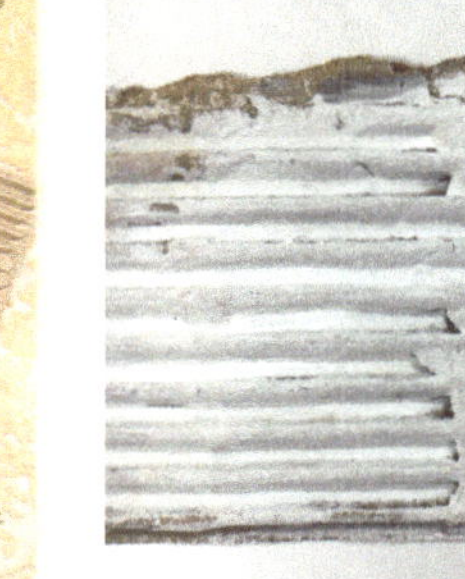

Gesso over corrugated cardboard pieces

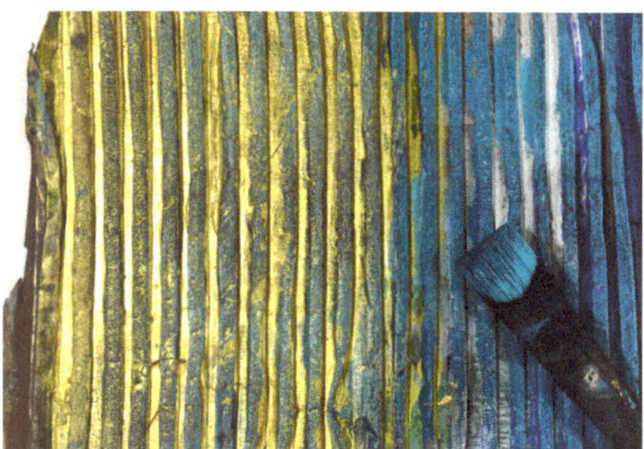

Apply a layer of paint over the cardboard

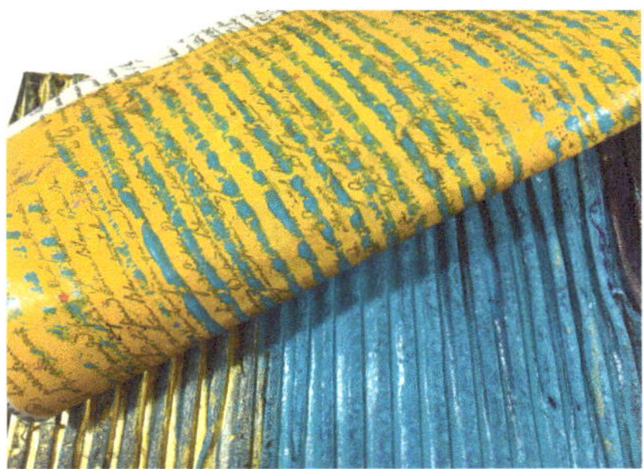

Press the paper onto the cardboard

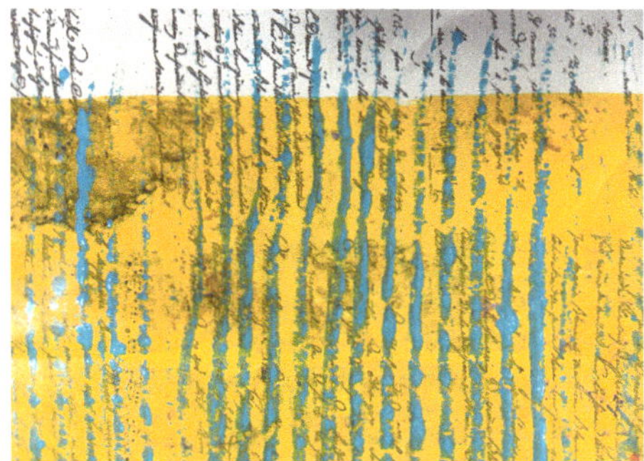

Corrugated lines over a yellow letter

Corrugated cardboard is something that arrives at your door on a regular basis if you are an *Amazon Prime* shopper like I am. If not, you can find free cardboard boxes from your local grocery store or COSTCO. This technique makes a wonderful second or third pass for your already embellished papers. The corrugated lines are much more organic and non-uniform once the cardboard has been pressed several times, it gets better
with age!

Separate the cardboard to reveal the corrugation in the middle. Coat the corrugated surface with a layer of gesso on both sides and allow it to dry. This prevents absorption of moisture from the paint, which will deteriorate the cardboard before it gains character.

Apply undiluted paint onto the corrugated surface with a brush. Press the cardboard in either the same or overlapping directions onto any paper surface, experimenting with different types of paper and colors.

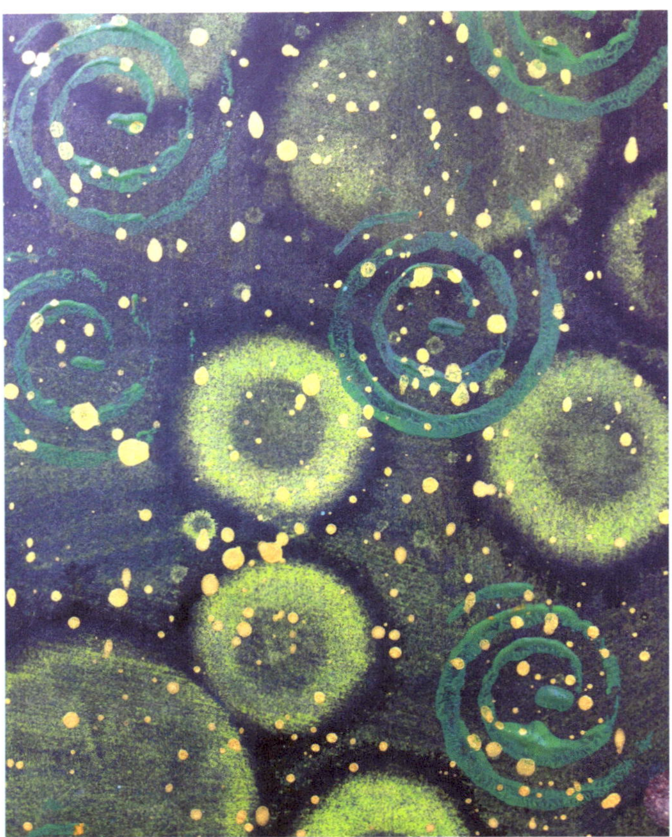

COMBINATIONS: Alcohol resist with splatter and hand-carved stamping on ledger paper

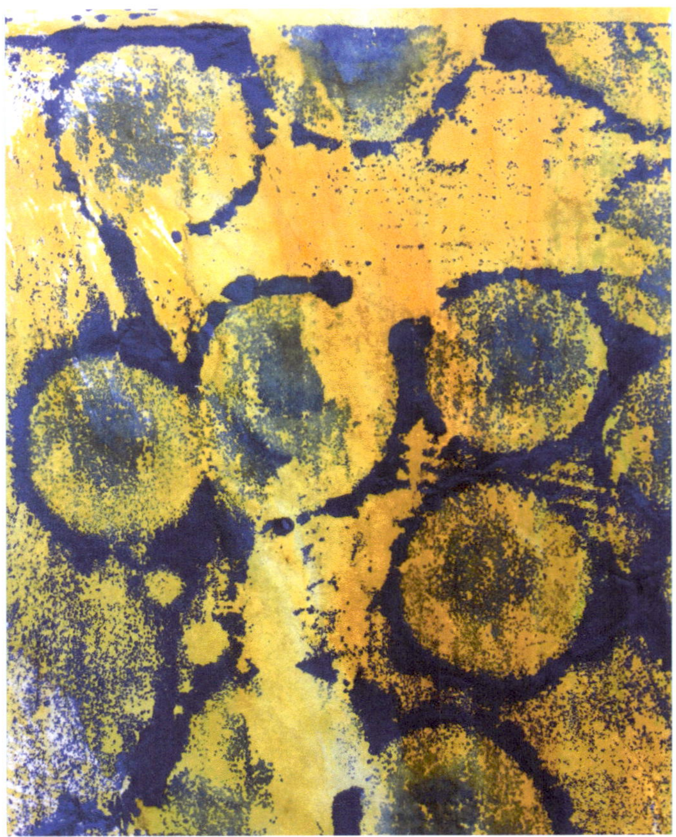

COMBINATIONS: A blotter paper type lift from the alcohol technique onto an absorbent rice paper

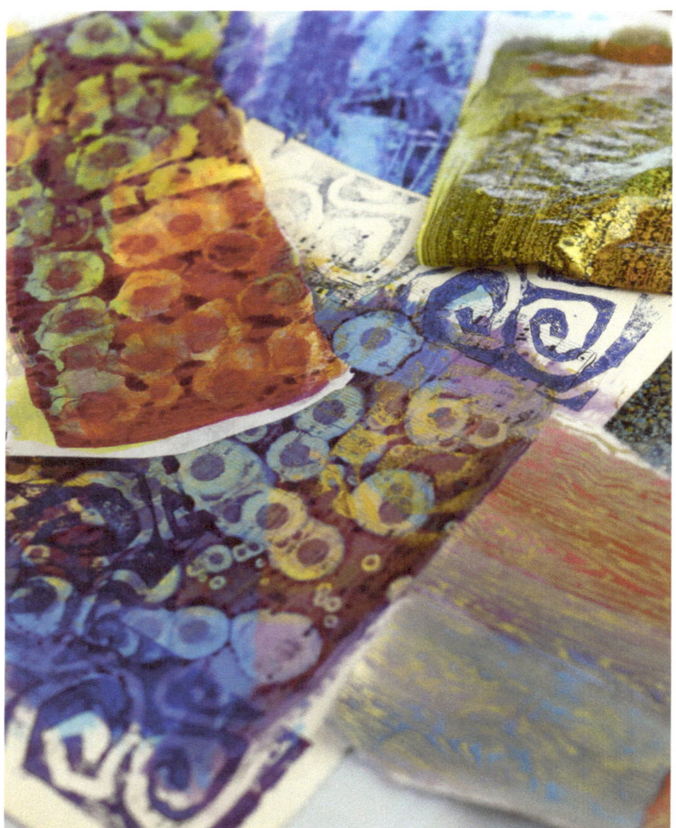

COMBINATIONS: Alchohol resist in various color combos

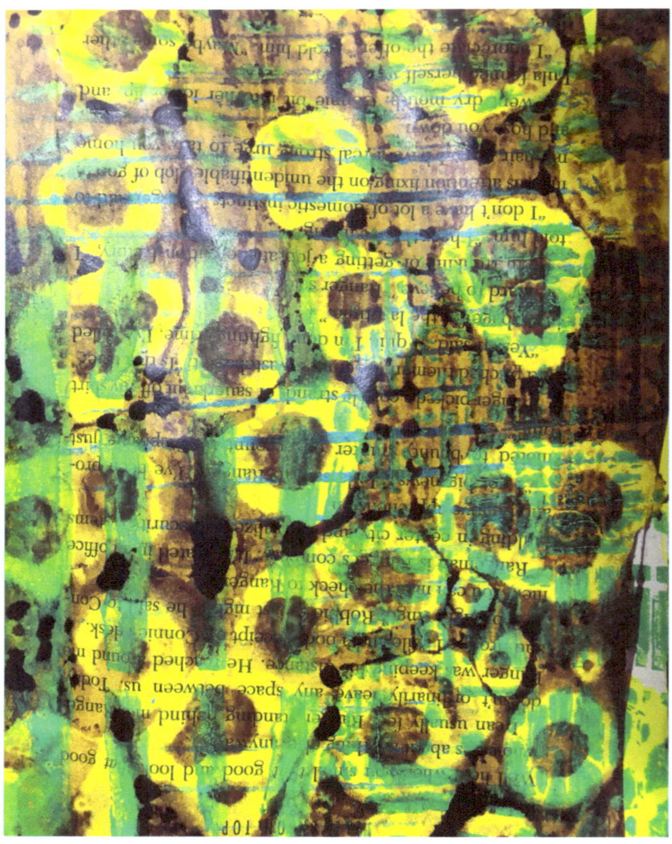

COMBINATIONS: Alchohol resist with cardboard stamping over an old book page

painting paper

Alcohol Resist

Materials:

- Household rubbing alcohol
- Eye dropper
- Acrylic paint
- Nonabsorbent paper that does not soak up the paint

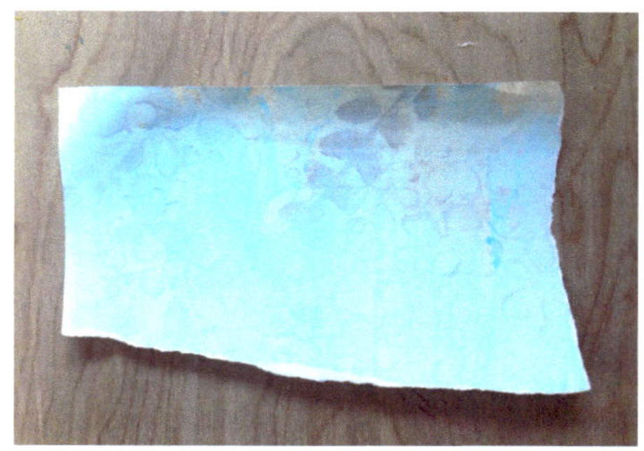

Wallpaper painted a light color and allowed to dry completely

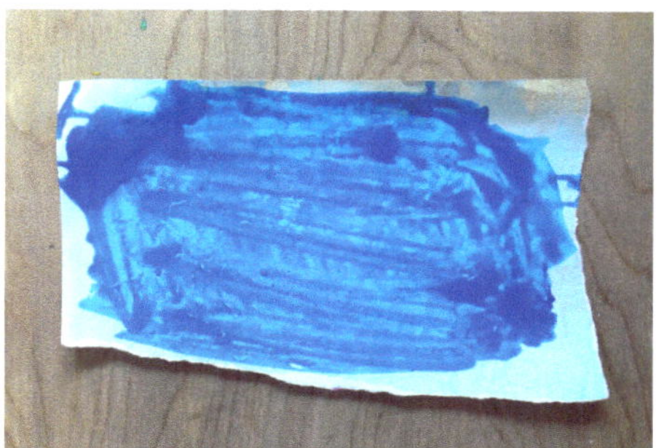

Overlay with a darker color, slightly watered down fluid acrylic paint

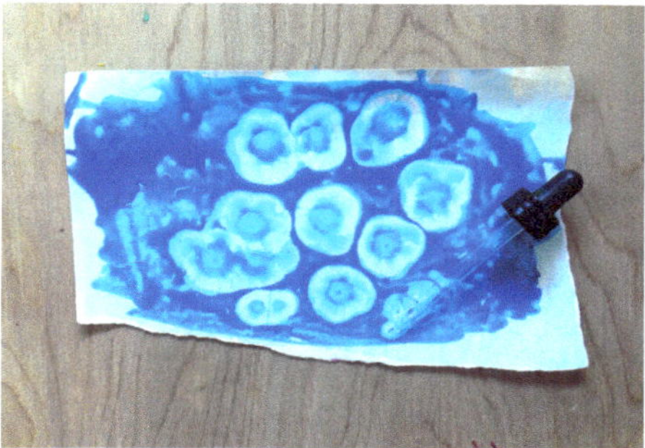

Working quickly, drop alcohol into wet paint with the eye dropper

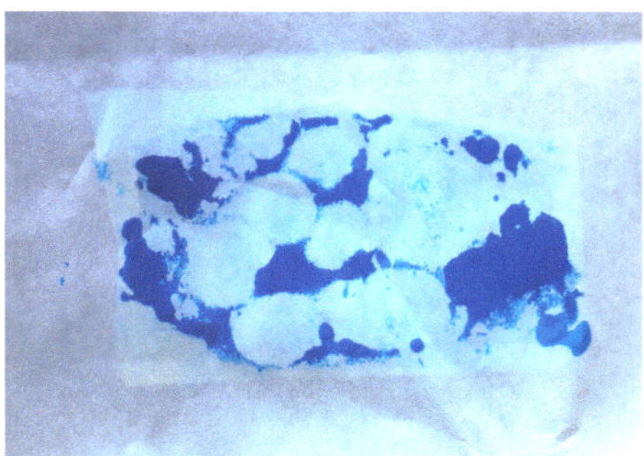

Option: blot off the paint with an absorbent rice paper and a light touch

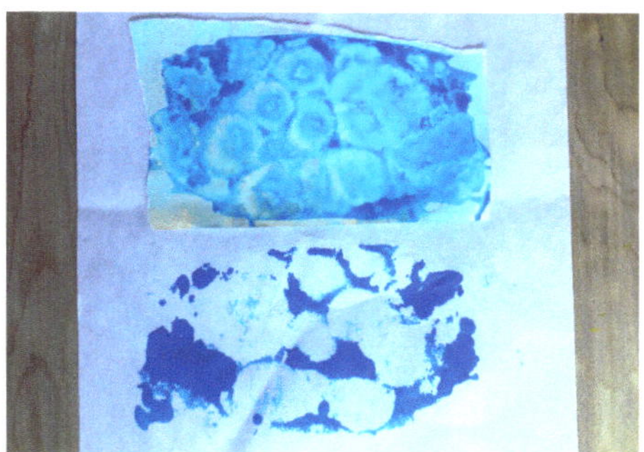

The alcohol pattern is transferred to the rice paper and can obscure the original effect

Rubbing alcohol from the first aid aisle (non-diluted isopropyl) pushes the pigment of acrylic paint away and can offer some wonderful resist techniques.

So many variables come into play with this technique: the type of paper and its' absorbency, the amount of water in the top layer of paint, and how dry the paint is when you drop the alcohol. It's best to experiment with this technique many times to get the best results.

Paint the paper with a light color paint and allow to dry completely. Consider using some of the additive techniques from previous pages.

Overlay a darker watered down fluid acrylic paint on the prepared paper and allow to dry slightly.

Drop alcohol from an eye dropper from varying heights and with varying force to form large and small droplets onto the paper.

Watch the alcohol resist push your top (wet) layer of paint away, revealing the lighter layer underneath. Too wet of paint on top will roll back into the resist space, too dry paint will not move. This technique requires patience and experimentation. If at first you don't succeed, try try again.

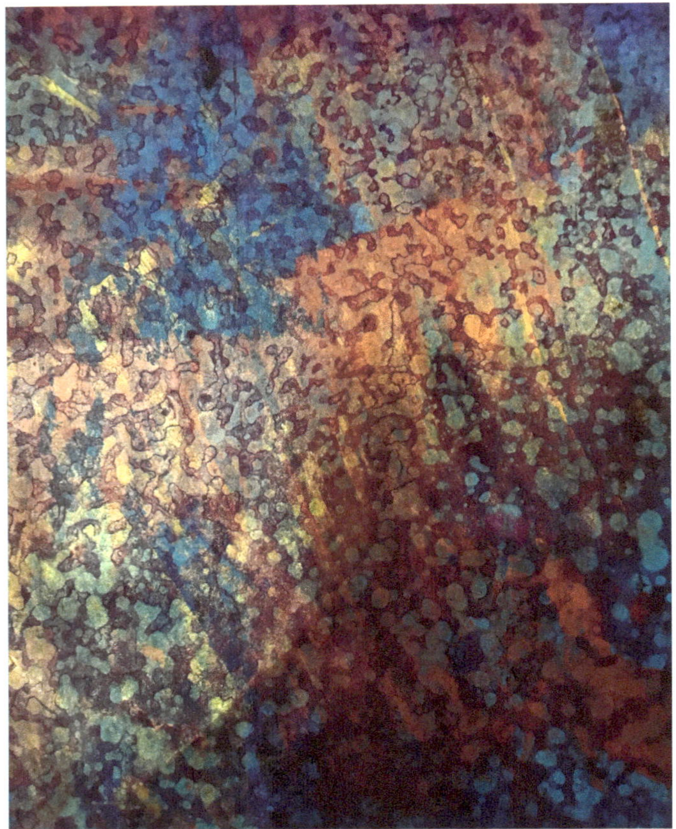

COMBINATIONS: Soap bubble resist over metallic plastic card scraping on deli paper

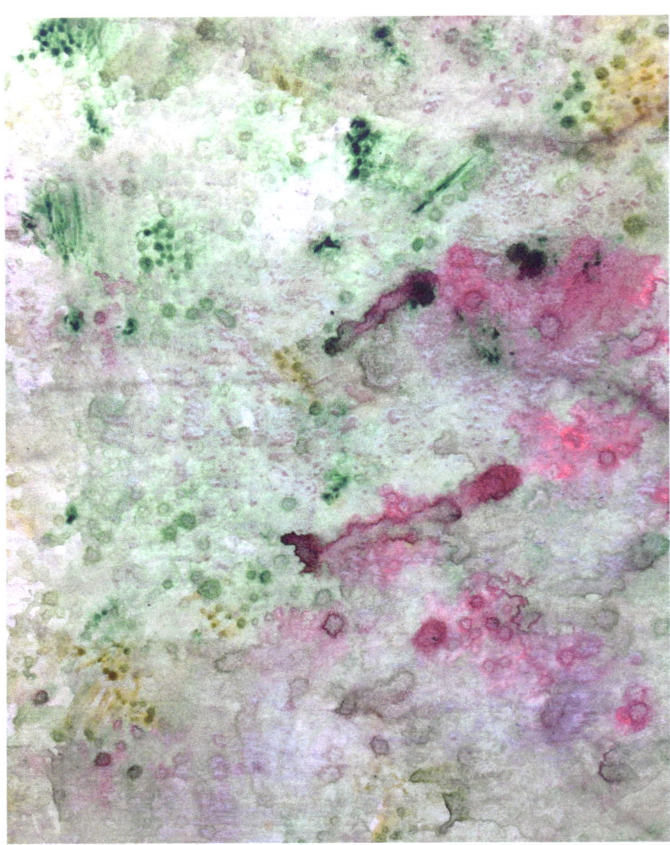

COMBINATIONS: Multiple colors of soap bubble resist on wallpaper, allowed to bleed together

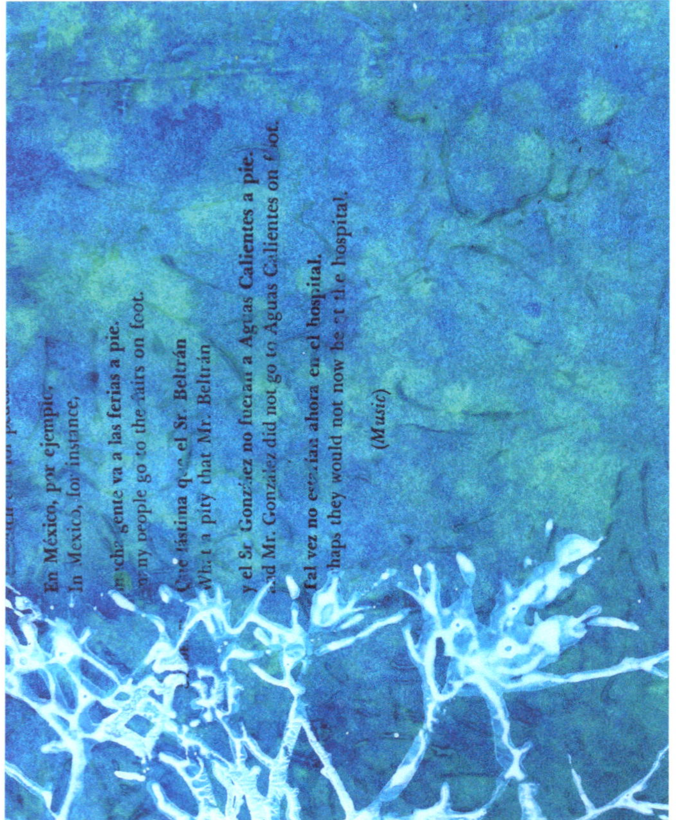

COMBINATIONS: Soap bubble resist over old book page with stenciled pattern in white gesso

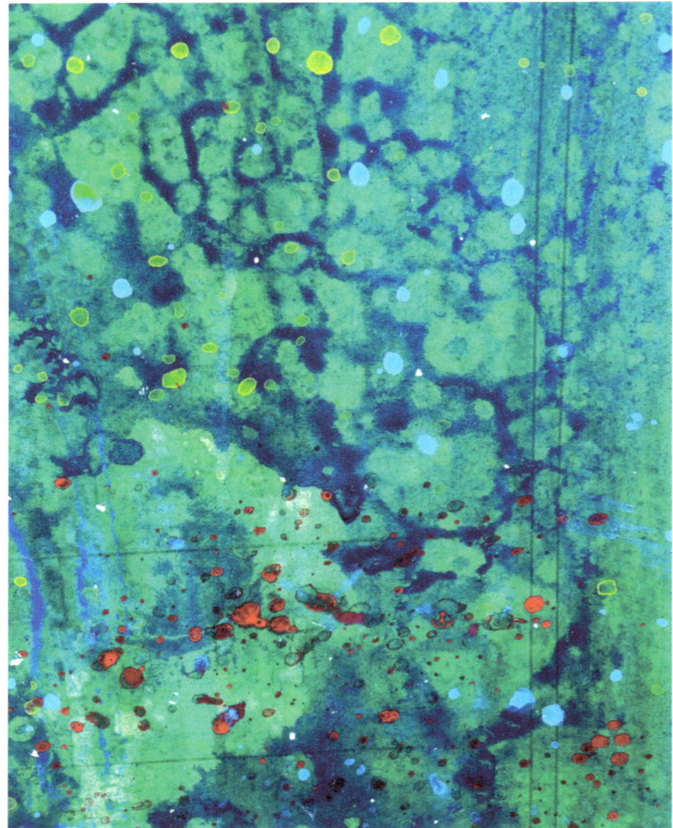

COMBINATIONS: Soap bubble resist over old ledger paper with splattering

painting paper

Soap Bubble Resist

Materials:

- Travel size spray bottle with a few pumps of dish liquid–Dawn works best
- Non porous found paper
- Acrylic paint
- Paint brush

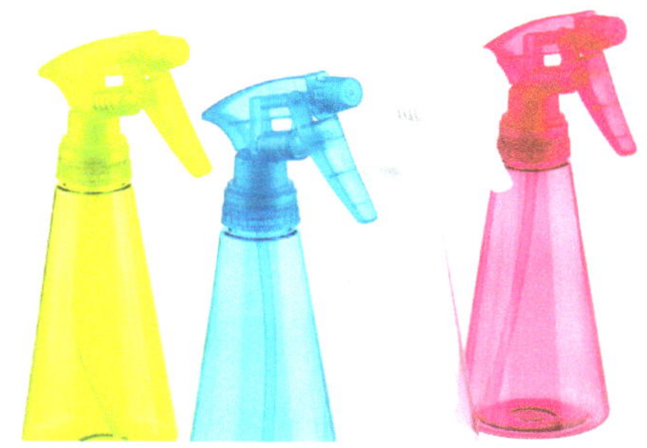

A few tablespoons of dish soap added to a spray bottle and shake

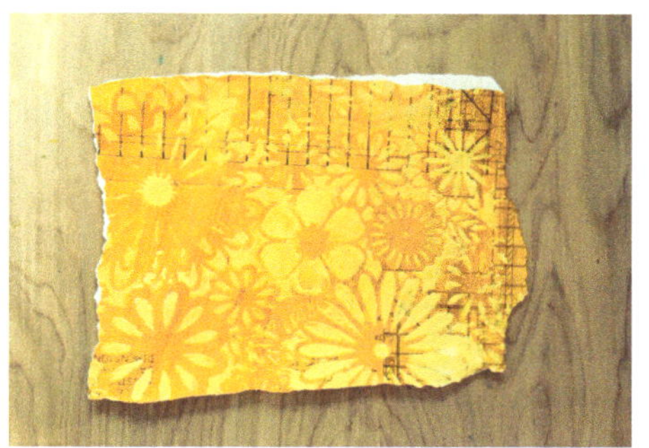

Paper embellished with a stencil pattern in light colors and allowed to dry completely

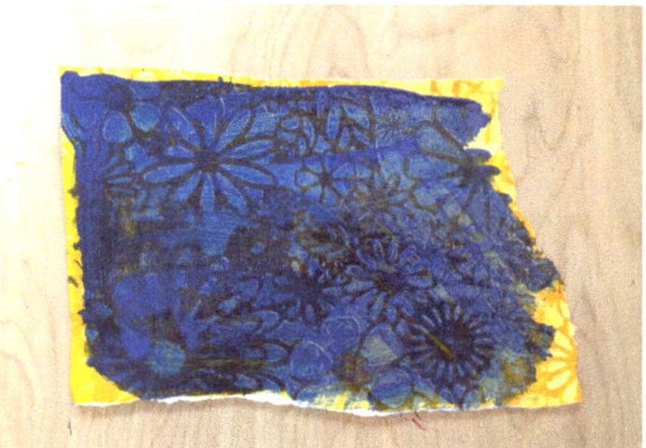

Paint a darker color over the top with diluted fluid acrylics–wet and watery

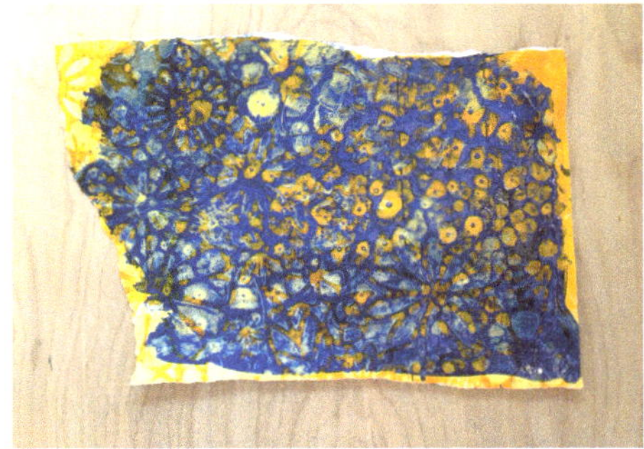

Working quickly, spitz the soap into the wet paint. A pattern will emerge as it resists

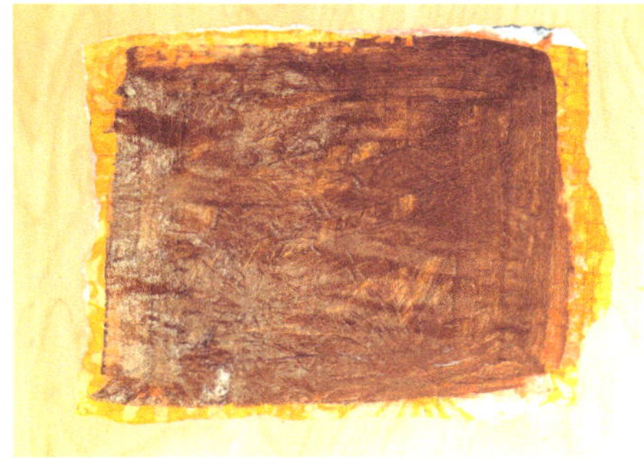

Different paper, paint colors, and water dilution can produce different effects

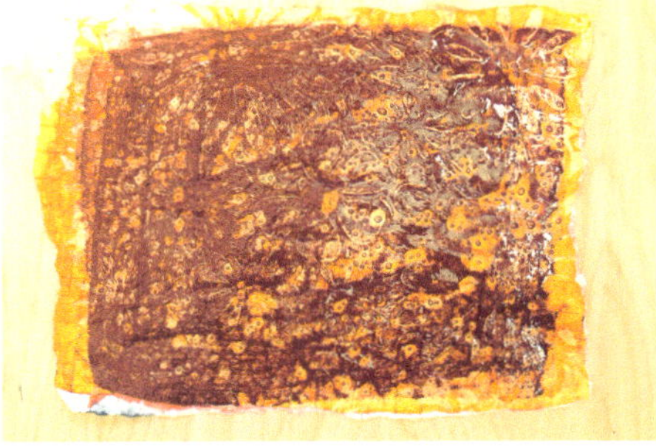

Working quickly, spitz the soap into the wet paint. A pattern will emerge as it resists

Use a piece of paper that will not allow the paint to soak all the way through. Coat paper with a light colored acrylic paint. Allow to dry completely.

Brush over the top of your painted sheet with a darker color of diluted fluid acrylic paint. (Much like the alcohol technique on the previous page).

While the top layer is still wet, gently spray the soap bubble mixture and allow the droplets to fall onto the paper. Try to spray the soap mixture up in air and let it fall straight down onto the paper in small droplets.

Watch the soap bubbles repel the top layer of paint in a small pattern of spots that sometimes continue to grow bigger and bigger.

There are many variables that come into play with this resist technique, so experimentation is paramount. The amount of water in the diluted top coat plays a role, the amount of drying time before spraying the soap bubbles plays a role, the color of the paint can even play a role. Experimentation is key.

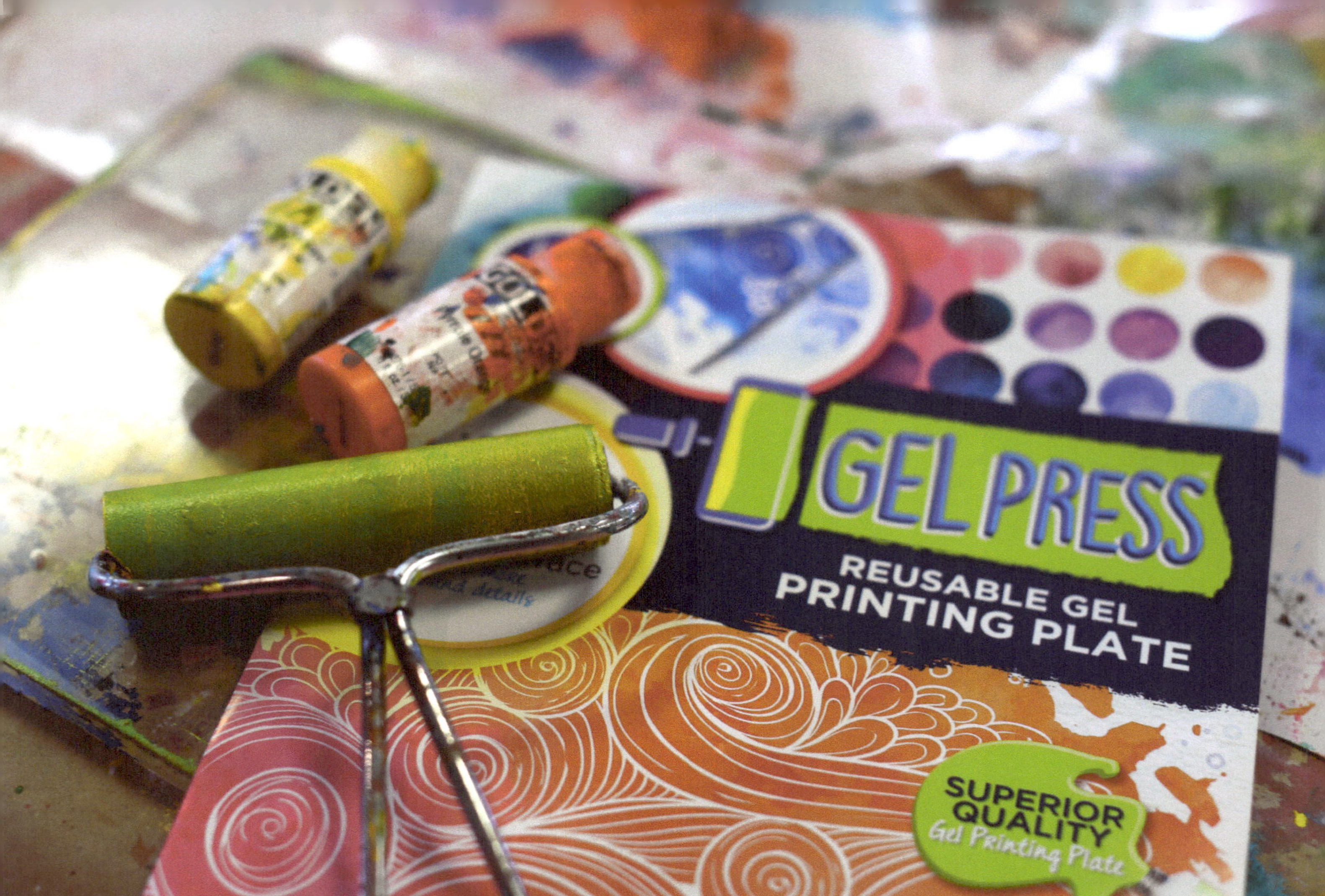

Gel Plate
monoprinting madness!

The Gel Press printing plate has become all the rage with mixed media artists, and yet I find at least two or three people in my Paper Paintings Collage Workshop who have yet to experiment with it. You are in for a treat.

This Gel Press printing plate looks and feels like gelatin, but is durable, reusable, and stores at room temperature. It doesn't take up room in your fridge like a home-made one, it's easy to clean and always ready for printing. Monoprinting on a Gel Press printing plate is simple and fun. The gratification is immediate, and the prints have endless creative uses.

It is my hope that you will experiment with all of the techniques in this book before you pick your favorites. The effects I get with some of my classroom demonstration papers make the students ooh and ahhh, but they don't necessarily always find them to be the techniques they choose for themselves. Why not invite some friends to join you? Clear a table top and have fun Gel printing papers together, then swap and trade and expand your inventory with the styles and color palettes of fellow paper painters . I've gotten some of the best papers in trade that I would have never made on my own.

color
combinations

Starting with light colors and working your way down to darker colors is the way to go with fluid acrylics, which are the paints I prefer in my process. Because fluid acrylics are translucent, a light color will not show up very well over a darker color. For this reason, I start light and every subsequent layer is a little darker. I also like to use colors that are next to each other on the color wheel for harmony, or colors that are across from each other for discord. I suggest experimenting with both to see what appeals to you.

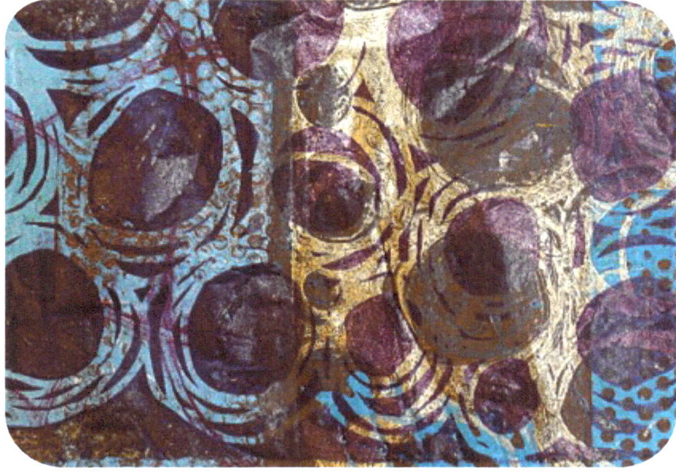

Harmonious colors start with light blue, to dark purple, to opaque gold on top.

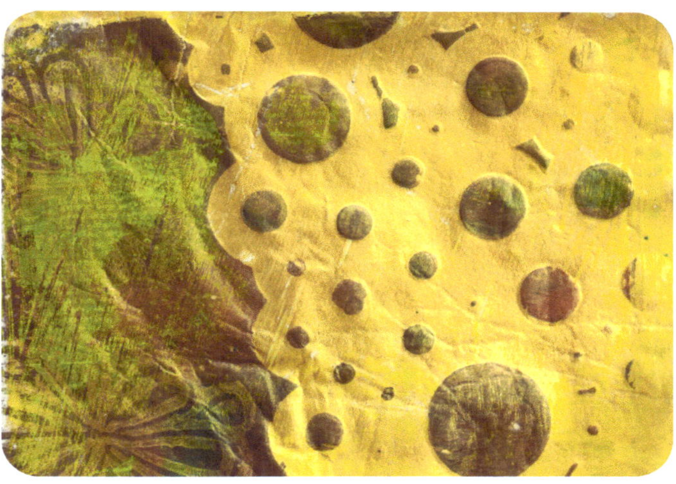

Creating an overall glow by utilizing metallic paint for the base and translucent, darker colors on top.

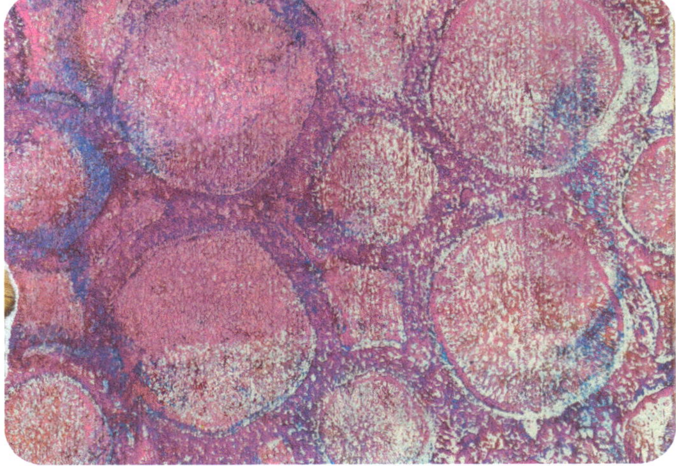

Creating harmony by staying with colors that are next to each other on the color wheel. Staring with magenta, adding darker purple.

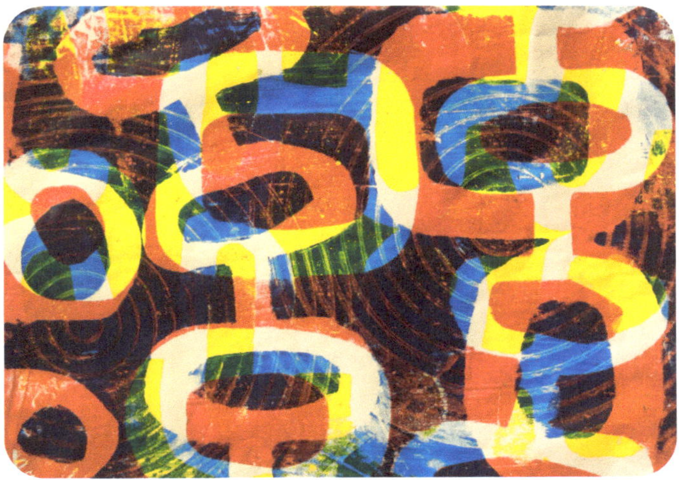

Creating discord with opposite colors. Starting with yellow, adding red, and lastly blue. Working light to dark, starting from white.

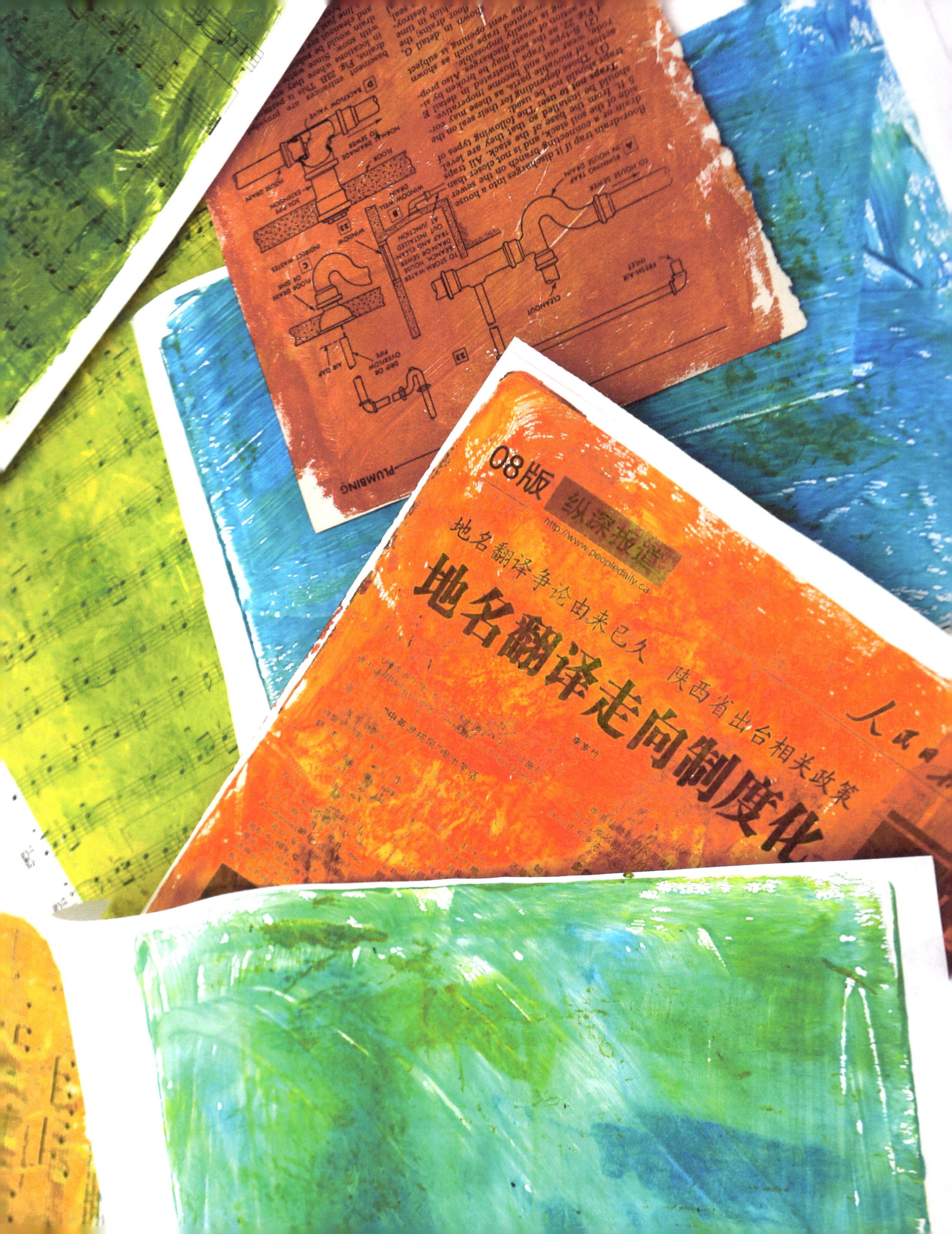
08版
纵深报道
http://www.peopledaily.ca
地名翻译争论由来已久　陕西省出台相关政策
地名翻译走向制度化
人民
PLUMBING

starting with light colored solids

I find, in fine art Gel printing, that starting with a light colored solid base is the way to go. I prefer not to have any high contrast white areas in my final prints, as I am hoping to achieve a painterly, fine art feeling. In order to eliminate the whites, without having to wash over the print post production, I always start with a solid base layer. I do not clean my plate between base layers, this process makes use of any residual paint on the plate from layer to layer. I call the leftover dried paint the crust. Your subsequent layers pick up the crust along with the newly applied paint–creating unexpected and beautiful results.

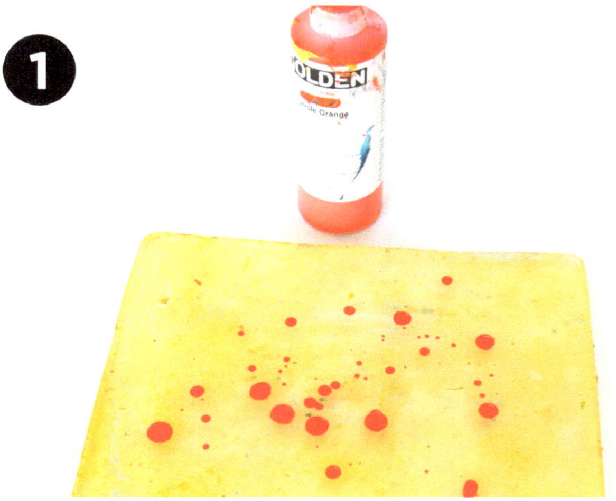

The brayer gives thin, even coverage for a few drops of paint applied directly to the plate.

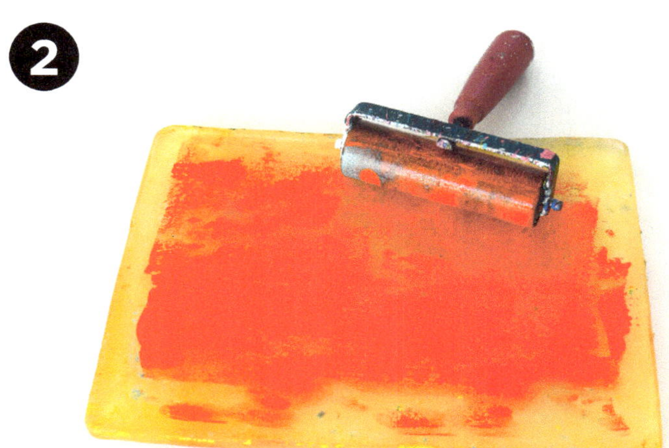

Roll the paint out to evenly cover the surface of the plate with the brayer.

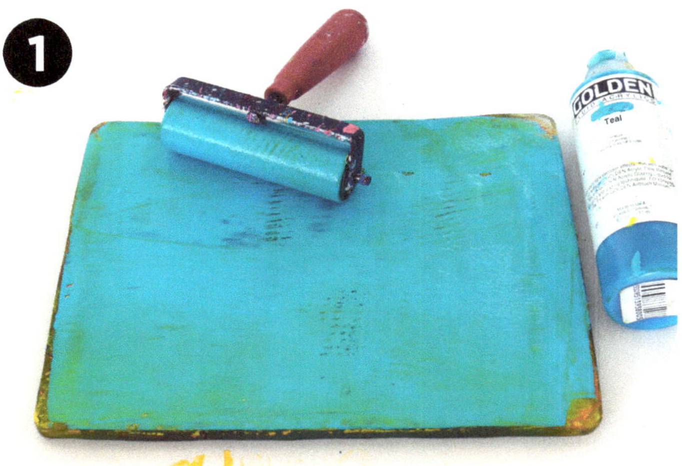

Start your printing process with a light colored solid.

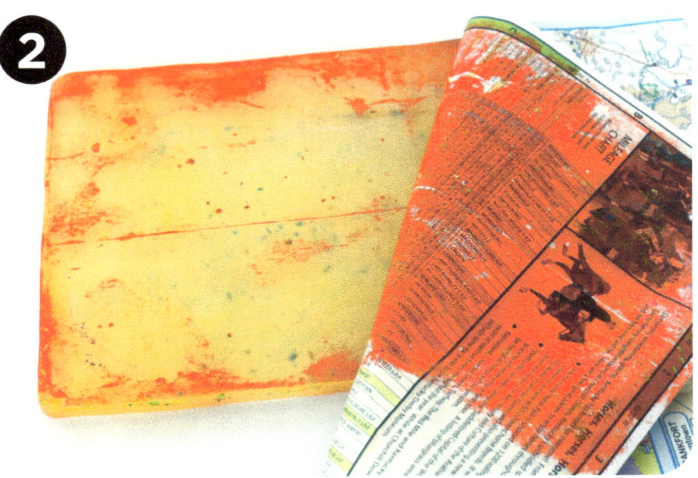

This will act as a base for subsequent, more complex layers

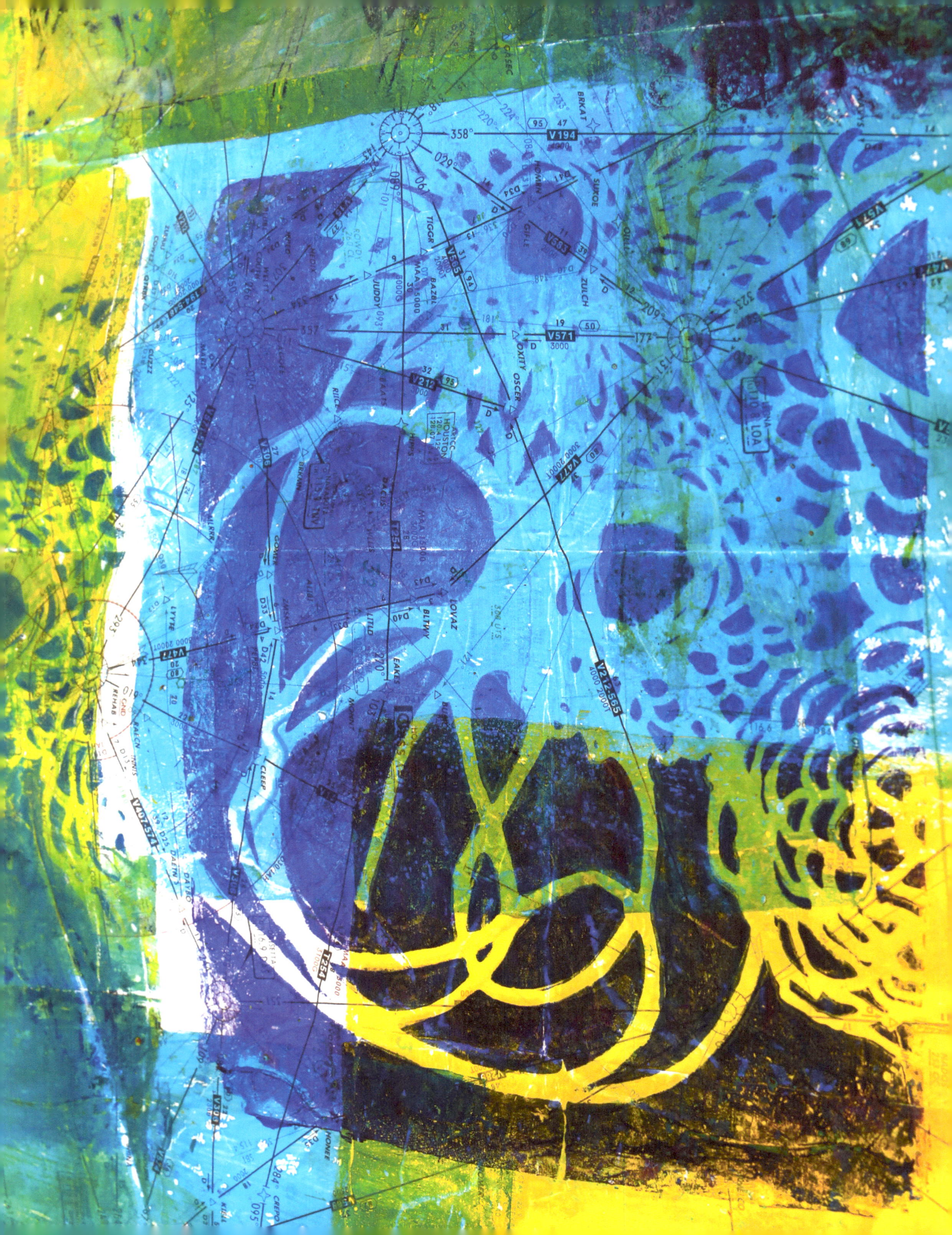

building layers

through translucency

Once you have your light colored base layer(s) printed on several small sheets of paper or an oversized sheet of paper, your goal is to start multiplying prints over and over with the techniques to follow in this book. Because Fluid Acrylics are translucent, every Gel printed layer you apply from here on out is going to show through and multiply with its predecessor. My typical rule of thumb is to combine a minimum of three layers in my Gel Prints, this creates rich papers for collage with lots and lots of depth. Varying the techniques of your layers creates even more visual interest. That being said, stencils tend to be the favorite technique of the Gel Press printing plate for my workshop students. My advice? Be bold, branch out, try different things!

The idea behind starting with a light colored base layer is that your prints don't include the white of the paper, which offers high contrast and can appear busy. High contrast can be distracting in collage papers, apple red should be layers of rich reds, intense oranges, deep yellows; adding white to this palette would be distracting.

I often multiply a print made using scraping tools over a print made with stencils, and then layer that print over one made with hand cut masks. This is the multi layered Gel print process I use for creating collage papers.

Keeping in mind my palette, I'll implement three or more colors (working from light to dark) that are analogous (next to one another) on the color wheel. I love the combination of blues and greens (cool colors) layered over each other through different techniques.

Every rule is meant to be broken! Experiment with combining opposites across the wheel as well.

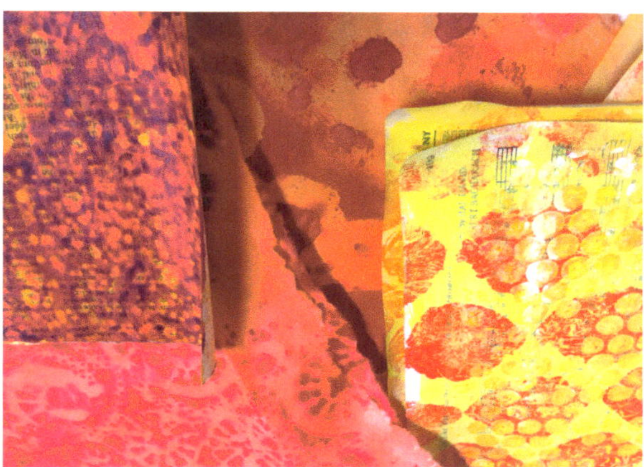

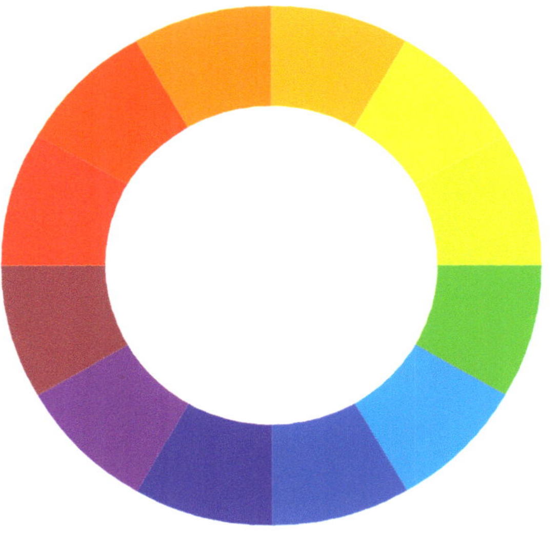

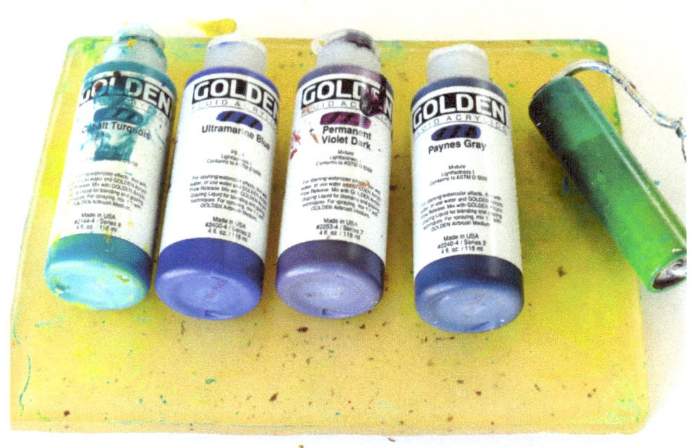

Making use of analogous colors.

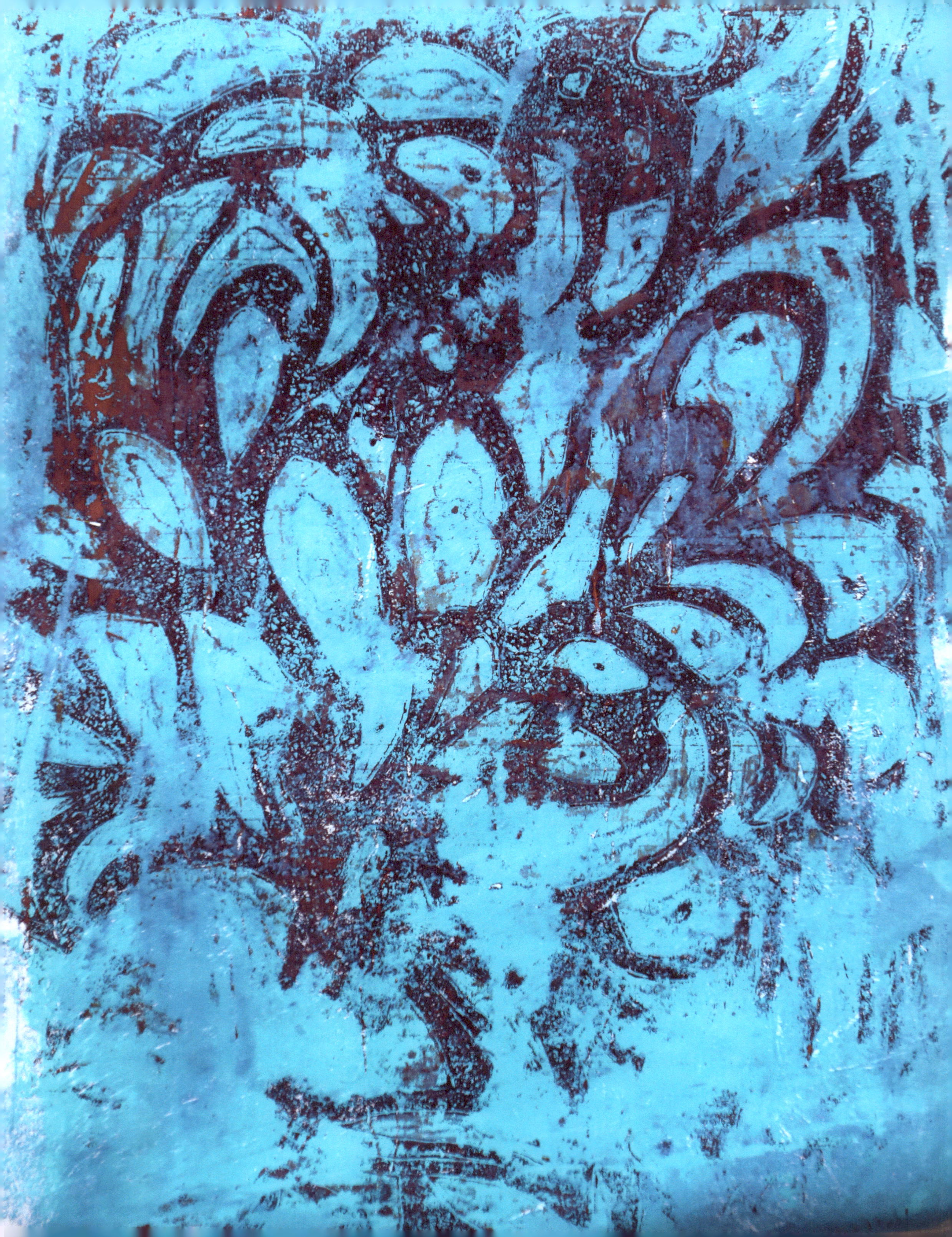

stencils

with ghost prints

Layering ghost prints one over the next (working light to dark) offers rich, painterly printed paper. The more layering the better, when you are trying to achieve painterly, fine art prints. Ghost prints can either be pulled immediately onto a pre-prepared light colored solid, or they can be pulled together with a second layer of paint.

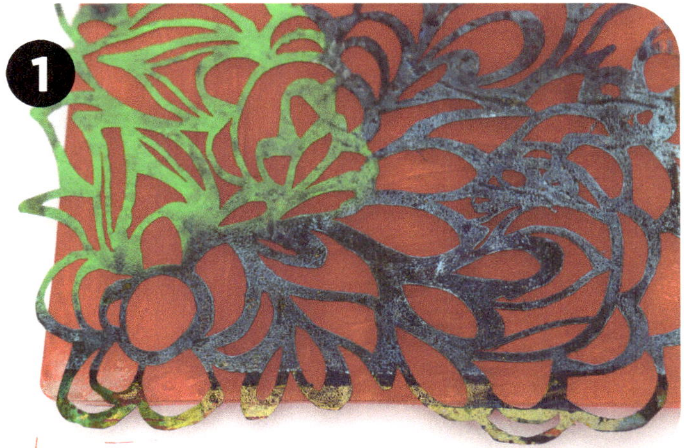

Lay the stencil over a thin layer of paint on the plate.

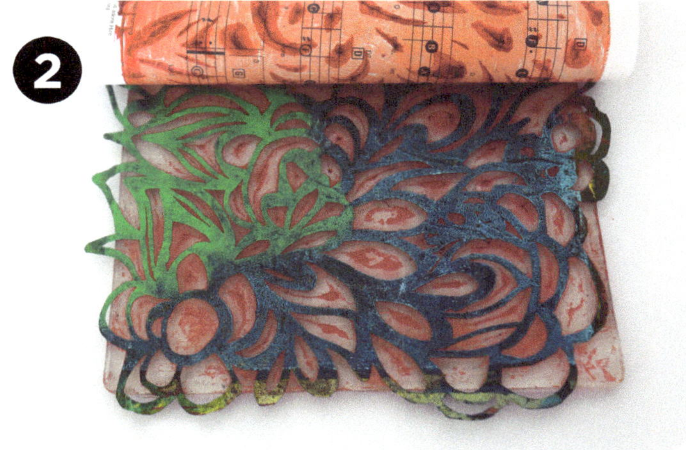

Press and pull a print from the plate

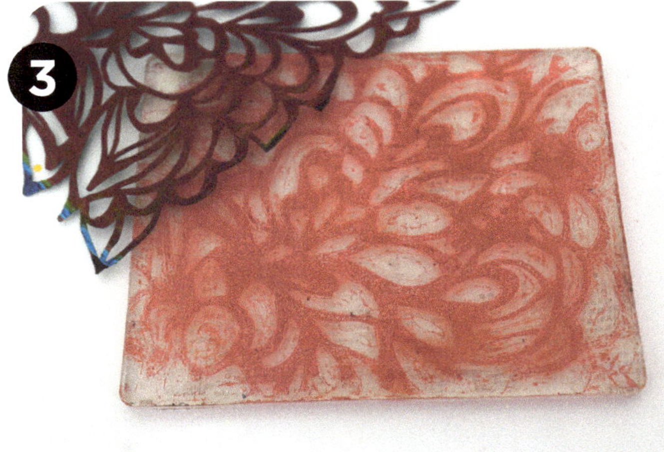

Paint left behind becomes the ghost print, or second print, after removing a stencil.

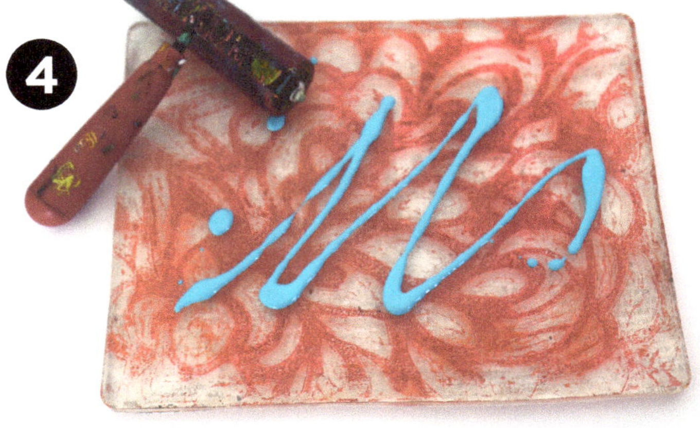

Add a thin layer of a lighter color paint over top of the dried ghost layer, pull the print of both layers together (left).

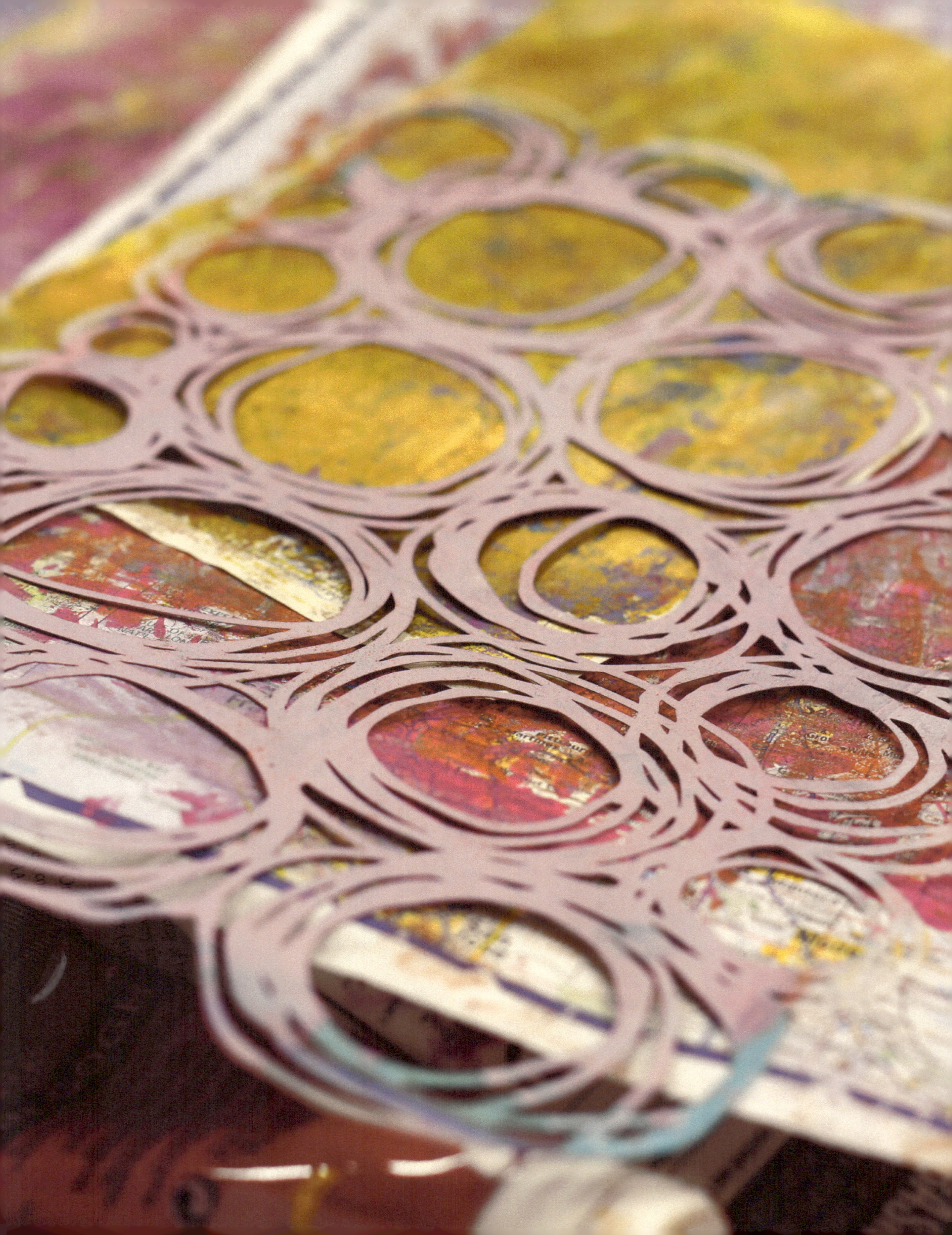

stencils

combining and layering

Layering stencil mask prints one over the next (working light to dark) offers rich, painterly printed paper. Combine stencils with elements such as leaves, string, and place mats for more diversity of patterning.

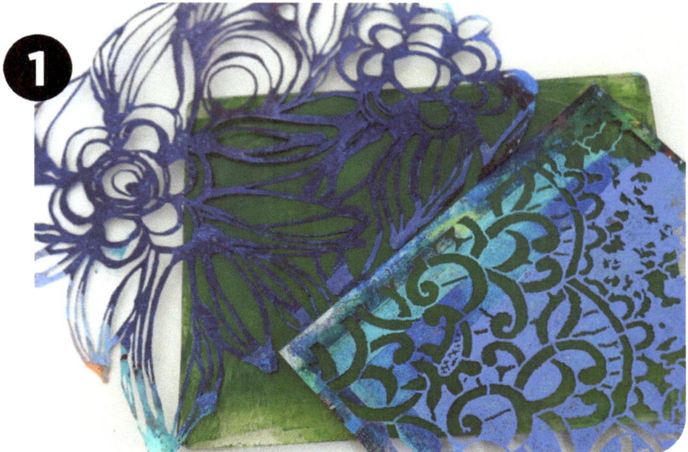

Combining two stencils on dark green paint.

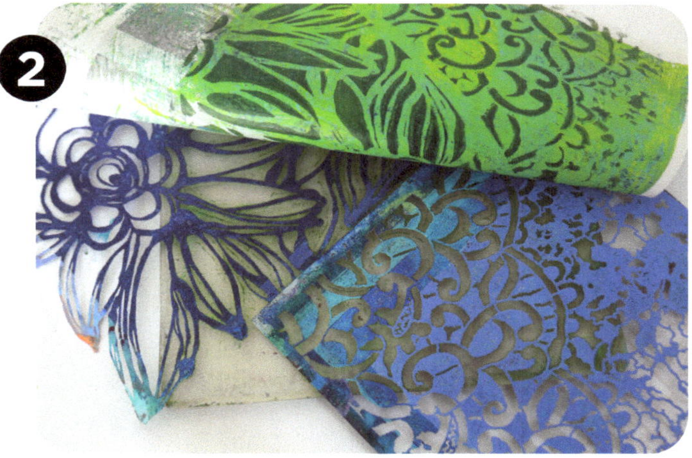

Pulling the multi stencil print on a light green solid.

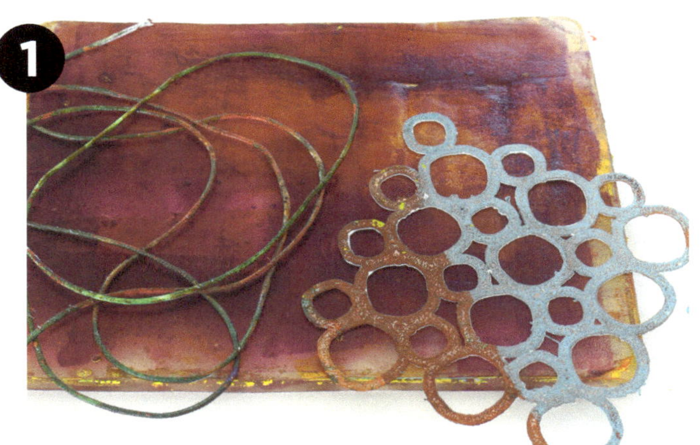

Combining a stencil with string (or other found masking material) on one print.

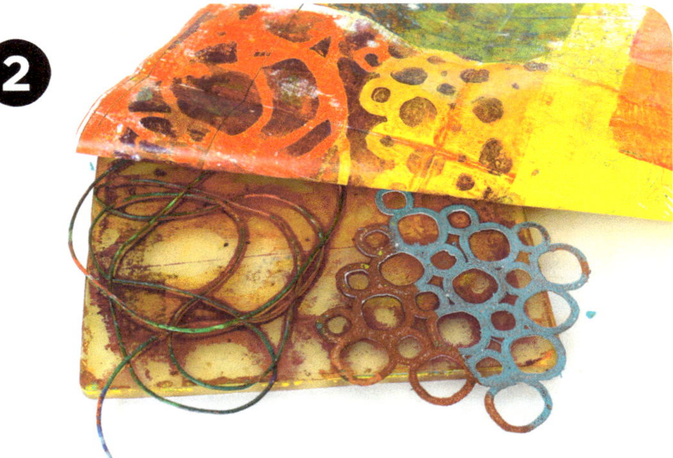

Pulling the print over a mixed solid base layer.

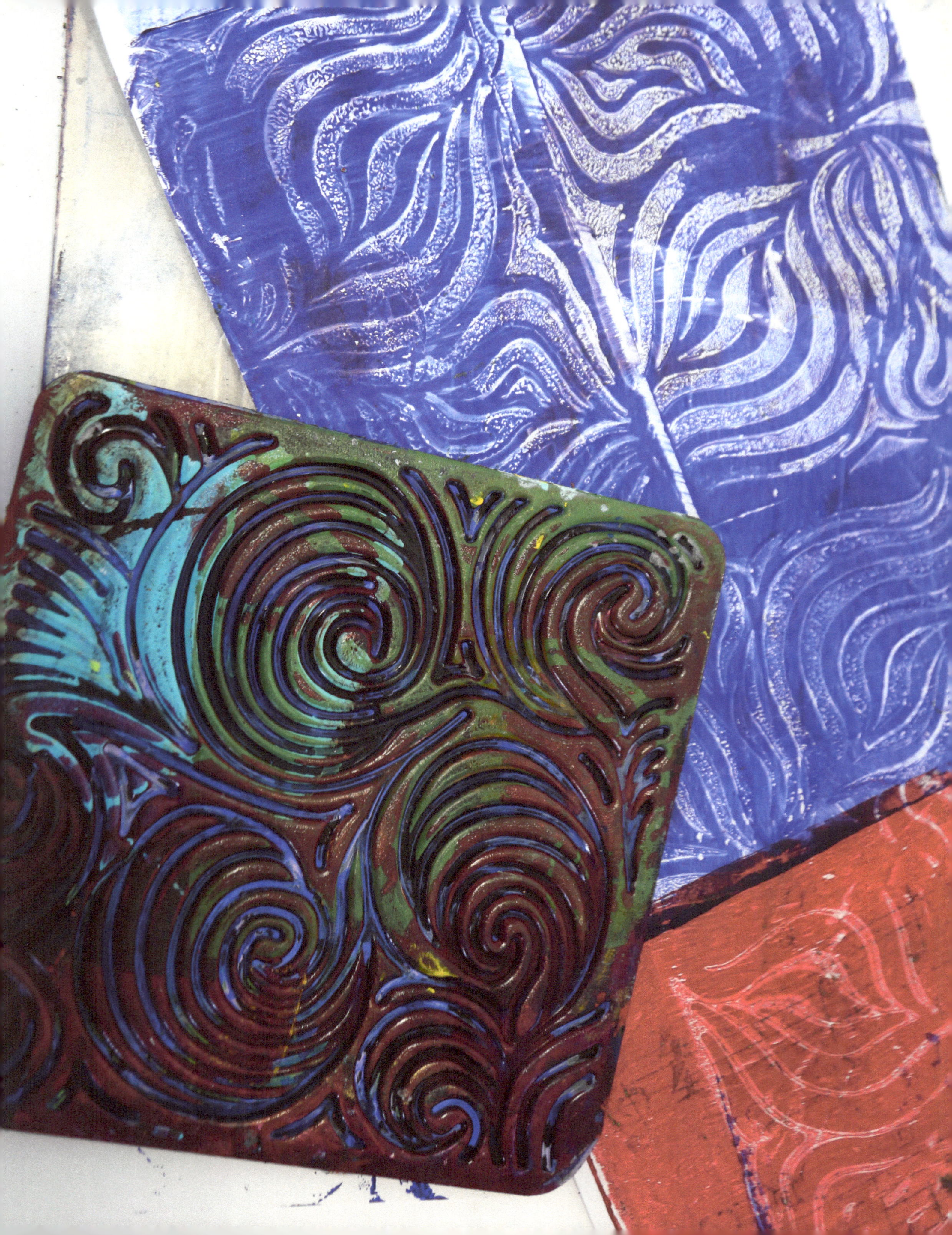

texture

plastic rubbing plates

There are many ways to apply texture to Gel Prints, commercially produced texture plates being just the beginning. Other elements that can be used include, the bottoms of shoes, the circle end of a paper towel roll, potato mashing tools, yoga mats, needle point mesh... The possibilities are endless. Look around you and start thinking about the everyday items in your life and how they would work when pressed into paint on the Gel Press printing plate. It's a whole new world.

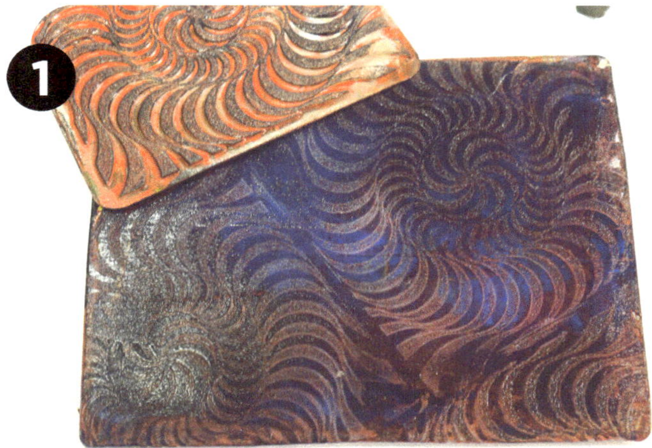

Press a clean, dry rubbing plate into a wet layer of paint to create a pattern by removing paint.

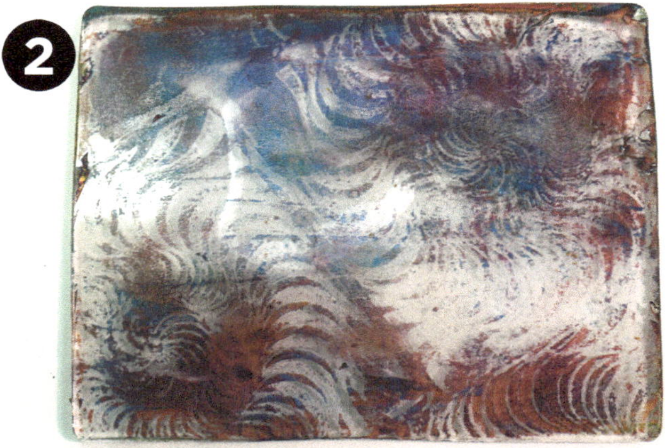

After the first print of the rubbing plate, let the residual paint dry on the plate.

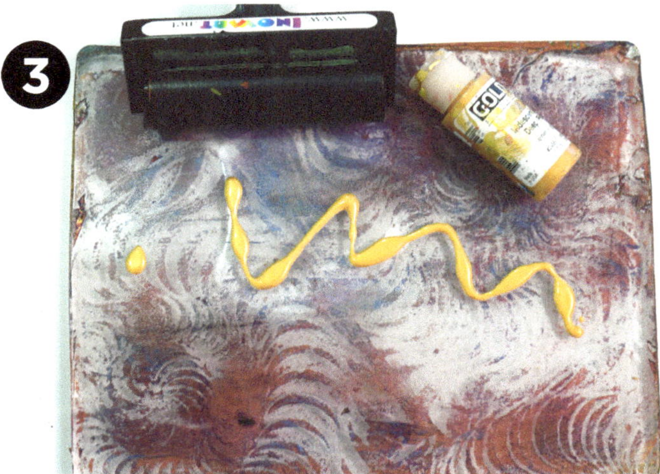

Apply a gold metallic over the residual paint.

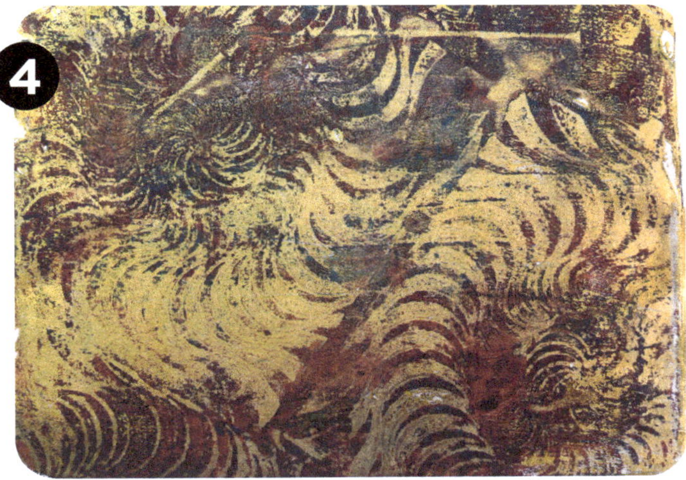

The gold metallic paint and the residual paint are pulled together to create one print, as shown here.

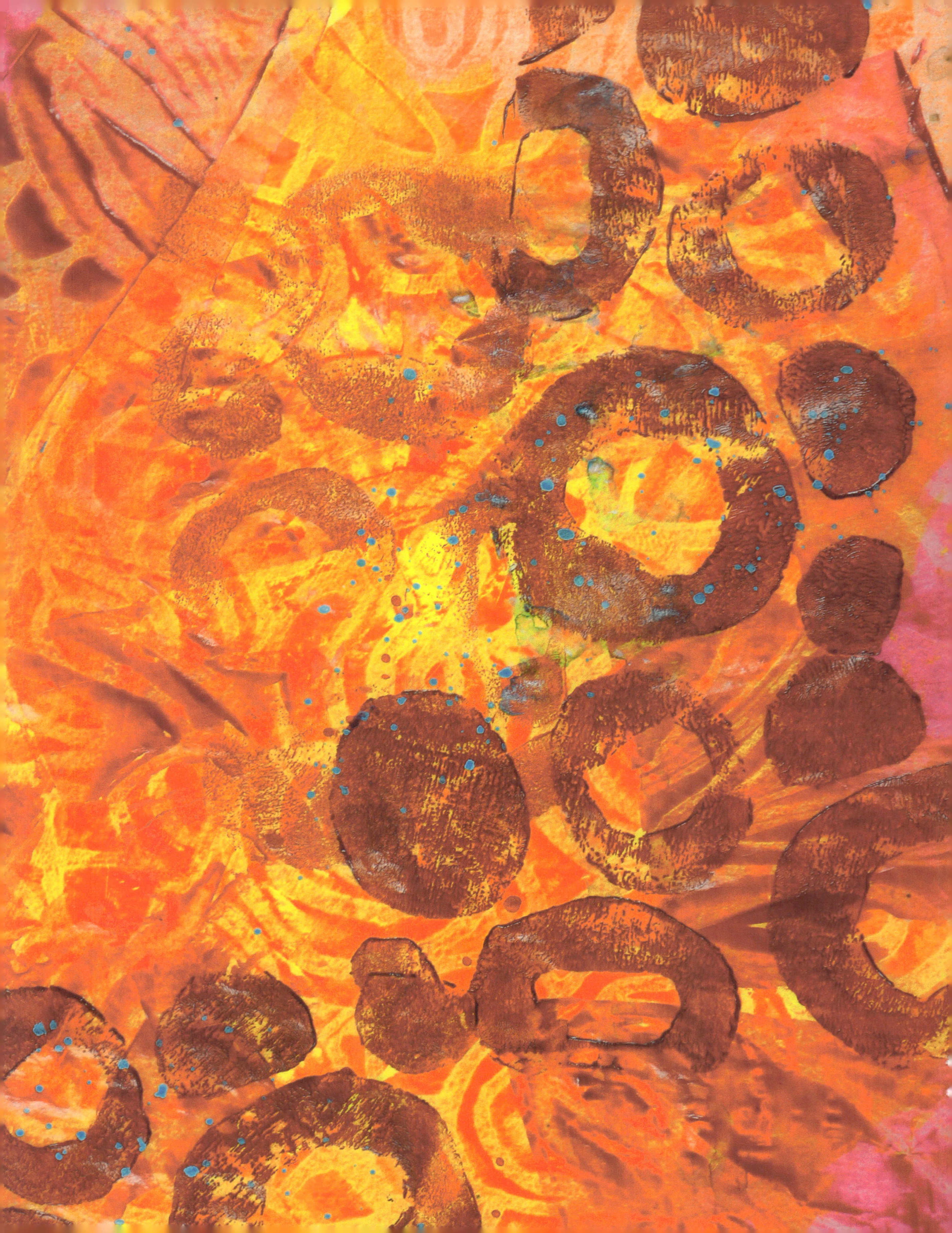

stamps

subtle subtraction

Hand-carved and commercially purchased stamps offer wonderful textures on the Gel Press printing plate. Pressing a stamp into the paint layer removes it subtly, revealing the pattern in a painterly impression. Overlapping and combining stamps with other effects offers more variety and interesting results.

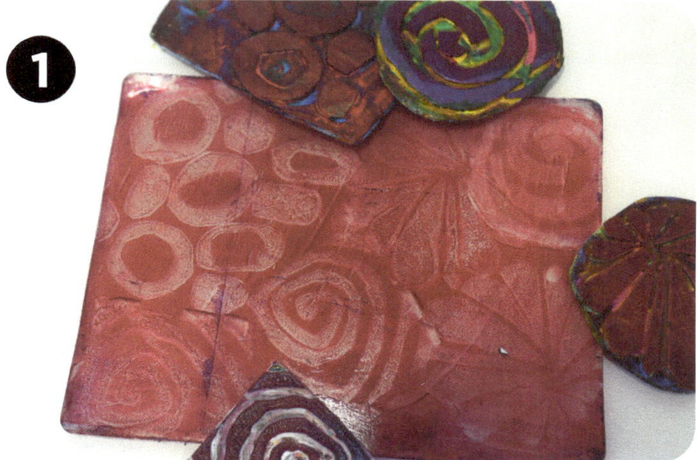

Removing paint with a clean, dry stamp pressed into it will create a subtle pattern on the plate.

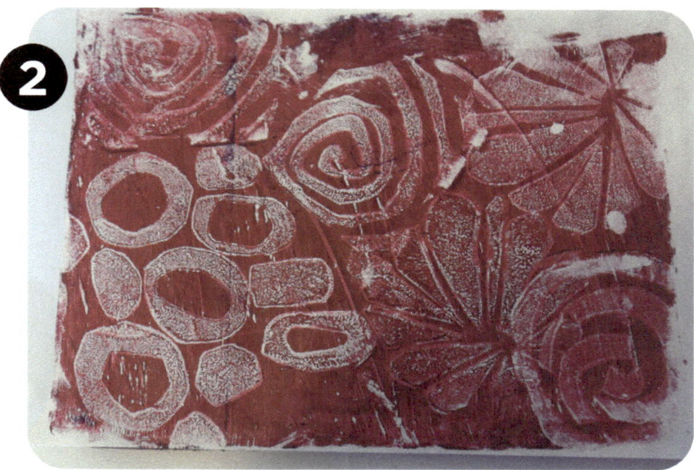

A print on white paper of the stamped plate.

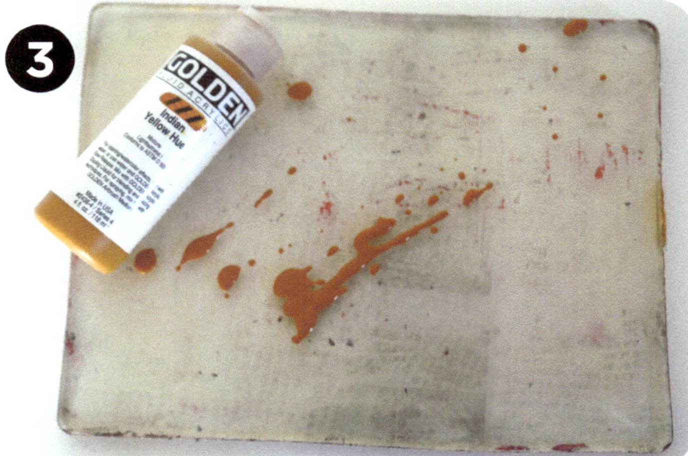

Set up the plate with a thin layer of light gold.

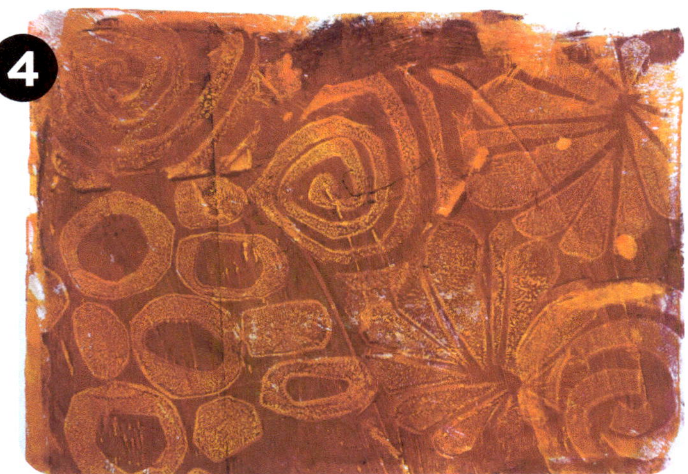

Overprint the light gold onto the pulled red print to tone down the whites.

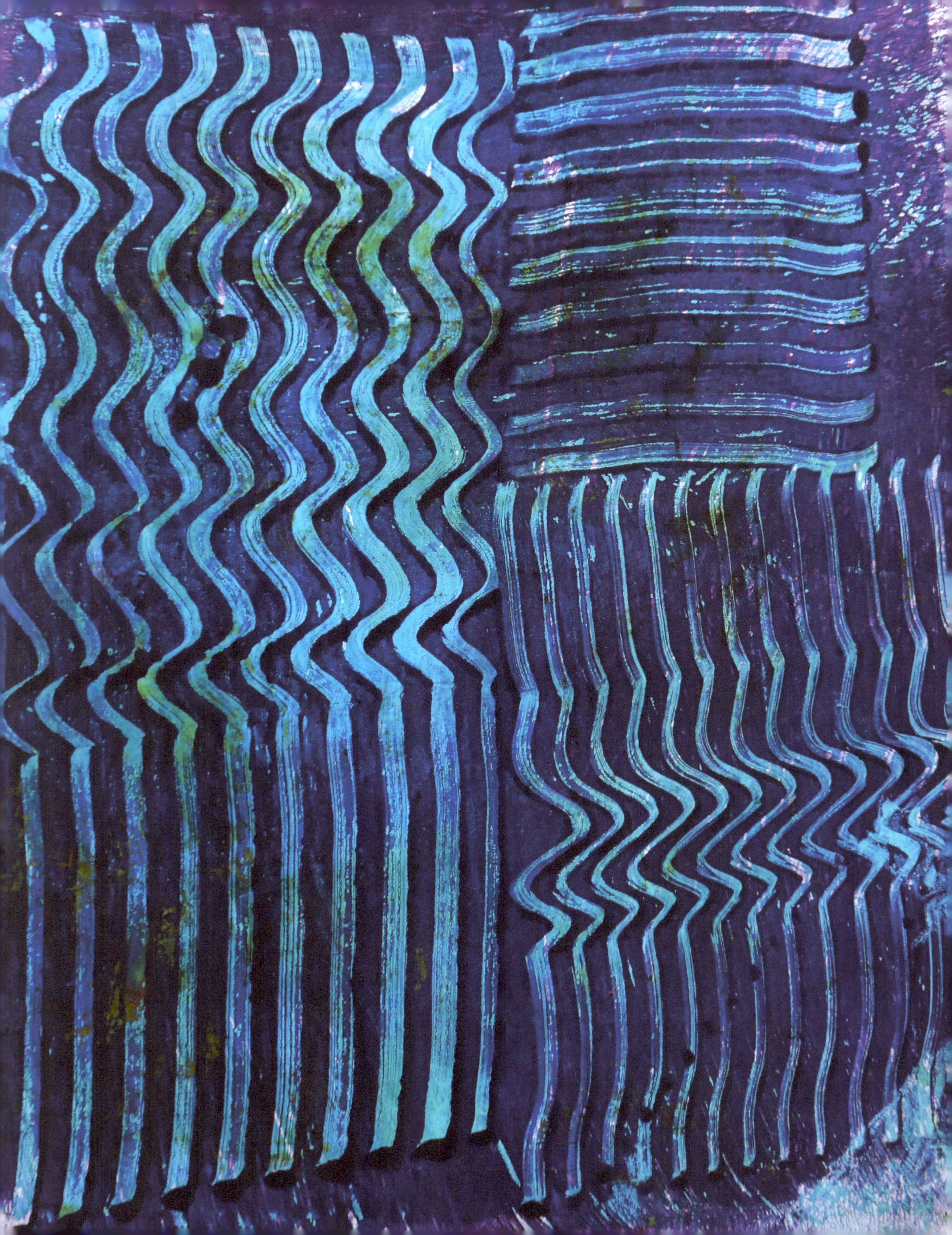

scrapers

catalyst wedges

Princeton makes a line of hand held wedge tools with teeth on two edges. They fit nicely in the palm of your hand and come in many different widths and patterns for scraping. The wedges work wonderfully on the Gel Press printing plate to scrape in straight, wiggle, zig zag or any combination of motions to create interesting patterns scraped out of (removing) the paint.

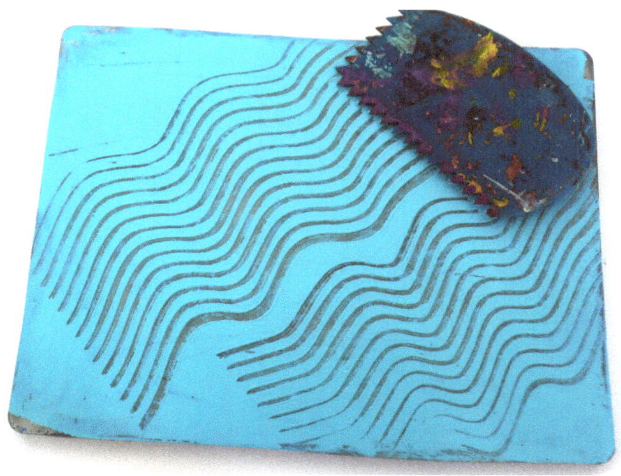

An examle of removing paint from the plate with the scrapers.

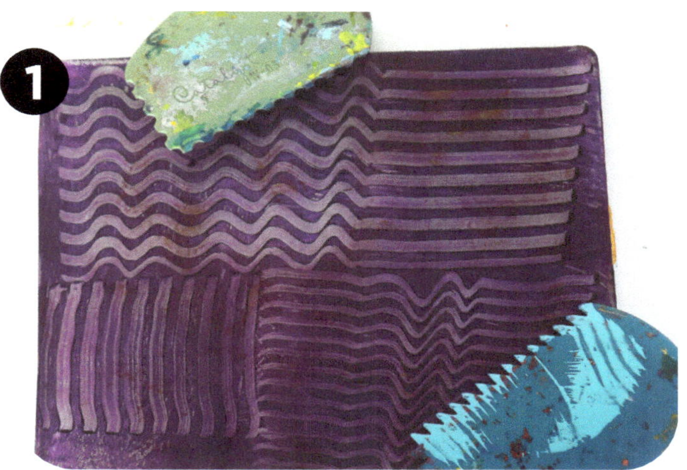

Apply a thin layer of paint with the brayer and scrape through the paint layer with the scrapers.

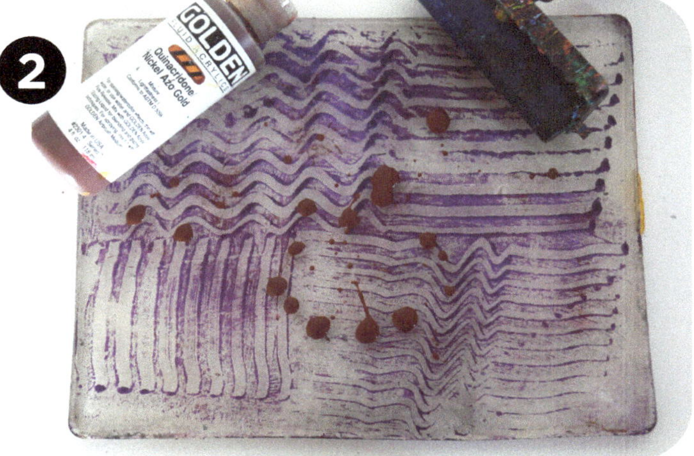

Apply a thin layer of light brown paint to the residual paint after pulling the first print.

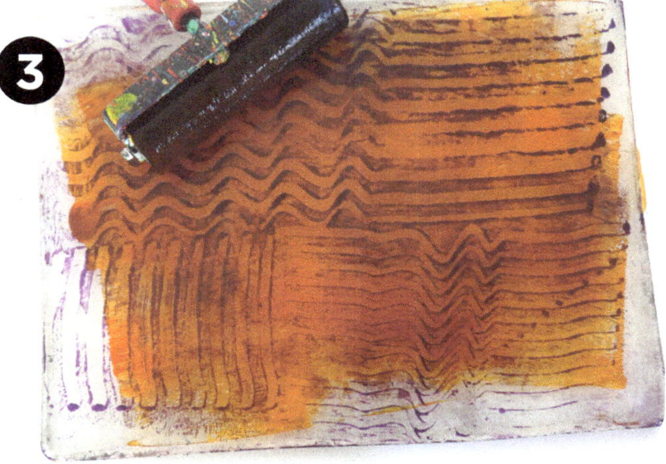

The brown paint and residual paint layer will pull off together for a subtle, painterly print.

... but in 1950 ... apartments were ava[ilable] ... for more people than in 1900 ... way, physical living in the 1950's ... than it had been half a century be[fore] ... was the despair? Was it because the 1950 ... fulfillment of prophecies made a cen[tury ago] ... that the end result of science and inven[tion] ... the machine's mastery over man and ... the very uniformity of every article that came to hand would take all the zest and variety out of life? That alone could not explain the despair, because ... labor-saving devices, food, clothing, and ... are merely tools with which life is lived. Rem[brandt]'s paint brushes could not have ... in kind from El Greco's or Pic[asso's] ... with these very similar too[ls] ... painters portrayed very different ... Elear and Germany ... welcome ... highly ... in his own badge. Uniform[ity] ... for uniformity in product ... in humankind.

... in America in the ... years of the century? Was ... individualist his grand[father] ... had been?

A lot of companies in my industry were started in ... years of the century as one man's ... said corporation president to Frederick Lewis Allen in 1952, "There was a fellow with an idea and some ... and the business was ... business ... the thing grew, and in the ... was uppermost and this man ... salesman. Later we began to see ... and a research man, or a ... man, would get the no[tion] ... become so complicated that ... special[ists] ... need is a team of people each ... one or more of these various special[ties] ... and the ... thing required of the head fellow is that ... be able to keep this team working as a well-balan[ced] ... He's got ... be a good captain ... the team. As chairman, i don[']t pretend really to know what the research people are ... it's my job to keep them going ... harmonious bal[ance] ... the rest of the outfit."

... this stress on the ... would have been puzzling ... individual A[merican busi]nessman at the turn of ... century, but i[t had] become so much ... order of thi[ngs] ... part of study ... sociologists, a ... told the story ...

... American ... how he lived, dressed ... mar[ried] ... black ... and part of ... american adult ... adult ... payroll of ... passion and highly sensitive to ... what the shop' thought about him.

According to David Riesman's study, *The Lonely Crowd*, the 1900 man was being replaced by another ... who was better suited to "a society in which the [pr]oblems not only of mere subsistence, but ... of [large]-scale industrial organization and produc[tion] [ha]ve been for the most part surmounted." The 1950 [mo]del, was the man trained to get along with the [group], who knew what the group expected and [w]anted. His values were the group's values, his goals [w]ere the group's goals. The voice that directed him [c]ame not from himself but from others—he was an 'other-[directed]' ...

Adult work[ing American]s were used to the idea of ... to being a ... ... would be no black mark against him ... [when the time] came for him to advance one step upward. Adult work-ing Americans had become hierarchy-conscious to an extent that far surpassed the old simple classification of "rich, poor, and middle class." And in this hierarchy-consciousness, the only kind of diversity that was ab-solutely safe was a diversity just like everyone else's diversity.

Was this new personality pattern the result of a brilliant plot hatched by diabolical ... of the giant corporations? A ... such a ... ment is not to the interest of ... group that ... to draw upon its ranks for its leadership. In one ... view, after the ... person heads returned to ... magazine that they ... ... dispensation. Certainly ... ... work along with another, but ... ... the time he's got to be himself, too ... ... the man is a self-deprived man ... ... being ... want and need intervals of fee[ling] ... powerful." wrote Margaret Halsey ... at Home. "They want and need power over ... ... government ... power to develop their talents ... ... direction those talents want to go. But ... ...'s magnificent conquests of Nature ... ... the mid-century American has not got ... of personal power."

... characteristically and traditionally would ... the reason for the feeling of despair ... neither science nor invent[ion] ...

leaves

positive and negative

Freshly picked leaves make lovely masks and positive prints. In Florida we have some HUGE leaves, but a combination of small and medium leaves work just as nicely. Experiment with different types, ferns always offer very interesting shapes.

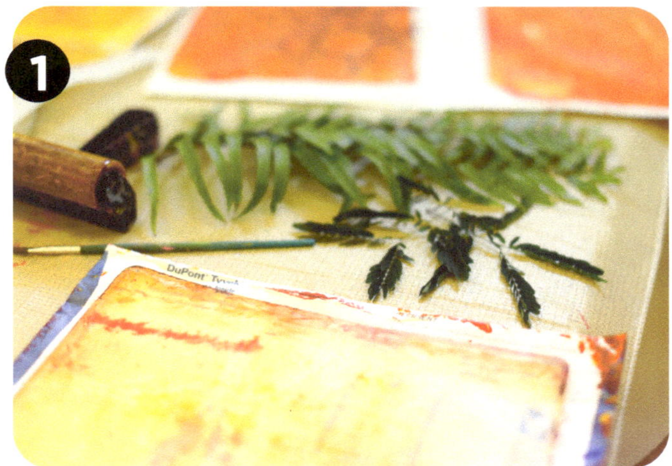

Leaves work beautiful on the gel plate, start with a light colored solid sheet

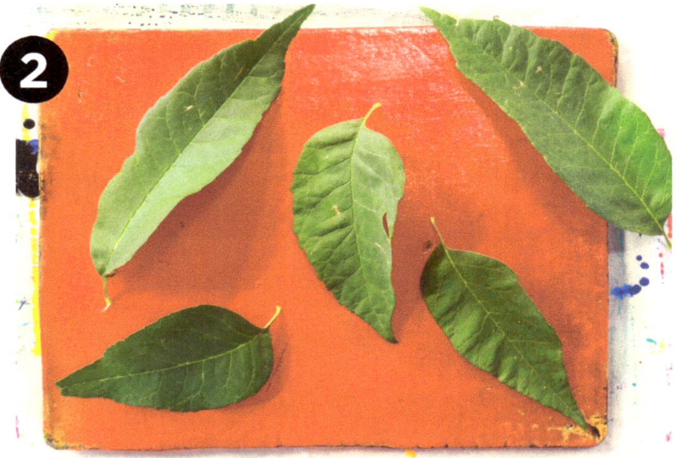

Lay the leaves vein side down into the paint

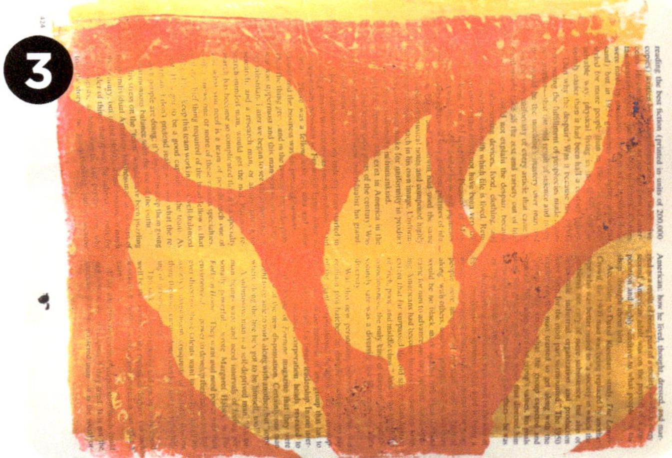

The first leaf layer in orange working over the pre-printed light yellow base layer.

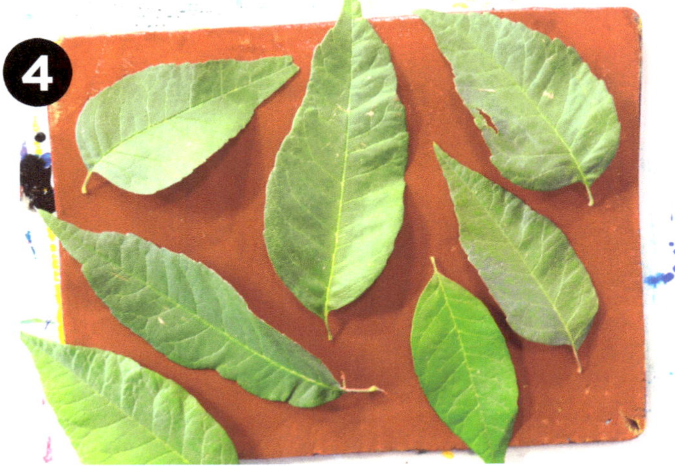

Change the position of the leaves on a slightly darker paint and reprint over the first leaf layer (left).

... that in 1868 Janssen ... hydrogen in the ... a "filler" that ... gen and so ... layer from ...

... the ... an opaque ... with a narrow open... ide enough ... the one red hydrogen line ... contained ... the sun's spectrum. If the en- ... were sl... moved across the rim of the ... would ... only the portions of the ... across which the spectroscope was ... spectroscope oscillated rapidly back ... image would appear continuous; and ... would be seeing the entire form of the ...

... Hale had entered MIT, his father ... spectroscopic laboratory ... taught himself ... and housed it in a ... complete library ... observatory ... -two ... just put off ... ly in 1890 ... set to work ... on his new com... solar explor... married that ... in the spring ... year began his active work with the spec- ... On May 7, 1891, he made his first suc... otographs of the solar flames, and went on ... in addition ... hydrogen, the flam... ... improve... his wife ...

... markab... ... to be closely connected ... other photographs enabled him to ... analyses of these darker portions that ... from deeper levels of the sun ... en, the University of Chicago was founded at ...

... on form ... on ... to complete the pu... University of Chicago ... tation, he was able to appeal to several ... nessmen for their support. ... traction magnate who dickered ... the basis for Theodore Dreiser's novel ... agreed to ... in the money. No provision was ... either ... other equipment to house th... ... staff. Nevertheless, Hale se... ... took on the responsibility ... funds ... ... the dono... also ... and physicist ... ... out of his ... ... came world fam... by ... raise funds ... an enor... was essentially a ... retiring man ...

Hale's oldest ... suffered from re- peated attacks ... and then to be ... taken ... the murder ... Pasadena ...

leaves

positive and negative

Freshly picked leaves make lovely masks and positive prints. In Florida we have some HUGE leaves, but a combination of small and medium leaves work just as nicely. Experiment with different types, ferns always offer very interesting shapes.

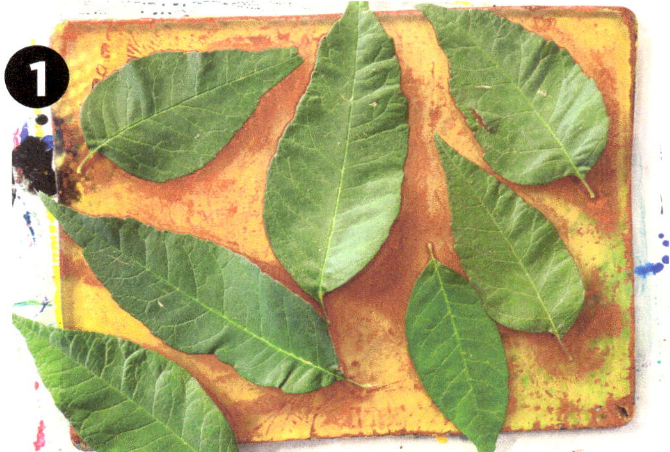

The leaves have trapped paint underneath after the first print is pulled.

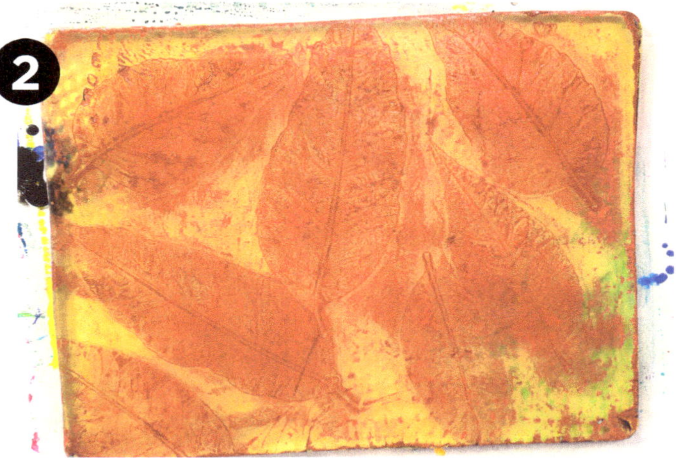

Gently removed the leaves to reveal the ghost print with excellent vein patterns.

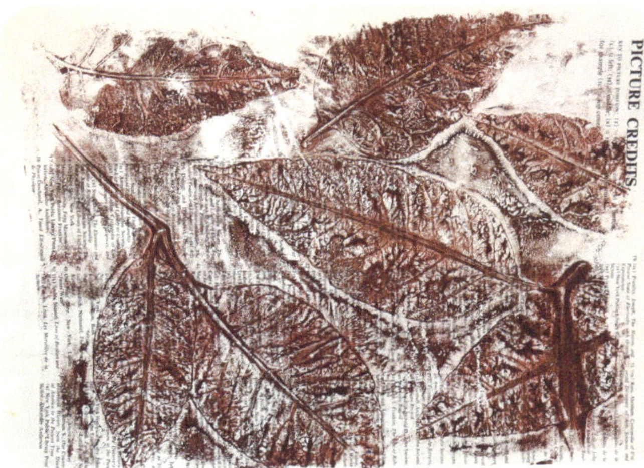

Example of a positive leaf print with trapped paint

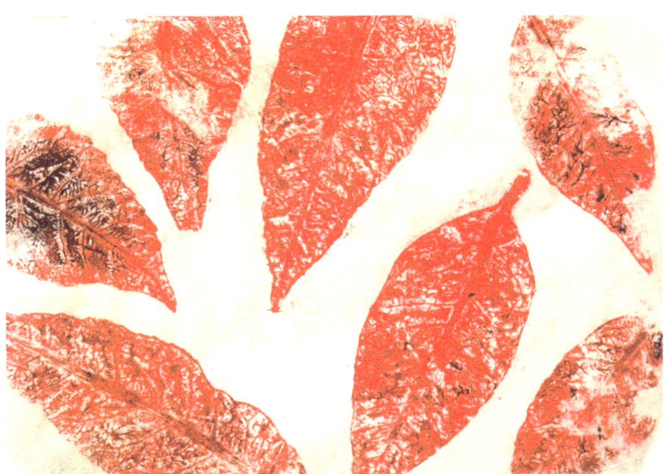

Example of a positive leaf print with trapped paint

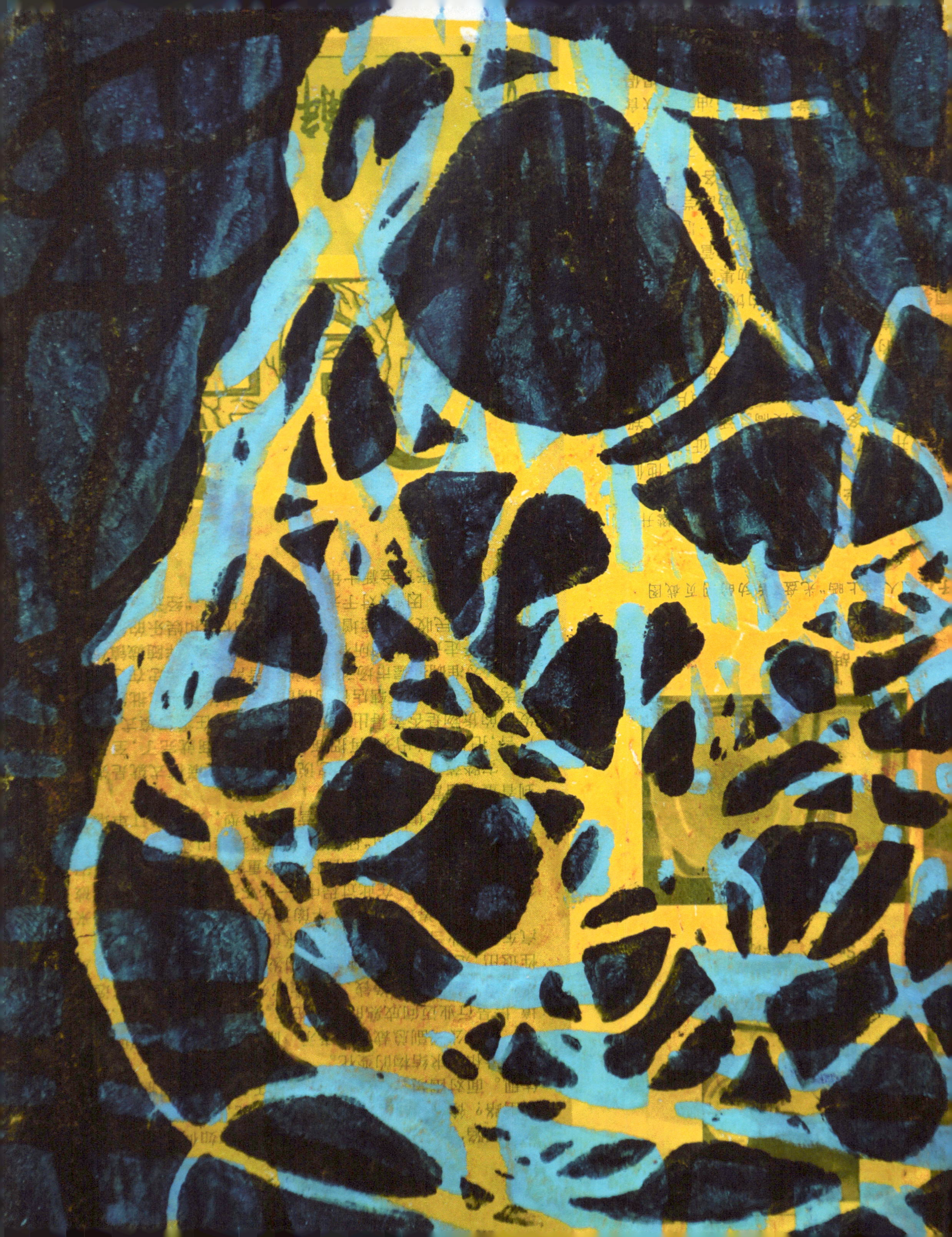

found objects

jute string and layering

A look around your home might reveal some wonderful objects for patterning on the Gel Press Plate. Here I am playing with jute string and taking advantage of adding it on top of some previous printed, lighter layers as well as using the ghost print from it to add on top of another light colored solid layer. Sometimes the most creative art materials are found outside the art supply store.

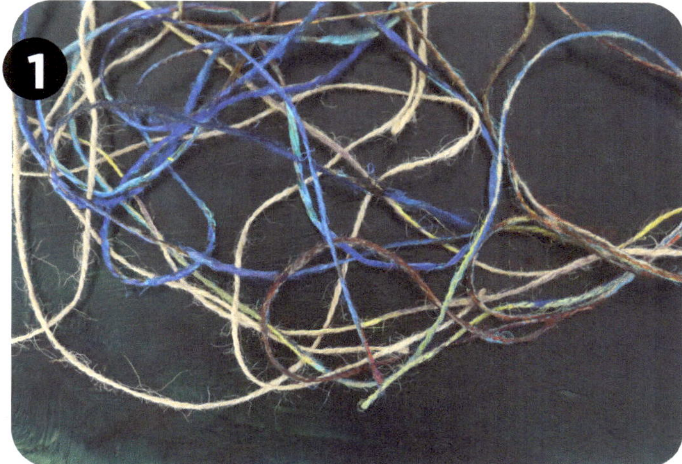

Jute string has a slightly fuzzy edge, it's thin enough to yield detailed line patterns.

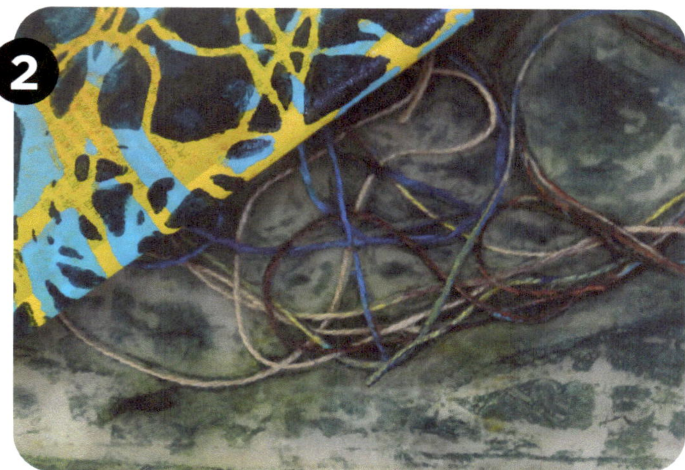

Pulling a print of the string on top of a prepared sheet.

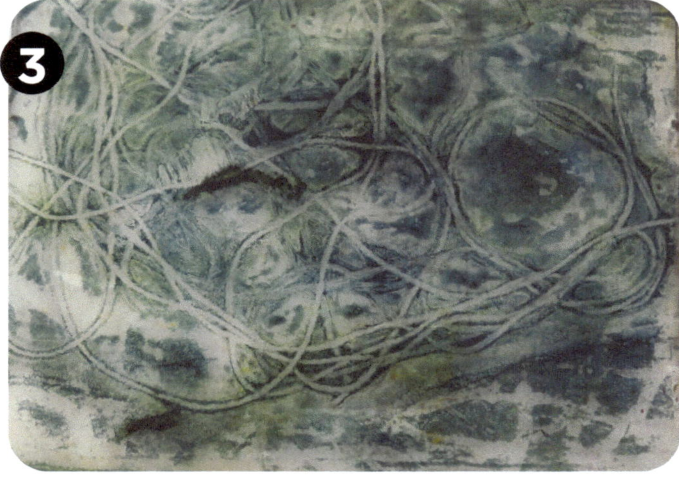

The ghost print after the first print is pulled, and the string is removed from the plate.

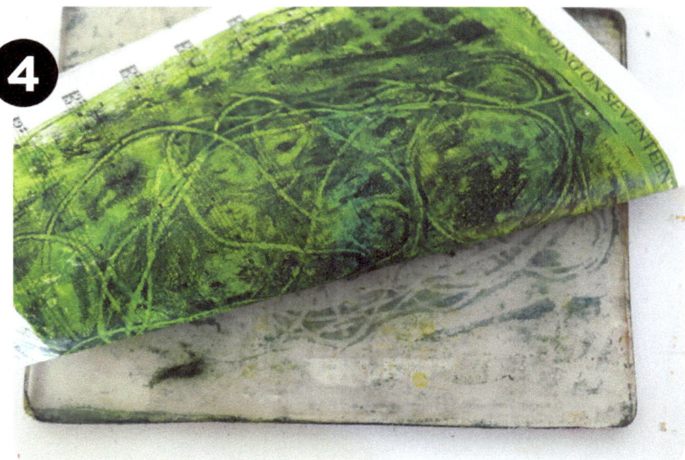

The ghost print applied over a light colored solid that was ready and waiting in the wings.

gel plate
found objects

mark making and imprinting patterns

Marks can be made in the plate from any blunt object. I like to try writing with the eraser tip of a pencil, the end of my paint brush, a credit card corner, or my finger. All of the marks you make into the paint will transfer to the print when you press it into the paper, some more subtle than others. There are many interesting patterns in unusual places, like the bottom of your shoes, tile samples, jar lids, flip flops, and plastic containers. Think beyond the commercial art supply rubbing plate, the possibilities are endless!

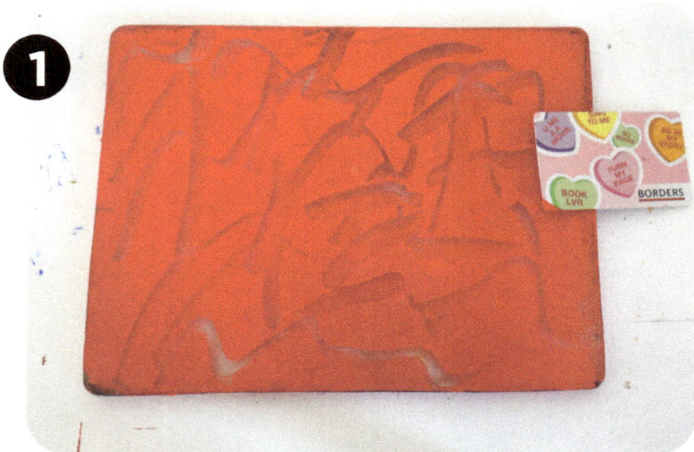

Using the corner of a gift card to make marks.

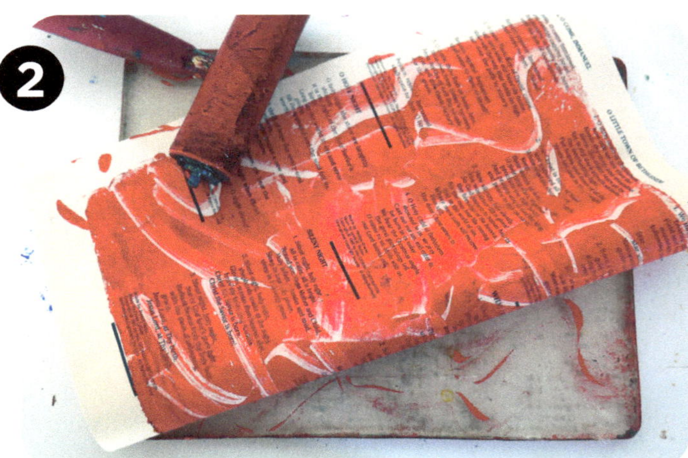

Pulling the print from the gift card pattern.

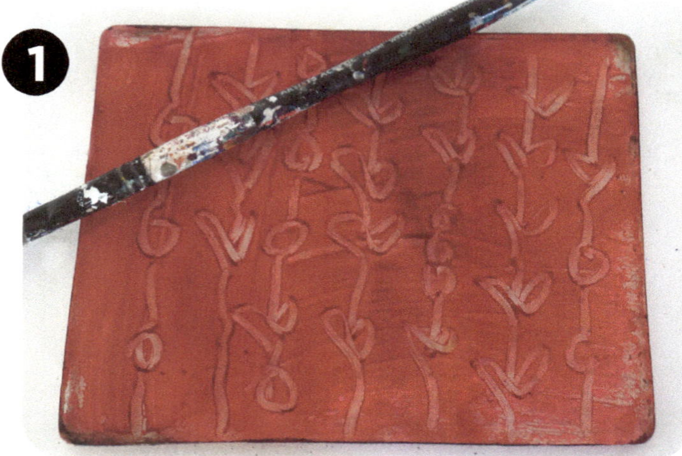

Drawing into the paint on the plate with the end of a paintbrush can yield spontaneous patterns.

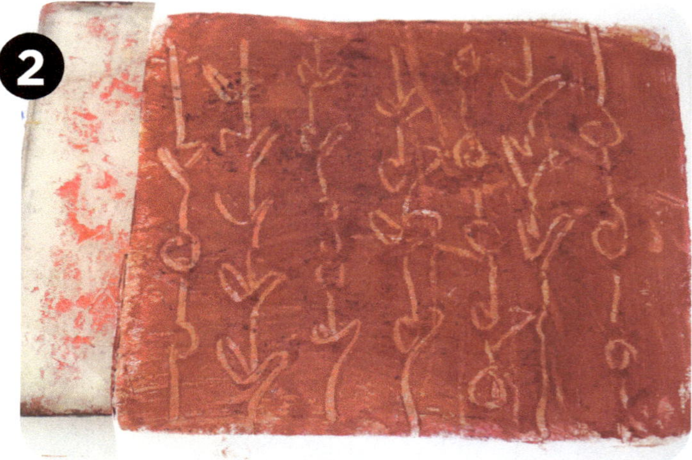

The print from the paintbrush marks. Note that the print is the mirror image of what is on the plate. Something to remember when writing letters.

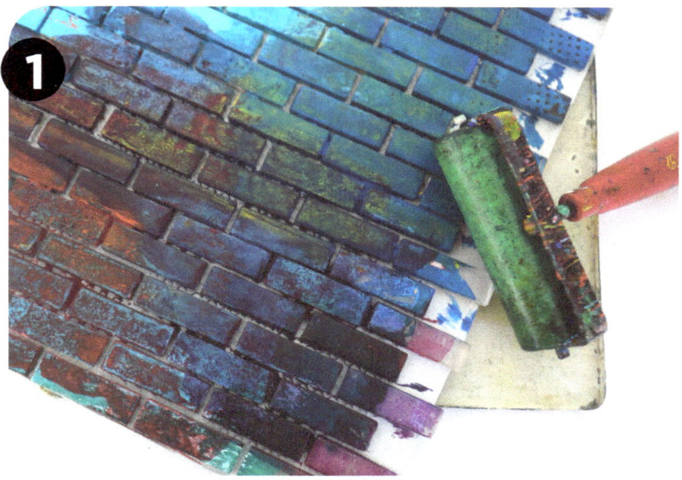

Tile samples from the hardware store in 12x12 sheets come in many different patterns.

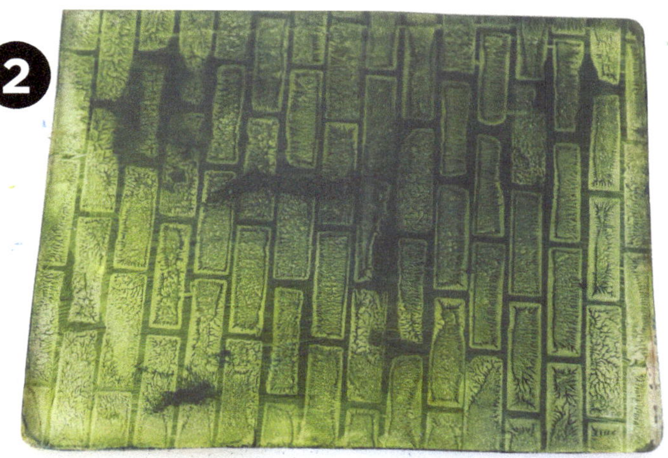

Tile can press into the paint on the plate to create subtle patterning.

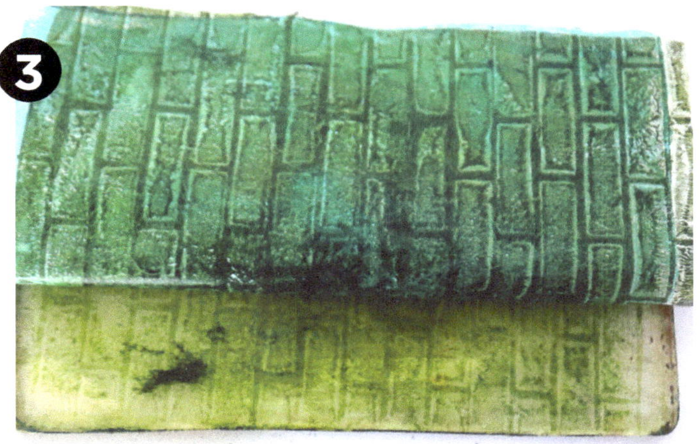

The print over a prepared light colored solid gives a two-tone subtle tile pattern.

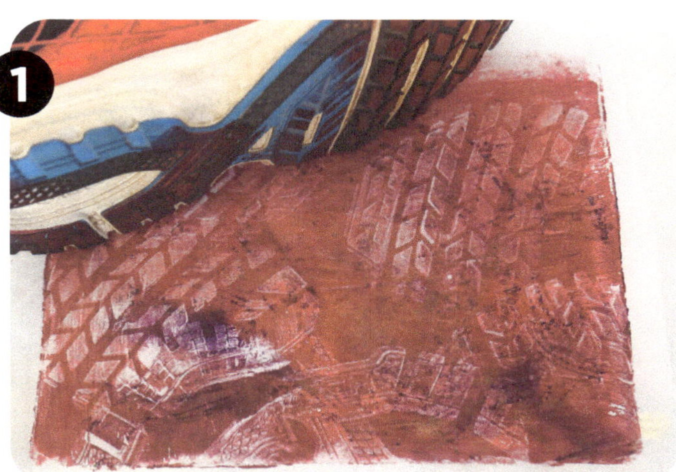

The pattern from the sole of my running shoe.

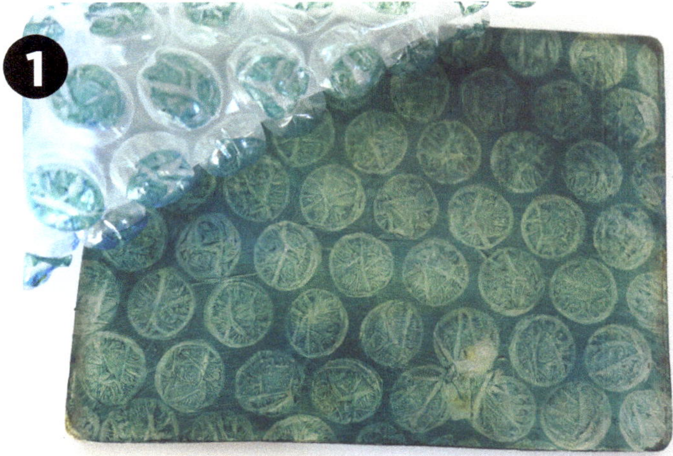

Bubble wrap from packaging comes in different sizes.

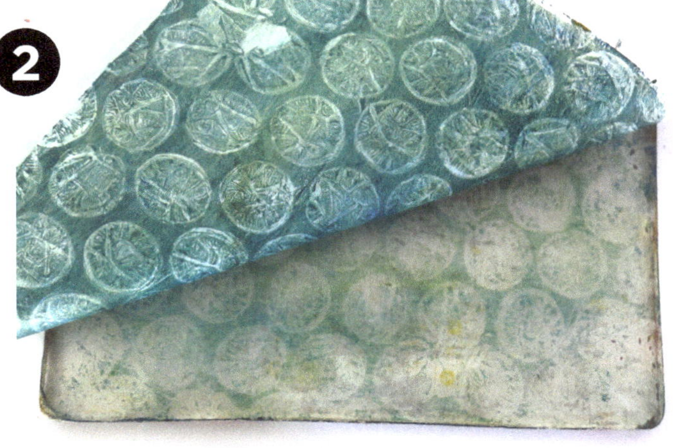

The print over a prepared light colored solid gives a two-tone subtle bubble pattern.

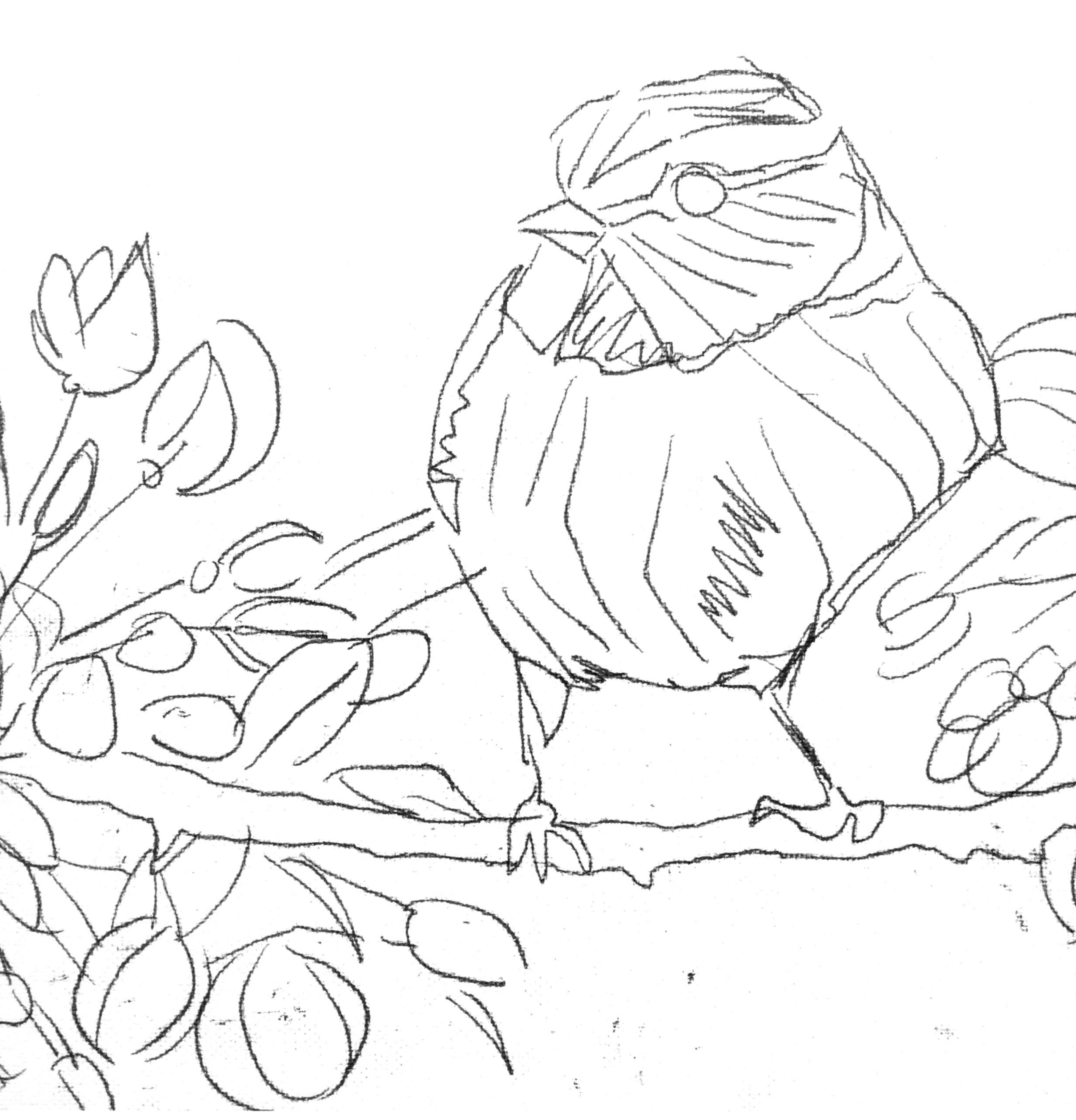

START
with a sketch

transfering your image

I always start with a pencil sketch before I begin painting. If you are not confident in your drawing skills you may use graphite transfer paper (shiny side down) underneath your sized-up reference image and basically *trace* your photo with a ball point pen. The graphite transfer paper works like old fashioned carbon paper... It transfers graphite to the substrate from the pressure of your pen! These marks can be erased and edited if needed.

Secure the reference image and the transfer paper with tape at the top so that it does not shift out of alignment. Lift the corner every now and then, to be sure you have not missed any areas of your sketch. My sketch (left) gives me all the info I need to make a good painting

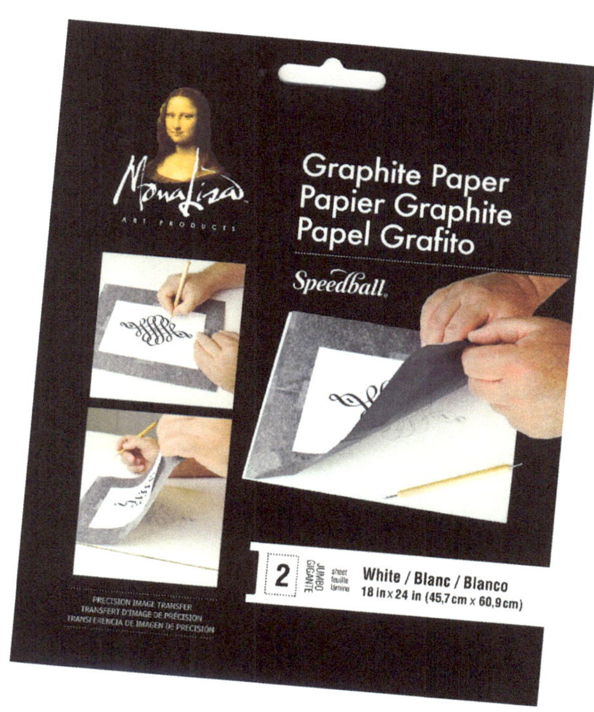

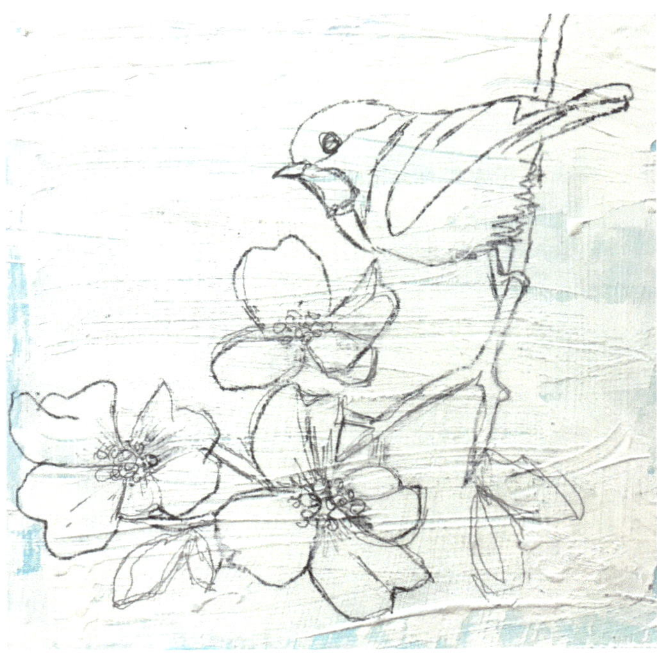

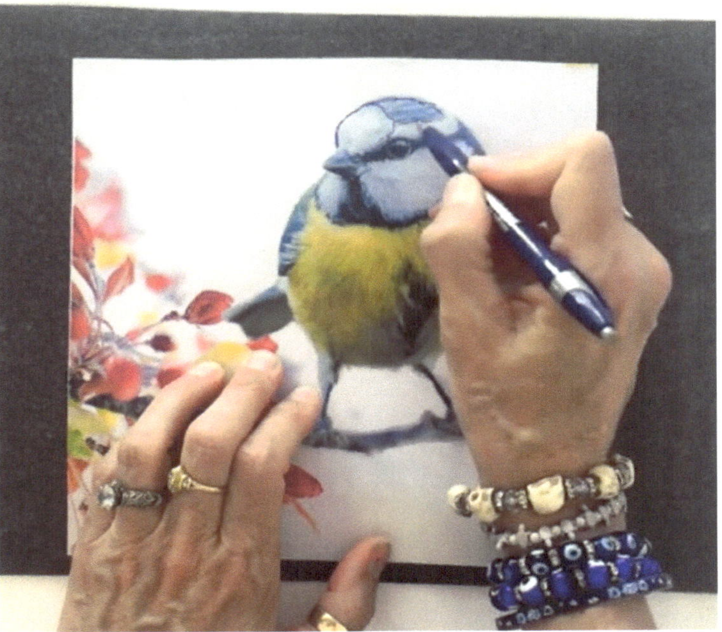

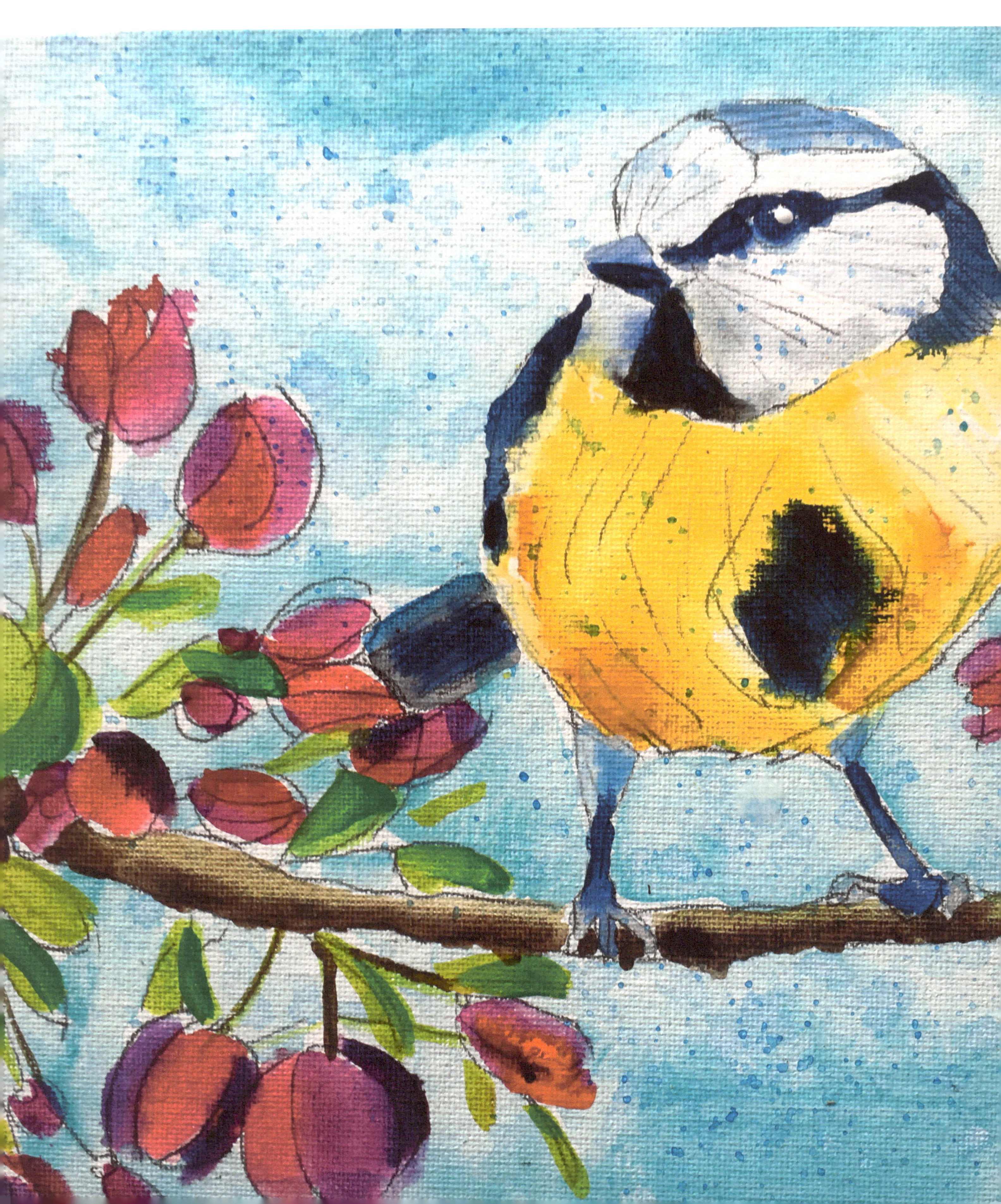

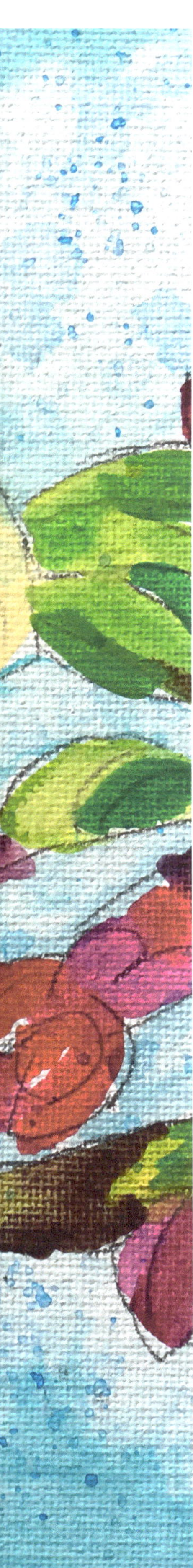

PAINT
your sketch

After the sketch comes the under painting, this painting should not be ultra detailed. I use the under painting process for two reasons: 1) I like to block in all my colors so that when I apply the paper over the top, if any spaces are left between bits of paper, the color of the painting is there, rather than the color of the canvas. 2) It is in the under painting process that I work out my values, what is light, dark, and medium tone. I also work out my colors. It's much easier and quicker to work out these challenges with paint than to have to work and rework the collage. Once I get the values and colors to my liking, I allow the painting dry completely.

I use Fluid Acrylics and Full Body Acrylics for the under painting. When I do drippy, splattered backgrounds, I use strictly Fluid Acrylics thinned with water, or Acrylic Gloss Medium. Sometimes, when working on wood, I like leaving the striation and grain showing through these drippy areas. When letting the wood show through it must first be primed with a clear product such as Golden GAC-100. Typically I'll either leave it natural tone, or stain it with a diluted fluid acrylic.

Don't spend tons of time laboring over your under painting – Do use it as an exercise to help you determine where your values are and what colors you will use in your collage. Be sure you have good shading, lights and darks, highlights and shadows.

I tell my students, *"Don't fall in love with your under painting!"* Do not take this to a level of finish detail that you love so much, you will not want to apply collage over the top.

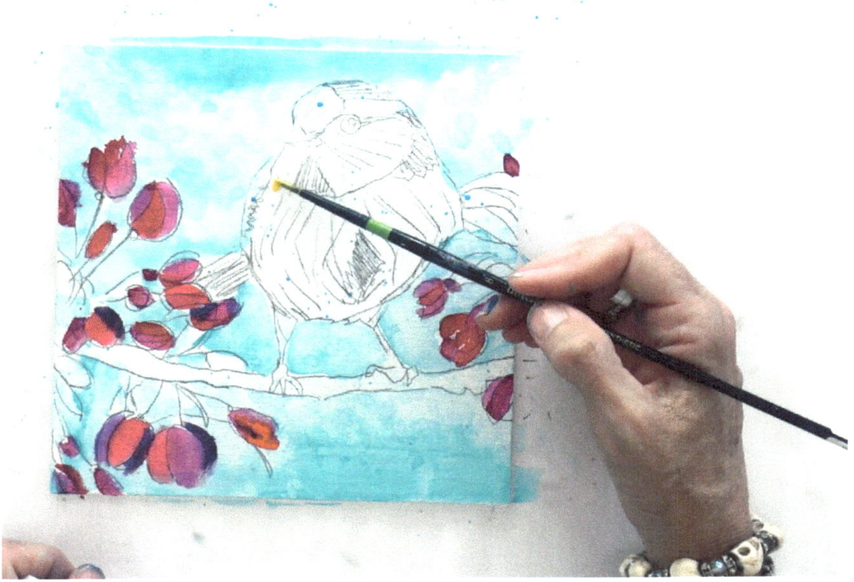

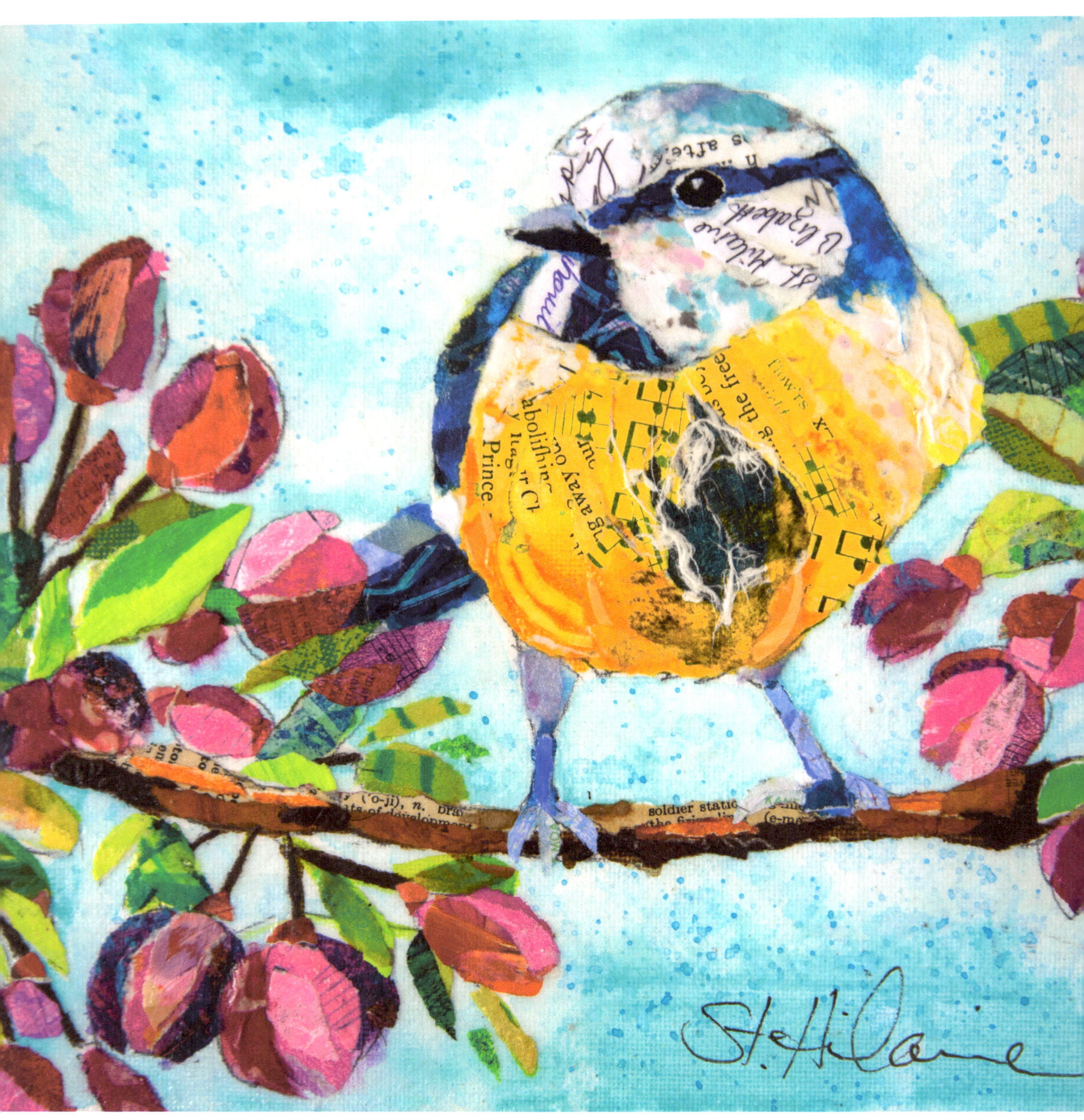

"Chickadee" Shading is very important to give the bird a 3-D feeling. Darker yellow at the bottom of the belly, lighter blue at the top of the head. The top of the branch is lighter than the bottom, and the flowers and leaves have a variety of lights and darks as well.

COLLAGE
application

My pieces of paper are torn, I never cut with scissors. I treat each piece of paper as a *brush mark*, therefore I do not want any hard edges. Even when I collage small birds, I create the pupil with a teeny piece of torn black paper, I even tear the highlight!

Consider making your shapes end organically, rather than having them cut off ubruptly like a piece of tape. An organic end that trails off naturally will visually flow into the next piece—just like a brush mark. We are painting with paper, so you want to follow the shapes, sizes, and direction of marks that you intuitively created in your underpainting.

I apply the glue to the board, place the torn paper into the glue, and apply more glue over top with pressure from the brush to make the paper lay down nice and flat.

Follow your underpainting in color and value, hold up your papers and be sure they are the right match before tearing and gluing them down, I call this *auditioning*. Once you start auditioning, you may find that you do not have enough colors or values in your paper palette, becuase someone once said…"You can never have enough paper!"

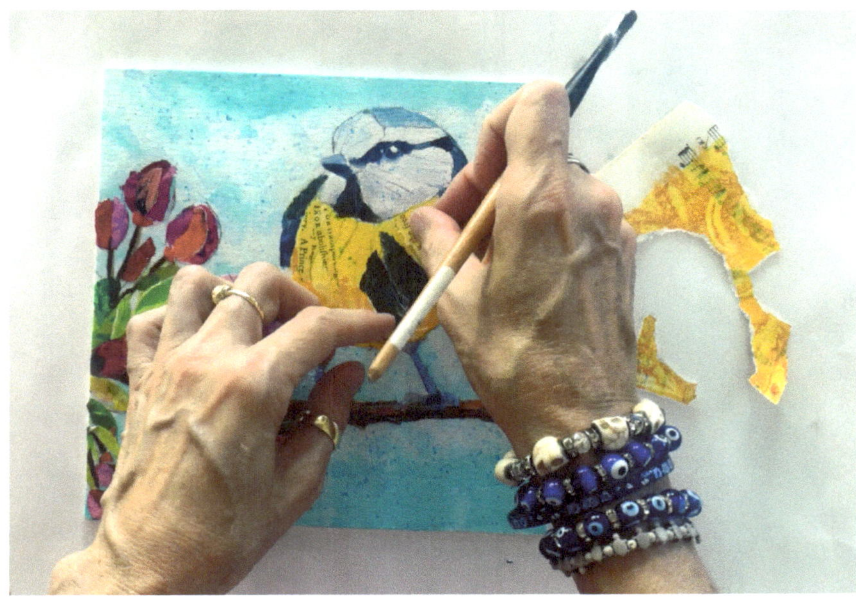

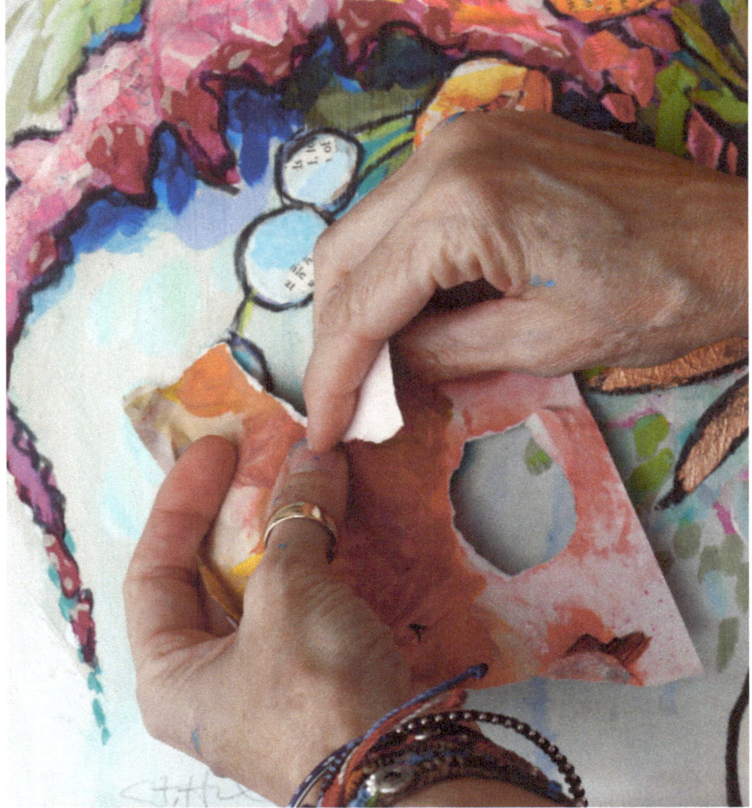

Eliminating and embracing white edges with tearing techniques takes a little bit of practice. Pulling the paper up toward yourself with your dominant hand eliminates white edges.

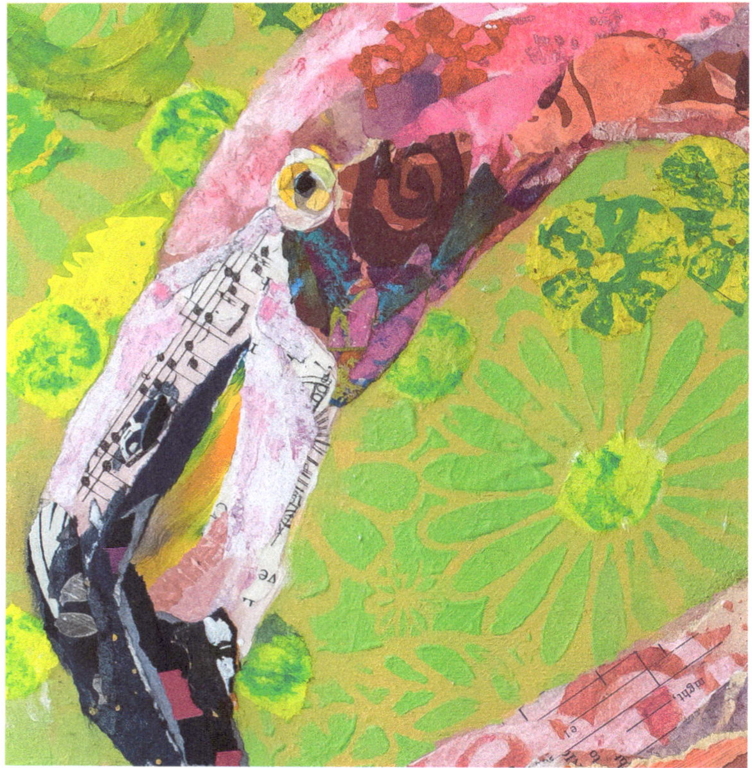

A bold pattern needs to go in the same direction as your brush marks, here you see the sheet music lines go down the length of the beak

eliminating white edges

1 Pull up, with your dominant hand, toward you to create the shape that you want

2 The white edges will be left on piece of paper in your non dominant hand

embracing white edges

1 Consider using the white edge of a paper for the seam between the top and bottom of the beak

2 Consider using the white edge of a paper for the rim around a tiny black bird eye

3. To achieve a white edge, turn your paper colored side down and follow the same steps from above

no scissors!

Every tear of paper represents a brush stroke in a Paper Painting, for this reason, we do not use scissors which would create hard edges that are not consistent with a painterly effect

directional patterning

1 Sheet music lines need to follow the form of the subject

2 Type and text needs to follow the form of the subject

3 Patterns need to follow the form of the subject

simple shapes

Suggesting vs Precisely Rendering

Breaking down forms into simple shapes is the best way to work in an impressionistic medium. Simple shapes give the eye enough information to make the visual connection, you don't need to render every feather on the wing, you can simplify it and suggest feathers with a pattern in the paper.

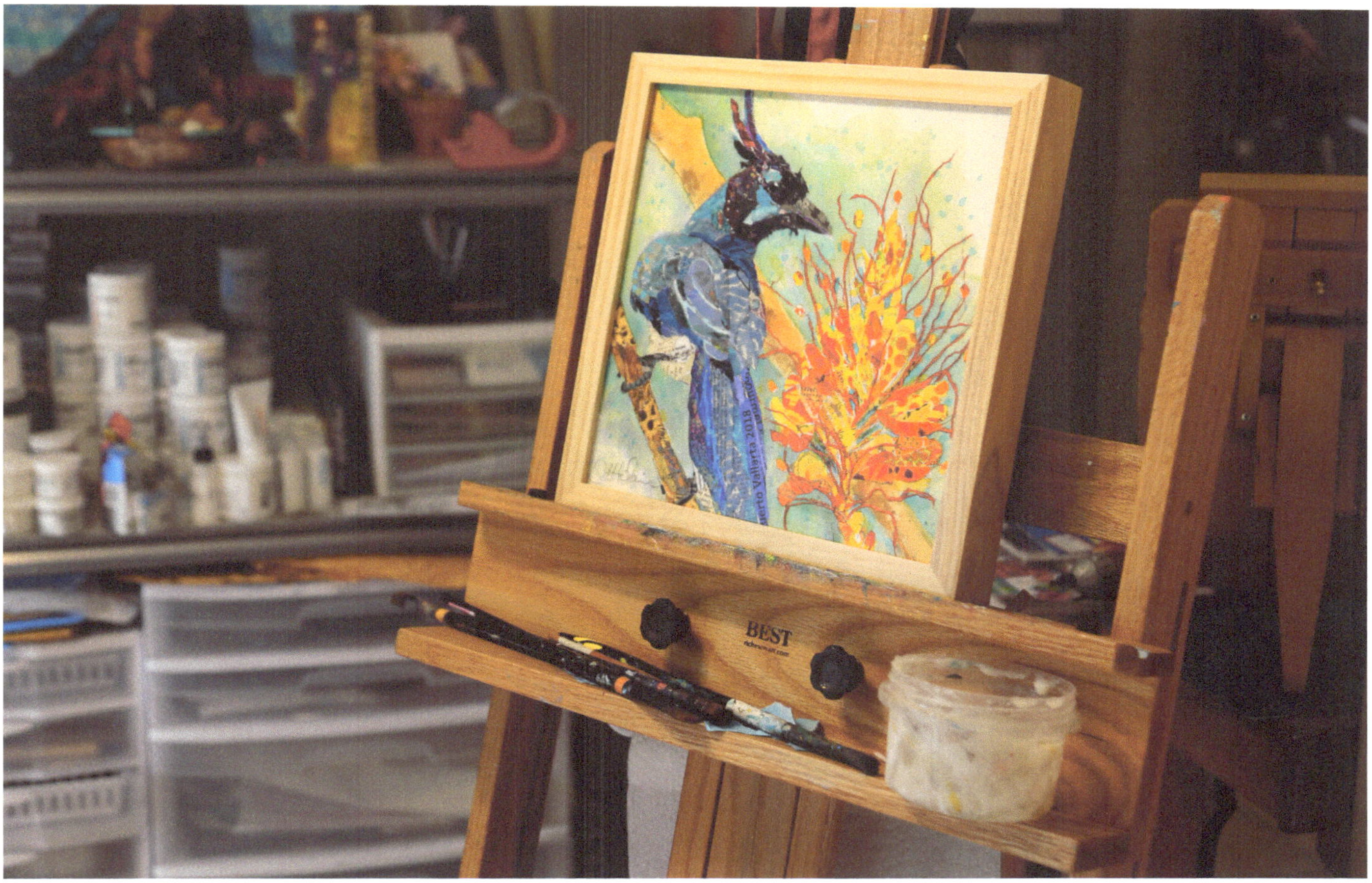

I work at an easel so that I can step back and evaluate my progress from a distance throughout the creative process.

applying the glue

1 Apply a thin layer of glue to the board
with a 1-inch filbert style brush

2 Place paper, one piece at a time into the glue

3 Press the paper down with the glue brush, applying
enough pressure to get the paper to lie flat, and applying
a thin layer of glue over the paper at the same time

4 Bring the glue in from all sides of the piece of paper,
making sure there are no loose edges

5 Examine the art to be sure there are no erroneous
lumps of glue, it dries hard and is not removable

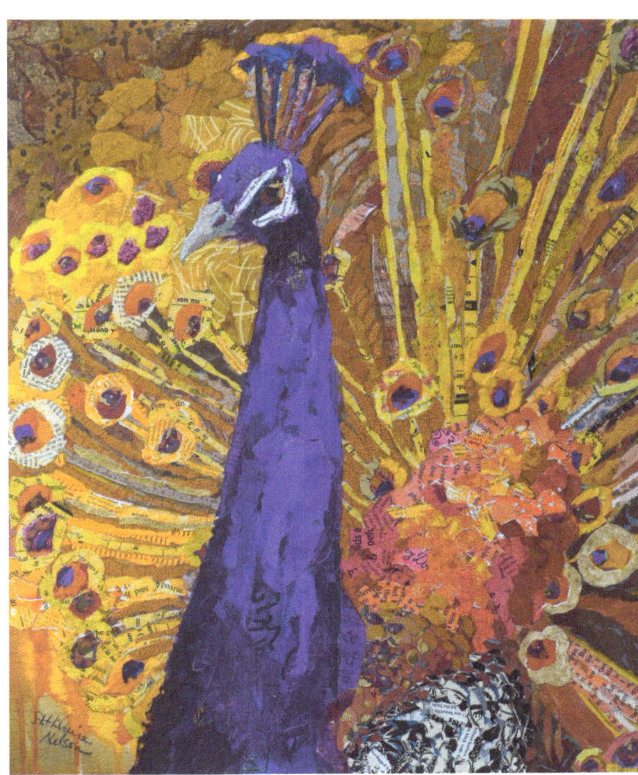

*Simplify the shapes to give the impression of feathers versus
trying to render every single swish of a peacock's tail.*

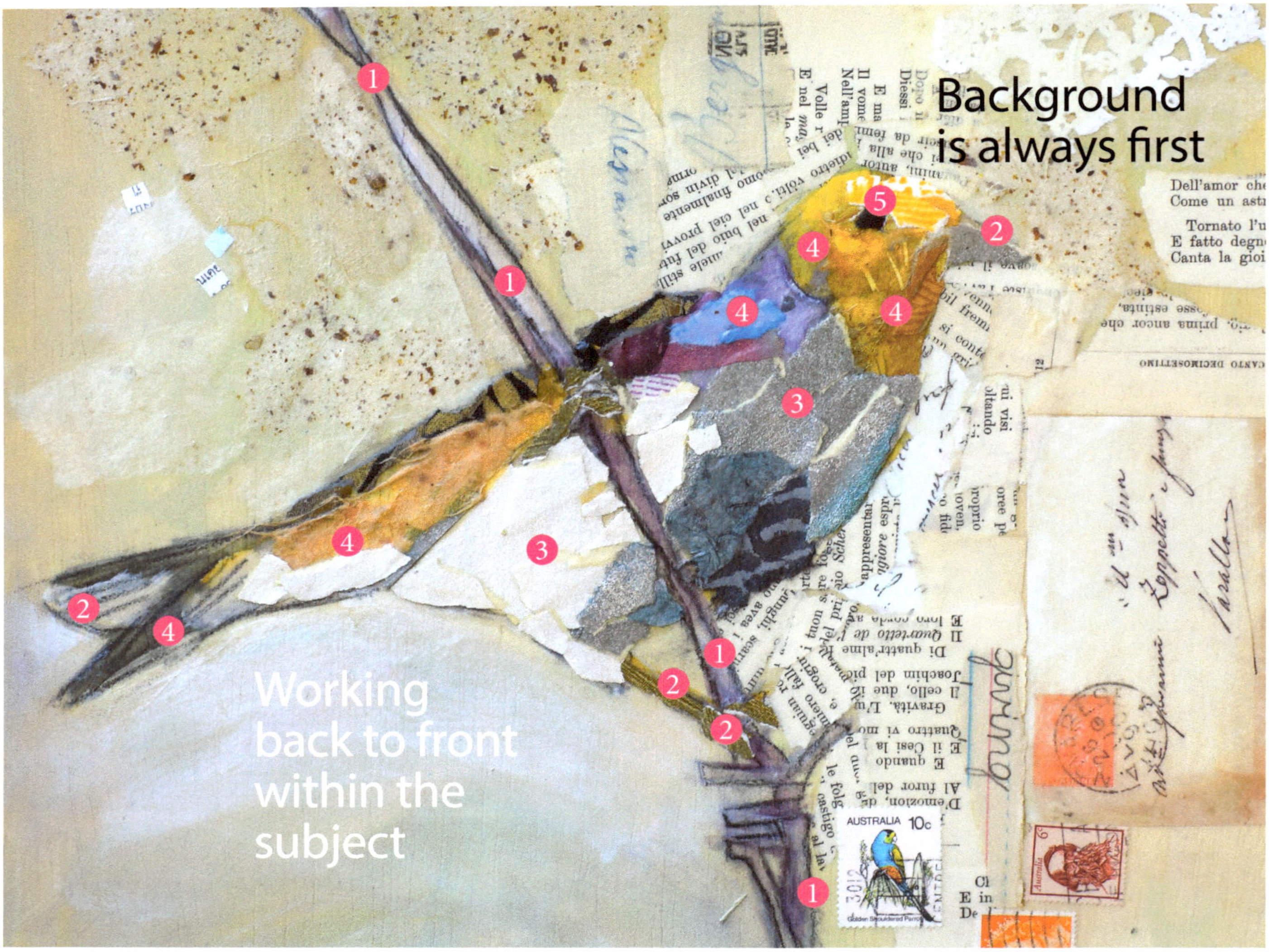

working back to front

Evaluate your composition and determine what is farthest back and what is closest to the front. Collage in that hierarchy, from back to front. The sky is behind the subject matter, the belly of the bird is behind the wing, the eye and the beak are on top of the head...

1 Overlapping edges visually come forward

2 Larger tears of paper visually come forward

3 Heavy texture visually comes forward

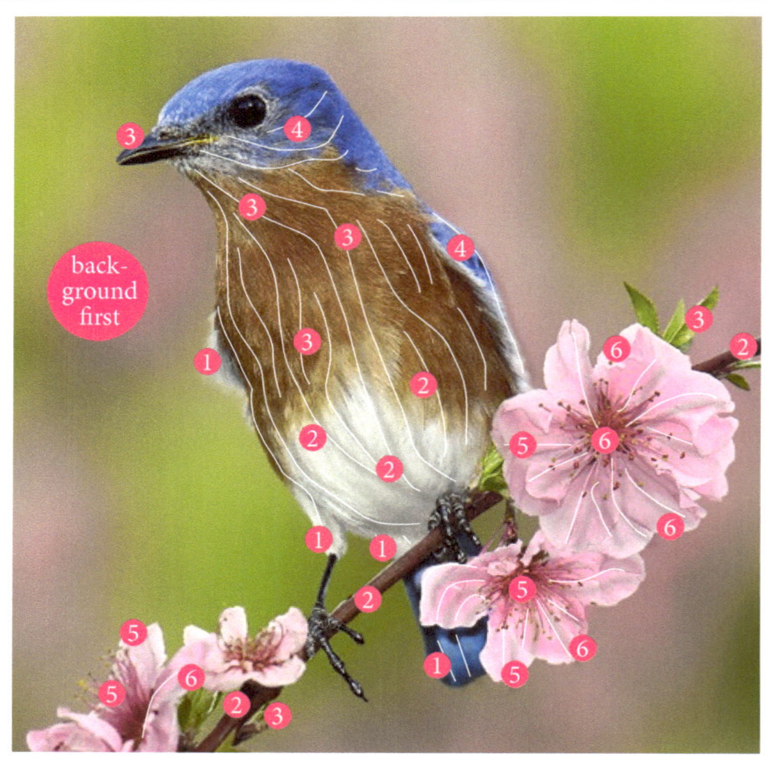

songbirds in collage

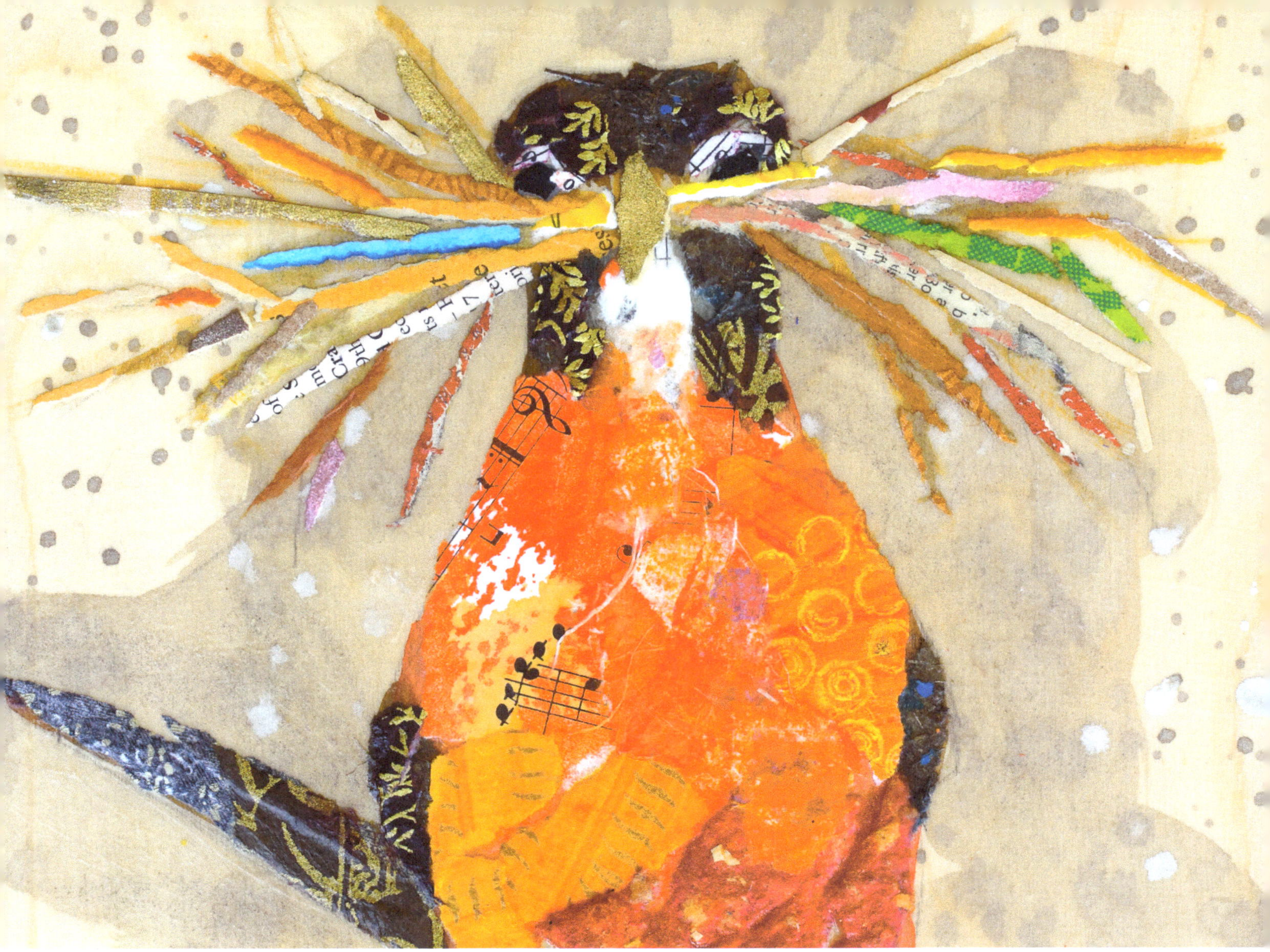

using arbitrary color

Don't be afraid to deviate from your reference photo and add some spice with colors that are not necessarily present in nature! This gives you the opportunity to infuse more color into your composition and WE LOVE COLOR!

Top Left "Finch on White"
Above: "Curious Bird"
Right: "Chick-A-Dee"

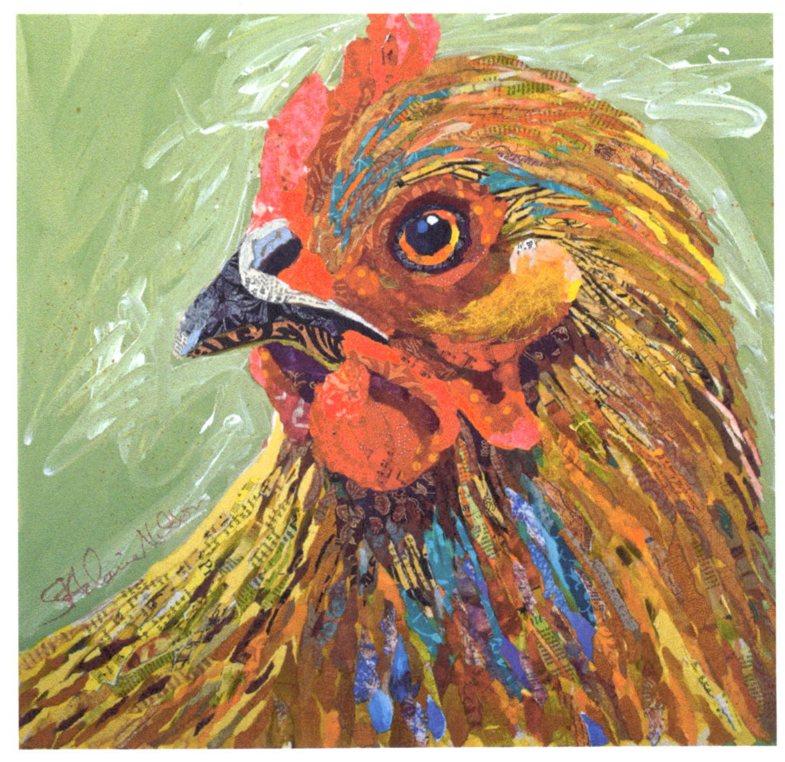

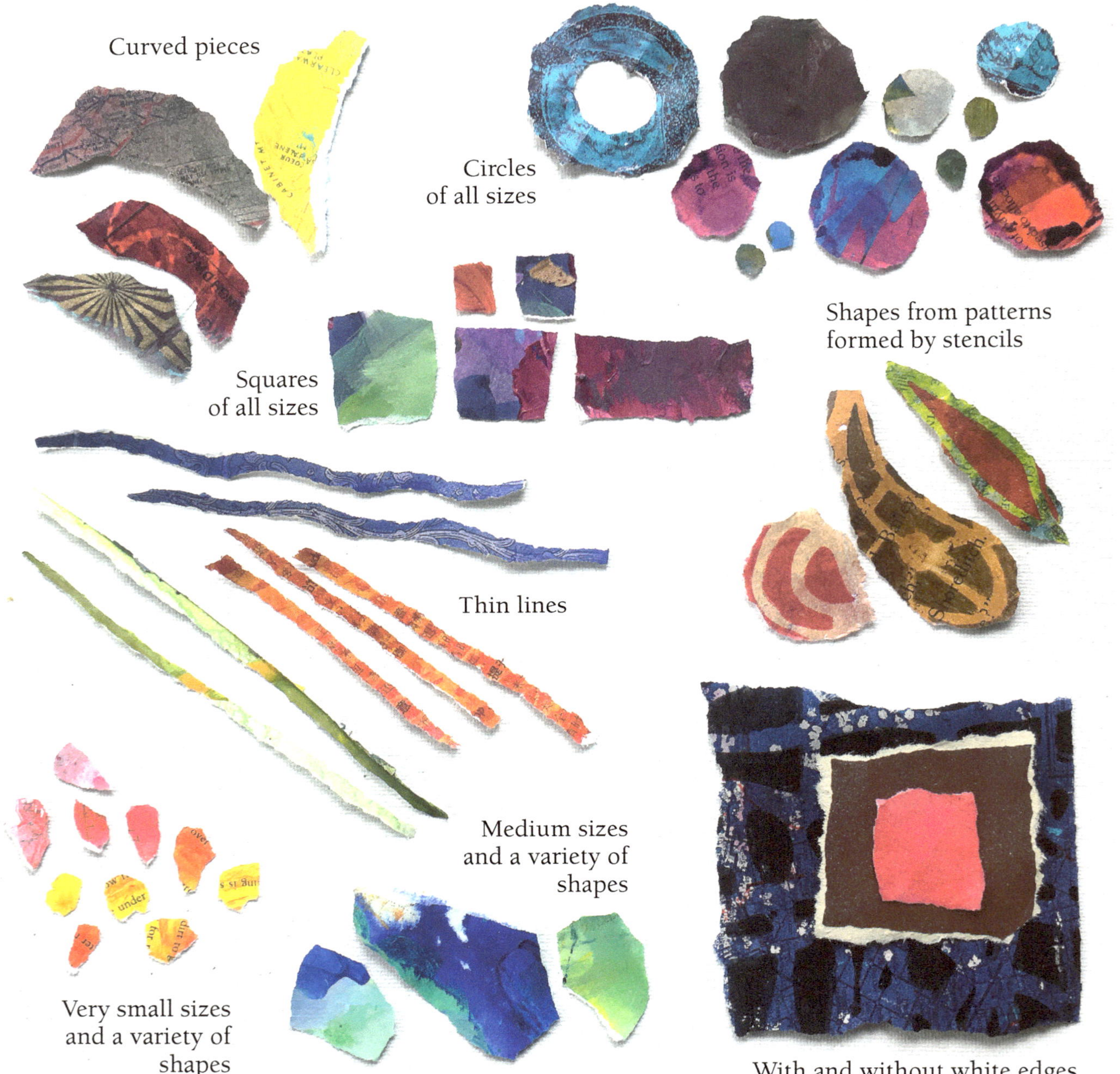

directional ripping

Directional ripping is basically following the form of an object with pieces of collage paper that have been torn into shapes that follow the direction of the brush marks from your underpainting. Practice tearing your paper brush marks in a variety of shapes and sizes.

Once you get a feeling for following the form with directional ripping and shading you will realize that this style of collage is much like traditional painting.

more white edges

Eliminating white edges requires pulling the paper UP while ripping– as you pull in an upward motion, the white edge is left behind. Practice pulling UP while ripping and rotating the paper so that you are always tearing in an upward motion. This takes a bit of getting used to–I suggest practicing on some scrap papers to get the hang of it.

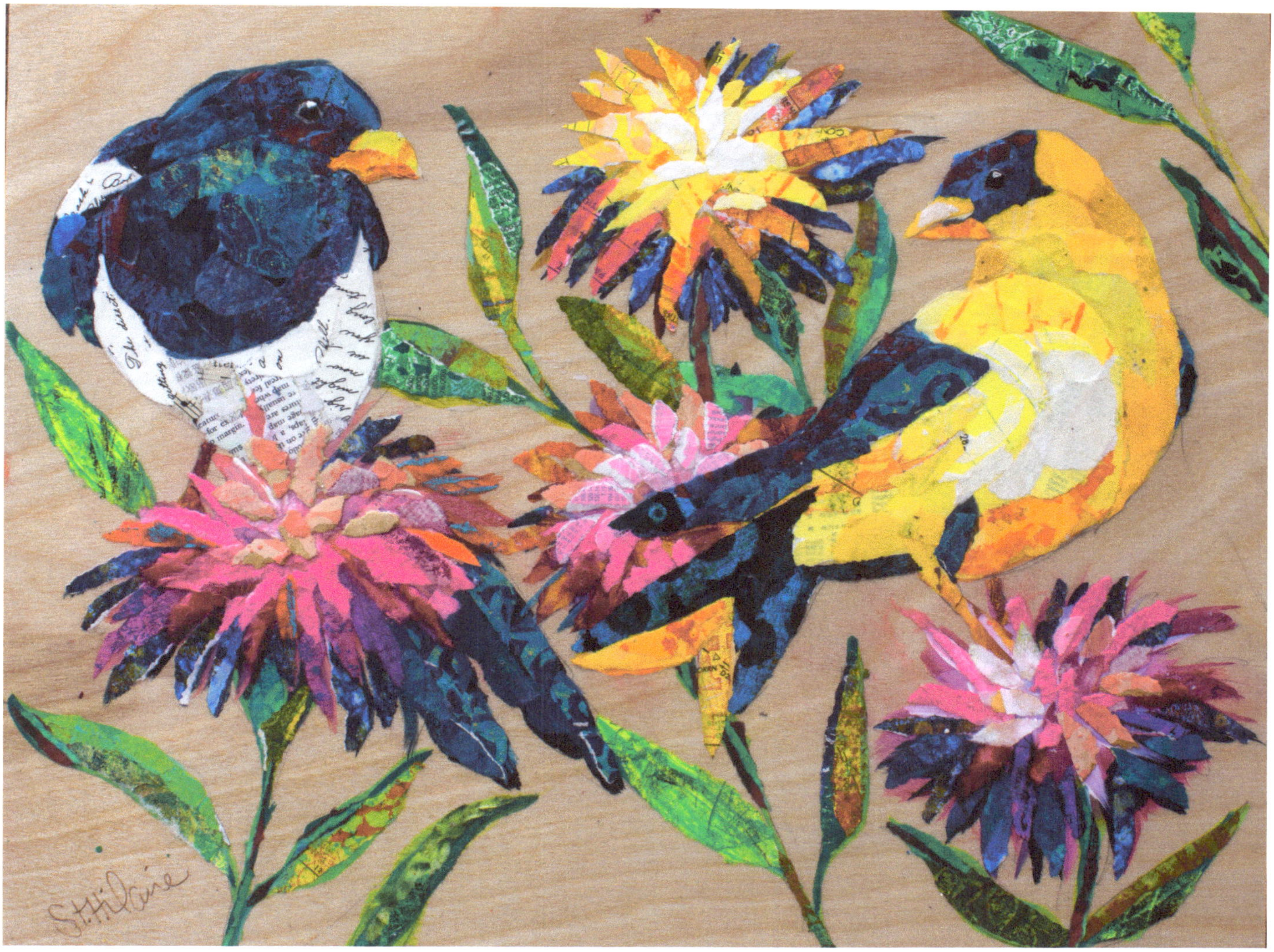

"Birds and Blooms" 16x14 is on clear primed wood panel, utilizing the wood grain for a background.

applying paper brush marks

Note how the torn paper curves around the shoulder of the yellow bird are following the form, the paper brush marks swoop up to the head and are elongated out to the tips of the tail. See how the flower petals are long and thin tears of paper, laid down in a direction that follows the form of the flowers, outward from their center. The black and white bird's chest has a feeling or roundness and volume as a result of the curved shaped papers that form a crescent shaper under the head and belly.

Painting with paper is just like painting with a brush, you must carefully tear each piece of paper, allow it to end in an organic shape, and apply it in a way that follows the form and volume of the subject in the same way you used your paint brush in the underpainting.

Paper brush marks should be torn to end organically vs. with straight edges like tape.

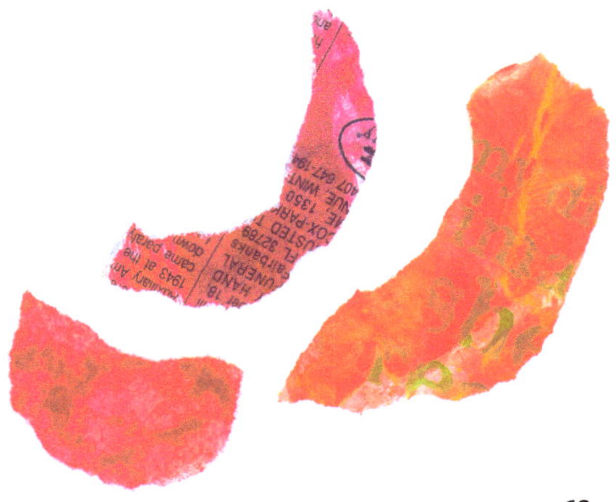

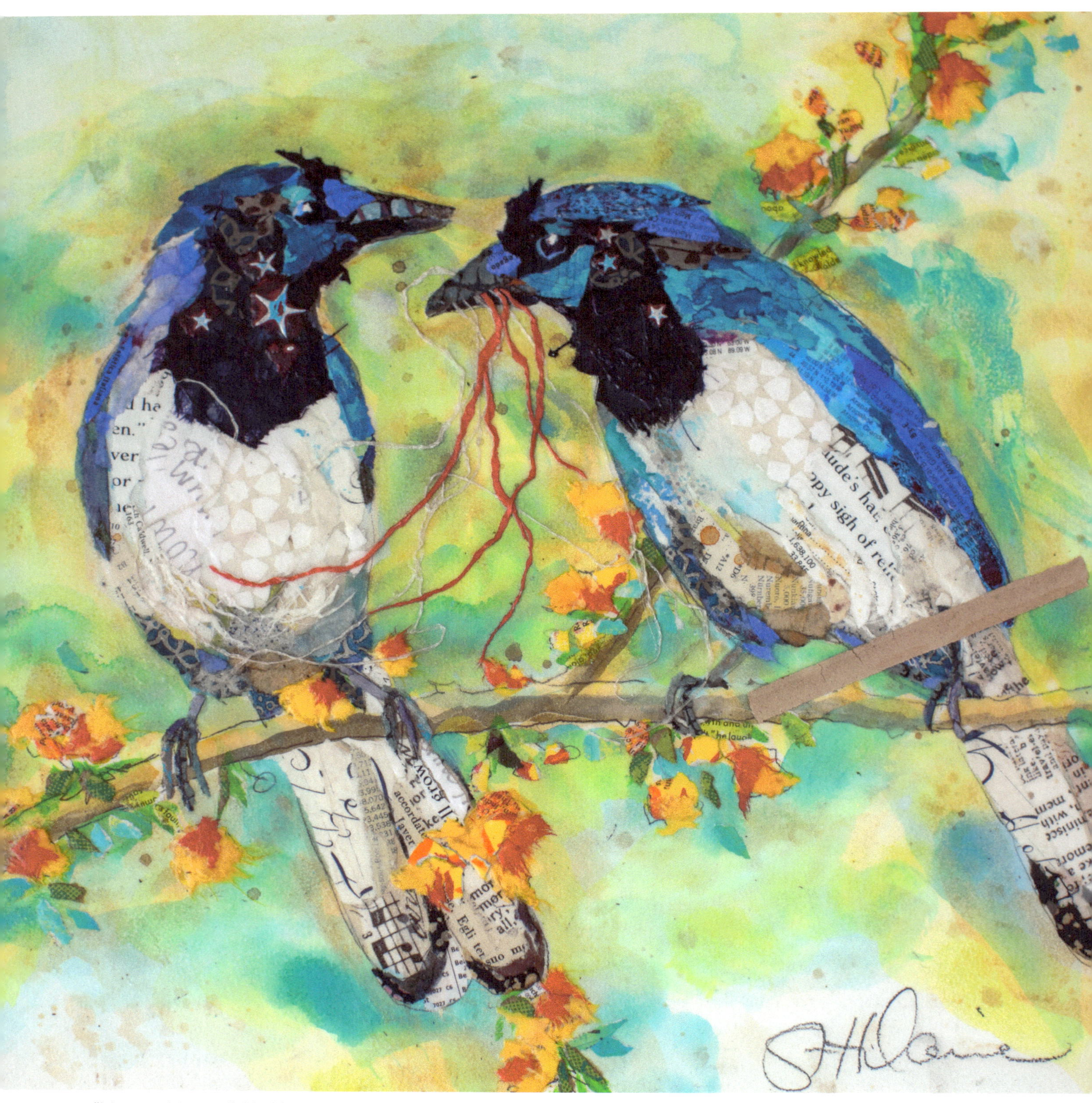

"Mexican Magpies" 12x12

White shading should be approached with different colors of white paper and text. Smaller text is more dense and appears darker, larger text with more white space appears lighter.

creating paper whites

White values are tough to shade, I like to use text and variety of paper color for this purpose. Not all whites are the same, different book pages are different shades of white, old books offer a nice yellow white, whereas new books offer brighter white. White can also be shaded with text. Small body copy that is close together appears darker than large headlines where the text is more spread apart. Utilize both paper color and text density to help you shade your white on white areas. Utilize your directional ripping to help define the form in your white on white areas, this will assist in areas with less shading.

Once paper is coated back and front with the Liquitex Gloss Gel Medium, it becomes archival as each piece is sealed off from the one above it and below it, as well as sealed from oxidation. A final coating of Golden UVLS Acrylic Varnish will seal and protect the collage. I use Golden Satin UVLS Acrylic Varnish and follow the direction on the label for application and dilution.

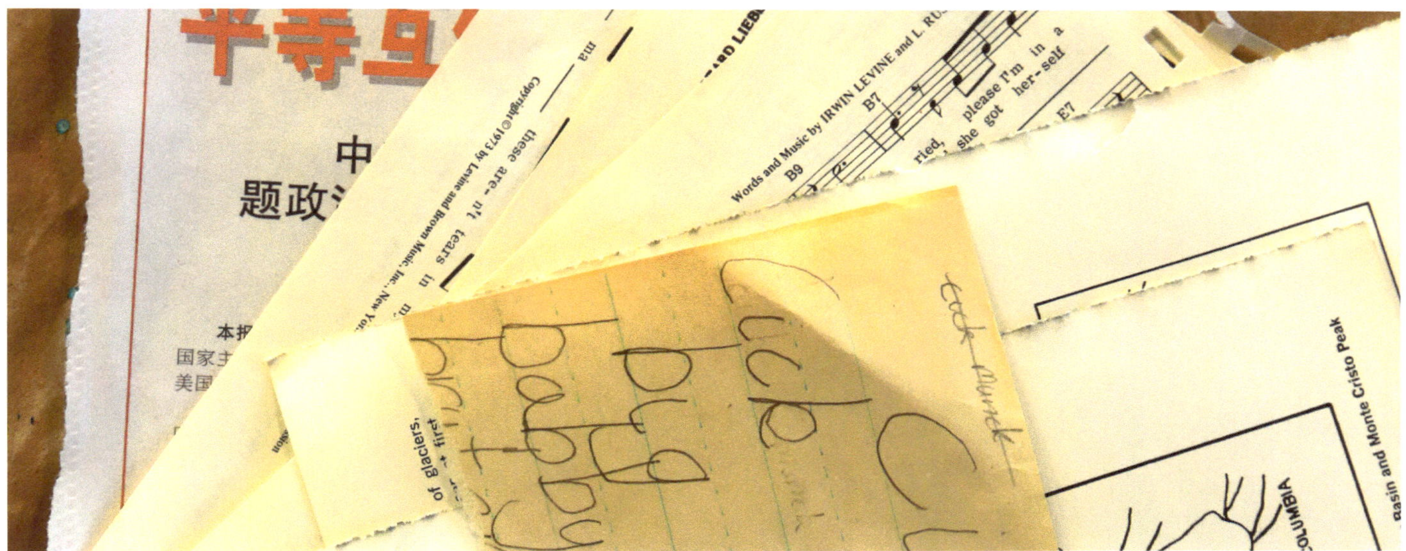

I have been known to use my kids' homework in my artwork, as well as old letters and ephemera from estate sales or the box under my bed from my childhood.

more points to consider

1. Large fonts from children's books offer more white space in and around the letters, this appears lighter

2 Small fonts from the body copy of a novel offer less white space in and around the letters, this appears darker

3 All white papers are not the same! Spread out your old books and examine the yellowing of the pages. Utilize the shade of the paper for shading in your white areas

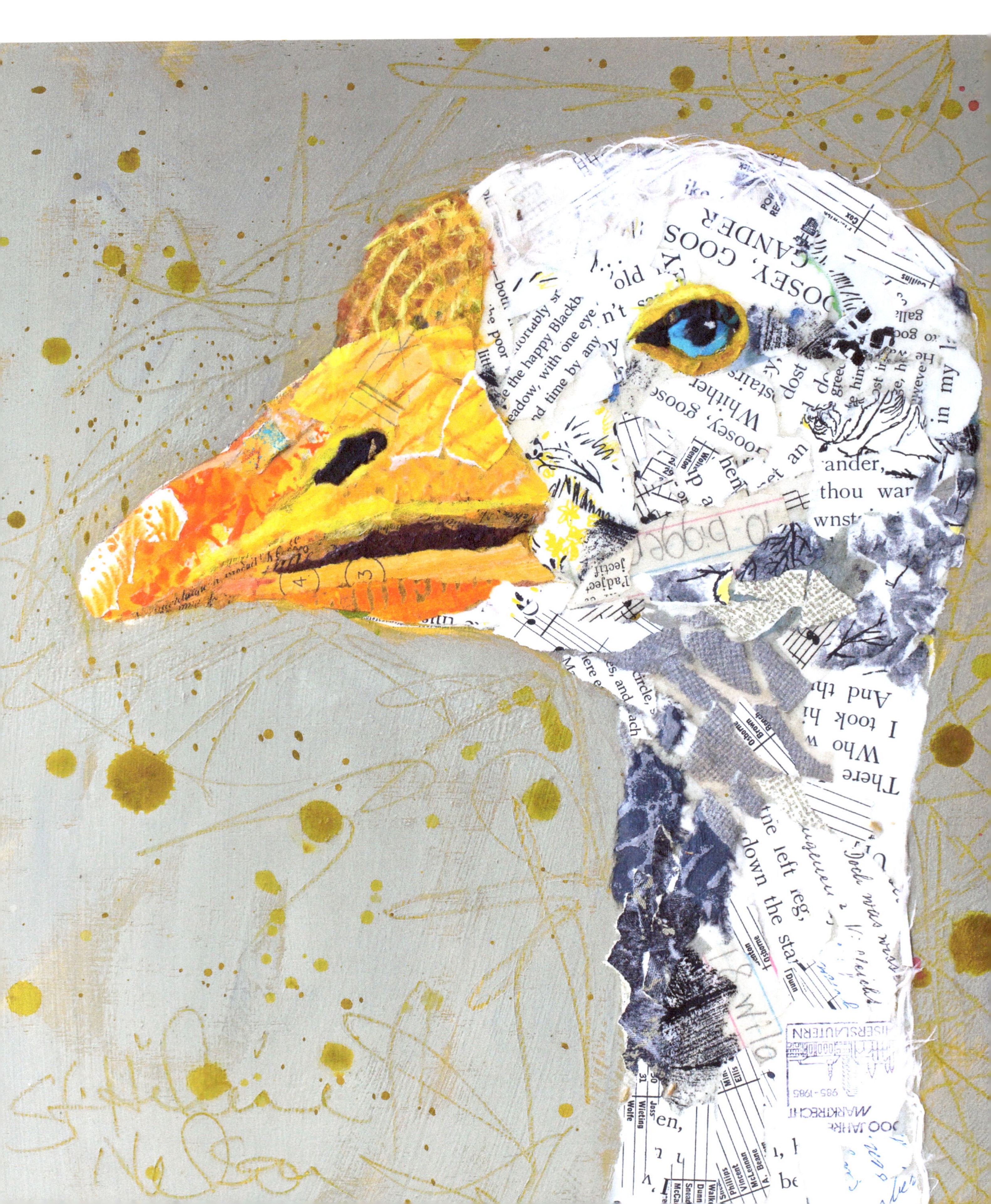

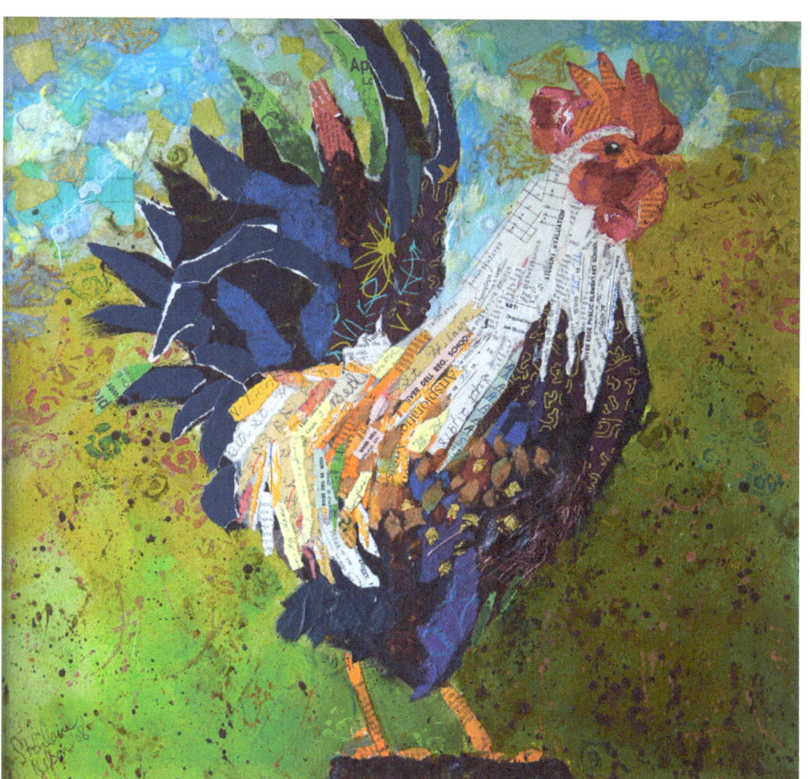
"Report Card Rooster" 20x20

"Goosey Gander" 10x12 (left) This piece utilizes a nursery rhyme to sneak in some related material that relates to the subject.

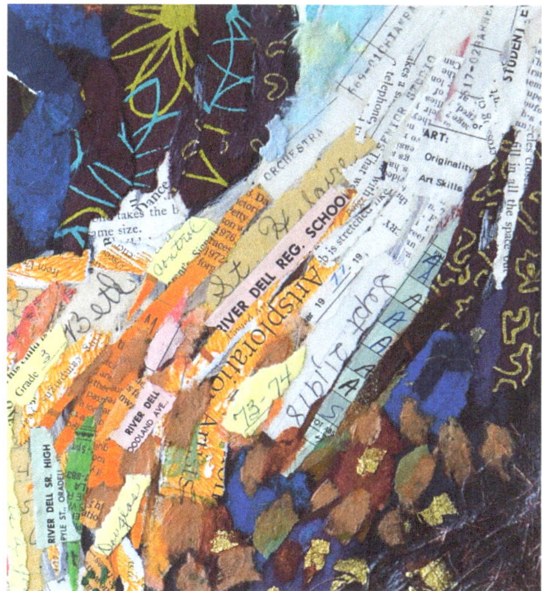

"Report Card Rooster" (detail) I created this piece for my kitchen, utilizing childhood ephemera from my grade school years.

related materials

It can be a lot of fun to try to find printed material related to your subject, and use it in your collages. I have found a book of nursery rhymes to be a wonderful resource for all of my barnyard animals.

Purchasing books especially for the occasion can be worth while as well. For my peacock series I did purchase a book of stories about birds, it offered me pages of text with words like "nest" and "birds" and even "peacock"and "feathers."

Nothing is off limits when it comes to materials you can include in your collages, remember to stain and tint all paper with Fluid Acrylics to offer a variety of colors and range of values.

Flea markets, yard sales, and eBay offer all kinds of materials that can be wonderful for collage: sheet music, postage stamps, old letters, cancelled checks, vintage children's books, foreign language books, and on and on. To be a good collage artist, you must be a good pack rat! (We don't say hoarder...) The key is organizing these materials so that you can find them when you need them.

Trading papers with other collage artists also opens up a world of opportunity. Often times others will create papers in colors and with techniques that you would not have considered or have not yet attempted, this brings new papers into your palette and opens up your creativity.

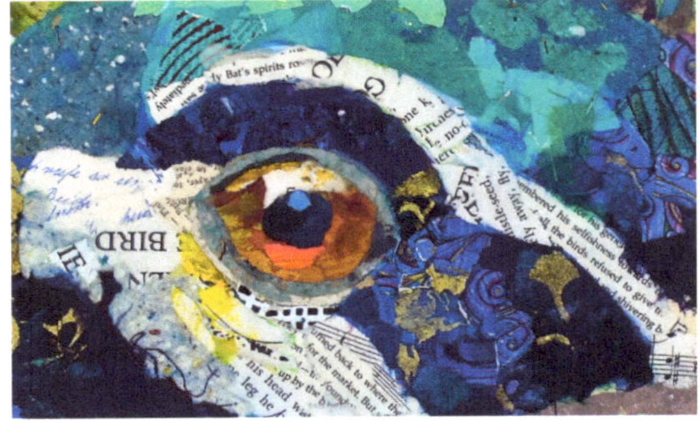

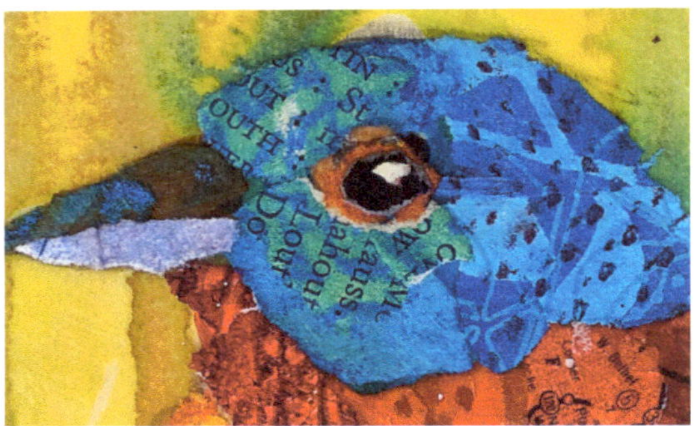

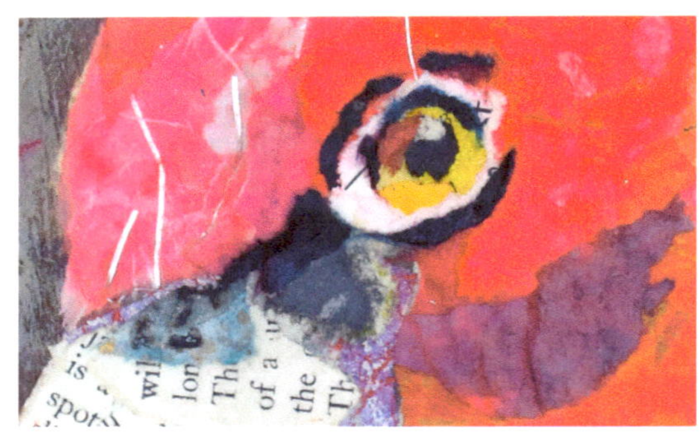

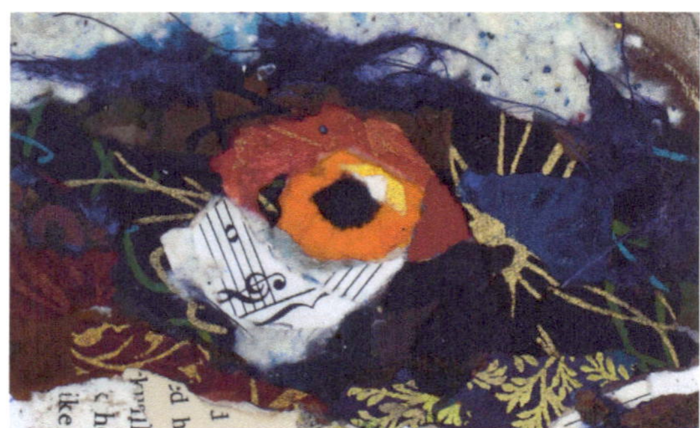

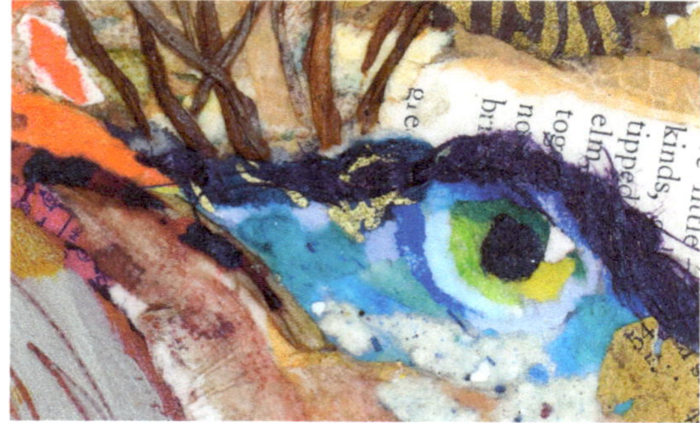

the eyes have it

Eyes add life to your subject, always include a highlight, even if it doesn't appear in your reference image, especially in the tiny black eyes of songbirds. Since the sun is your overhead light source, the highlight is typically positioned at the top of the bird's eye.

For larger birds with eyes that have more real estate, shading and multi color is the key. Eyes are always slightly darker at the top, under the brow bone. Be sure to render the color of the iris with a few different shades of the same color, this shading and multi color effect is how you achieve glossiness and lifelike eyes.

Note that the flamingo has two different shades of yellow, plus brown under the brow bone–then the pupil is added on top of the yellow, with the highlight going down last. I always create the highlight from a tiny piece of white paper, never painted. Typically I find a paper in my stash that has a slight "point" on it, and I "nip" that point off, with my fingernails to create a tiny tear for the highlight.

The green-eyed bird at the bottom is a nice example of shading under the brow bone, highlight at the top, and multi color greens with yellow in the iris.

Mr Peacock at the top has many shades of brown and orange in the iris, with those colors reflecting out onto the white feathers below the eye. Within his iris, there is a light blue highlight that is secondary to the white highlight at the top. Peacock eyes are my favorite.

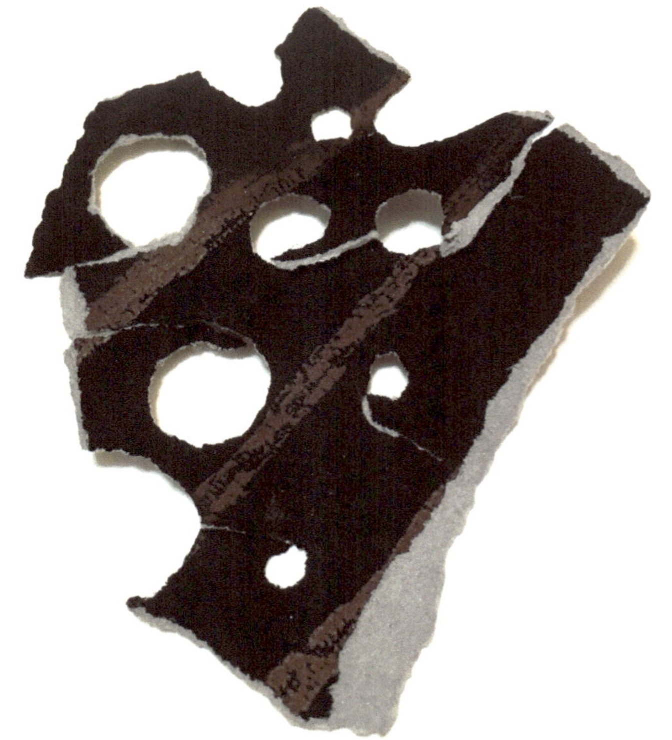

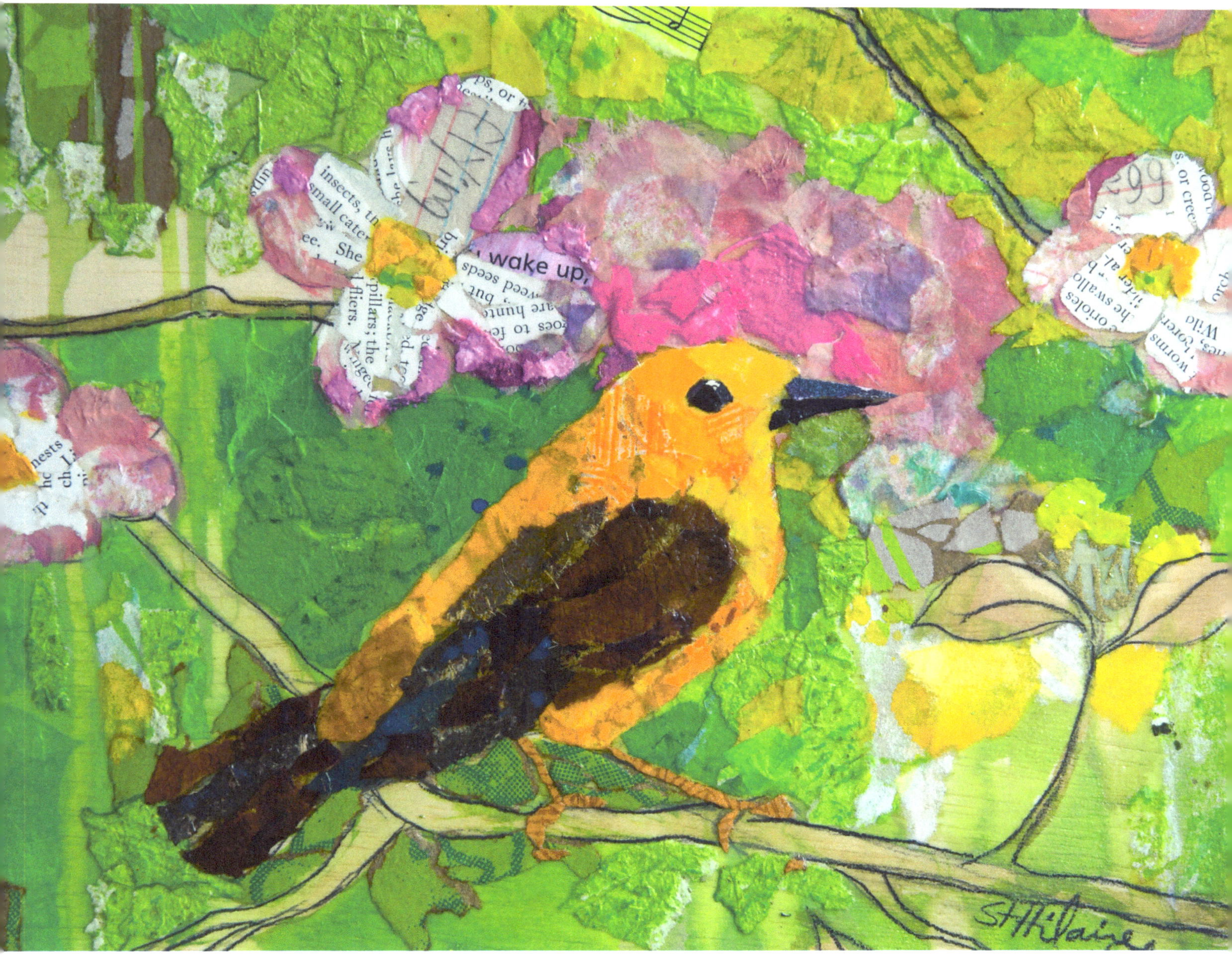

A highlight is imperative, even if it's not apparent in your reference image. I never add my highlight with paint... Always a very small tear of white paper.

Above: "Peeps and Tweets" 12x9

Below: "Zebra Finch Farewell" 10x10 (detail)

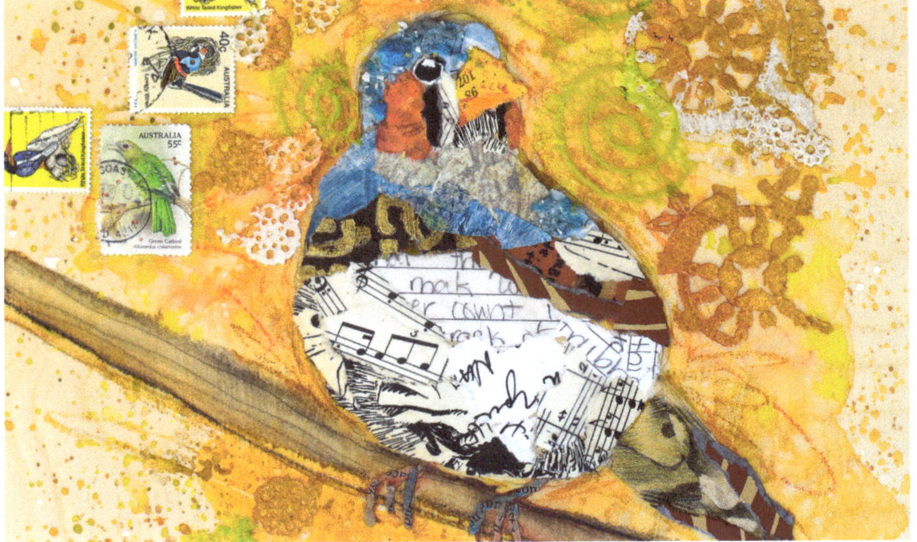

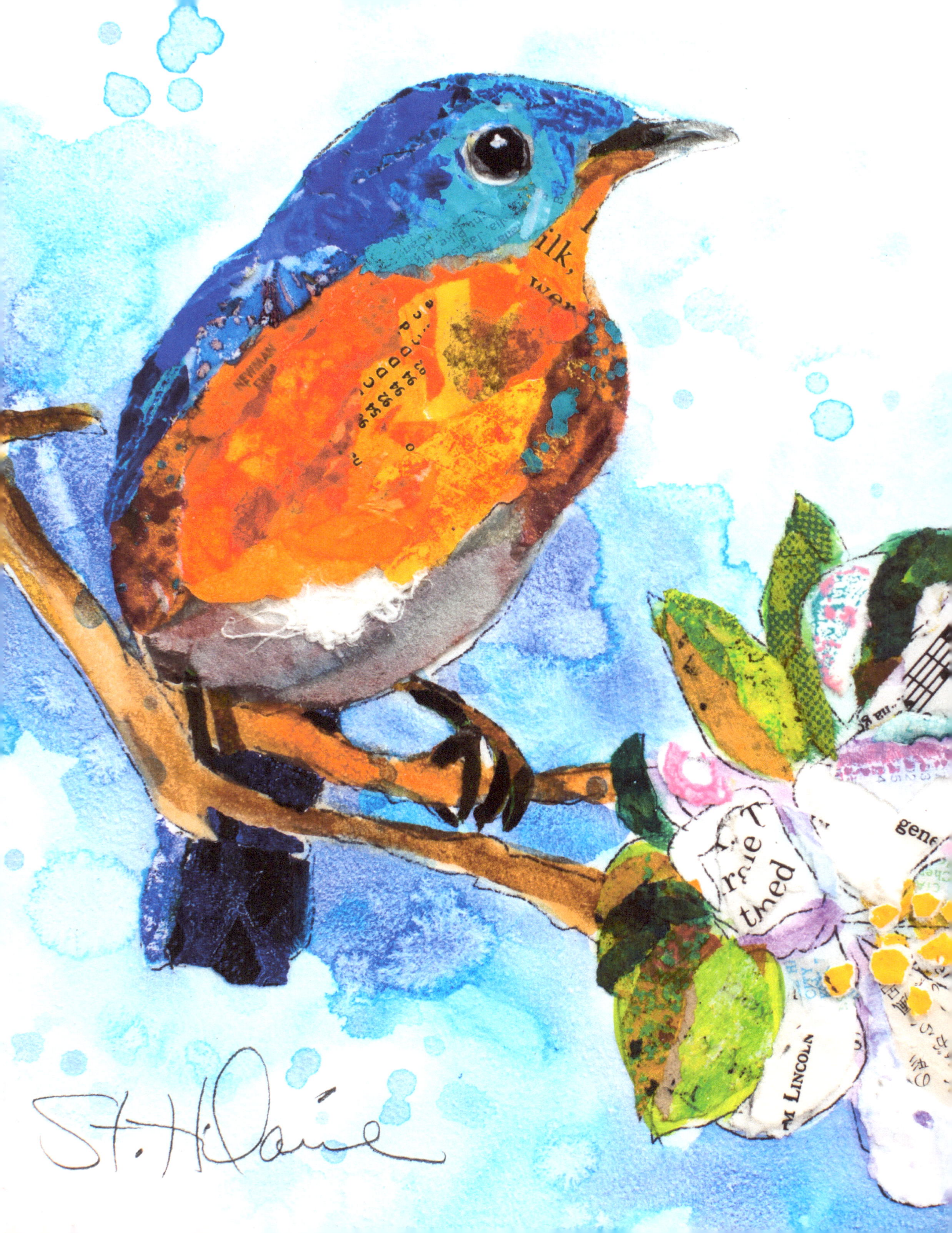
St. Hilaire

INSPIRATION *gallery*

leaving the background painted

Here's a wet and watery backdrop for my collaged Western Bluebird and florals (left). Often times I leave my backgrounds painted and collage just the subject.

Experiment with different combinations of painted, mixed media, and collaged backgrounds behind your birds, the combinations are endless!

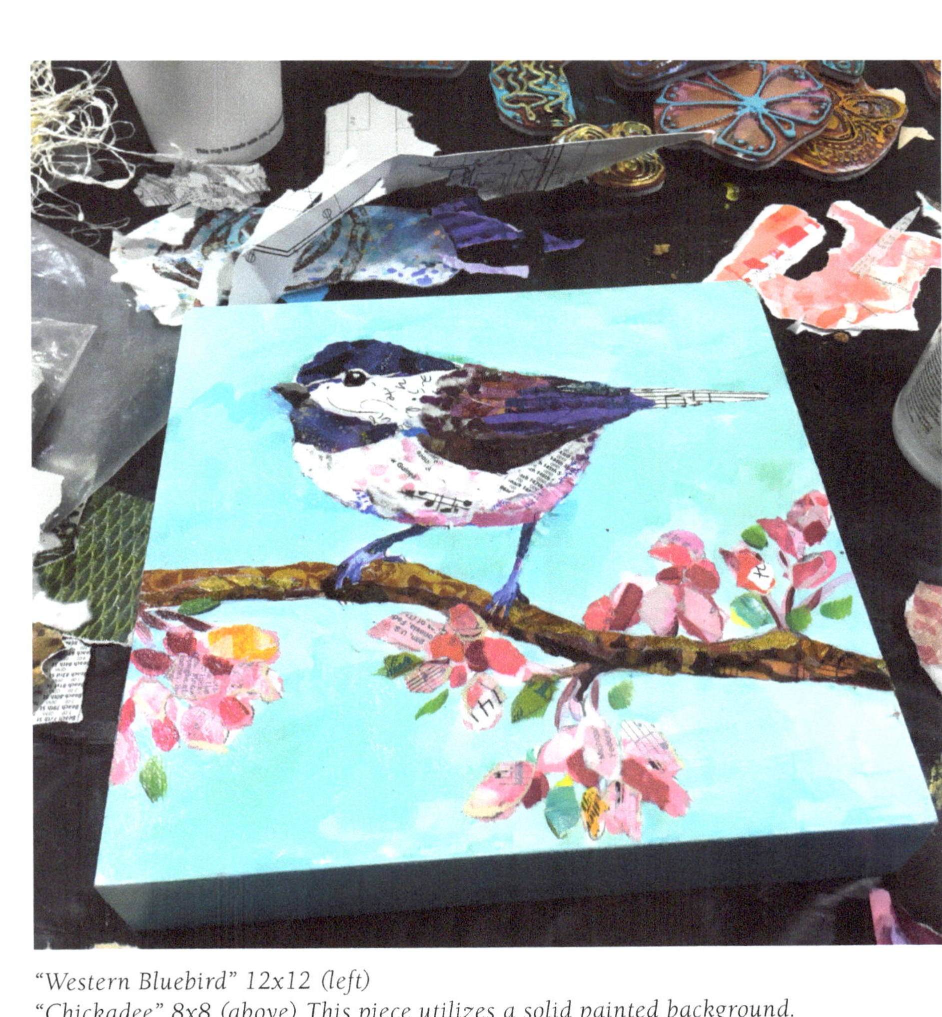

"Western Bluebird" 12x12 (left)
"Chickadee" 8x8 (above) This piece utilizes a solid painted background.

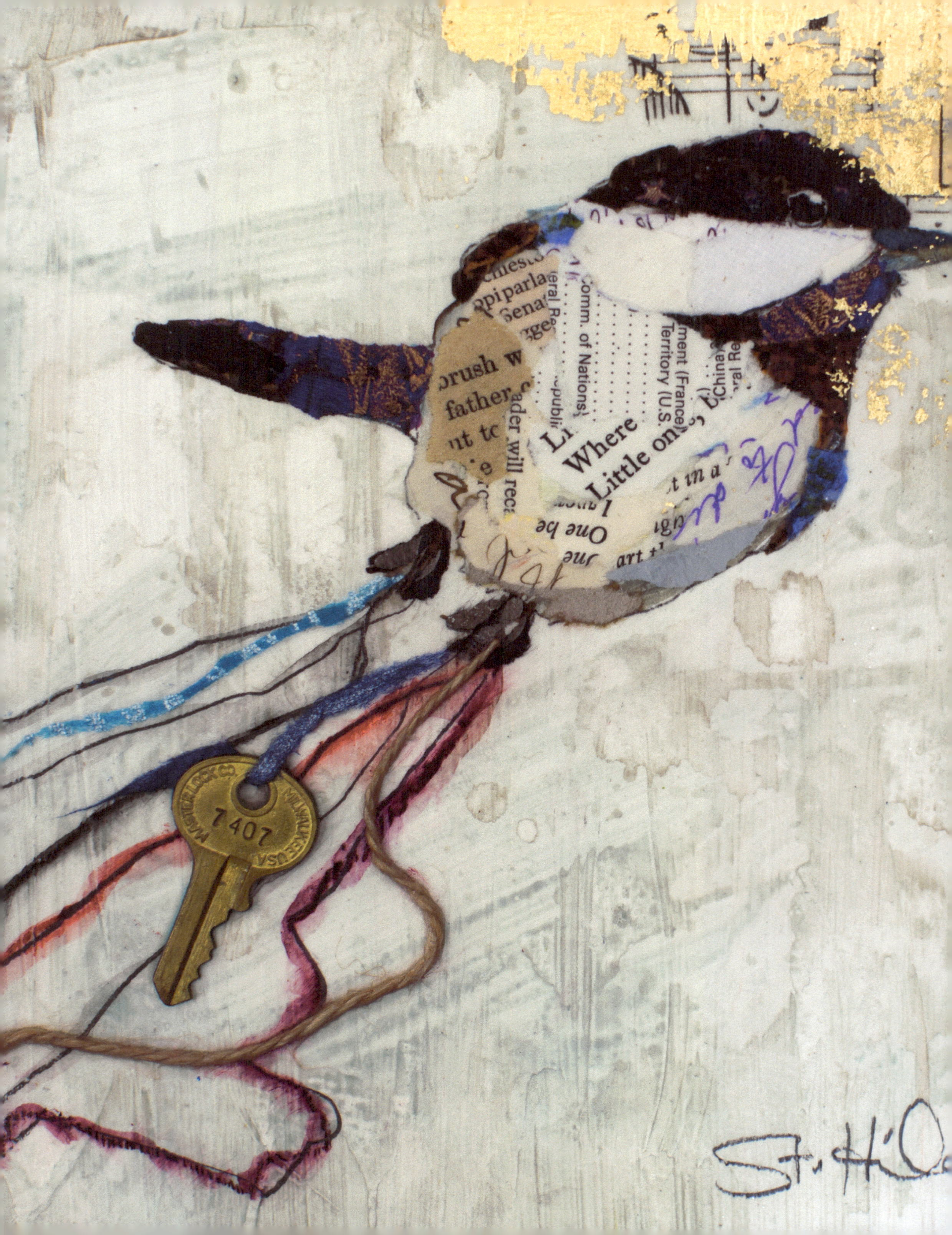

brush w
father
ut to
der will rec
Where
Little one
One be
art
Comm. of Nations
Territory (U.S.
Republic
China
ral Re
7 407

found objects

I enjoy adding string, and keys to my bird imagery as it reminds me of nesting. Here in this Chickadee collage, I have also added gold leaf and sheet music to the background.

You can see that I left the sketch lines amongst the strings, I felt they added depth and dimension and so I did not fret about gluing my string and thin strips of paper accurately on top of them.

The key was applied with the same Gloss Gel Medium that I use for the collage glue, cleaning off any excess that squeezed out when I pressed it in place.

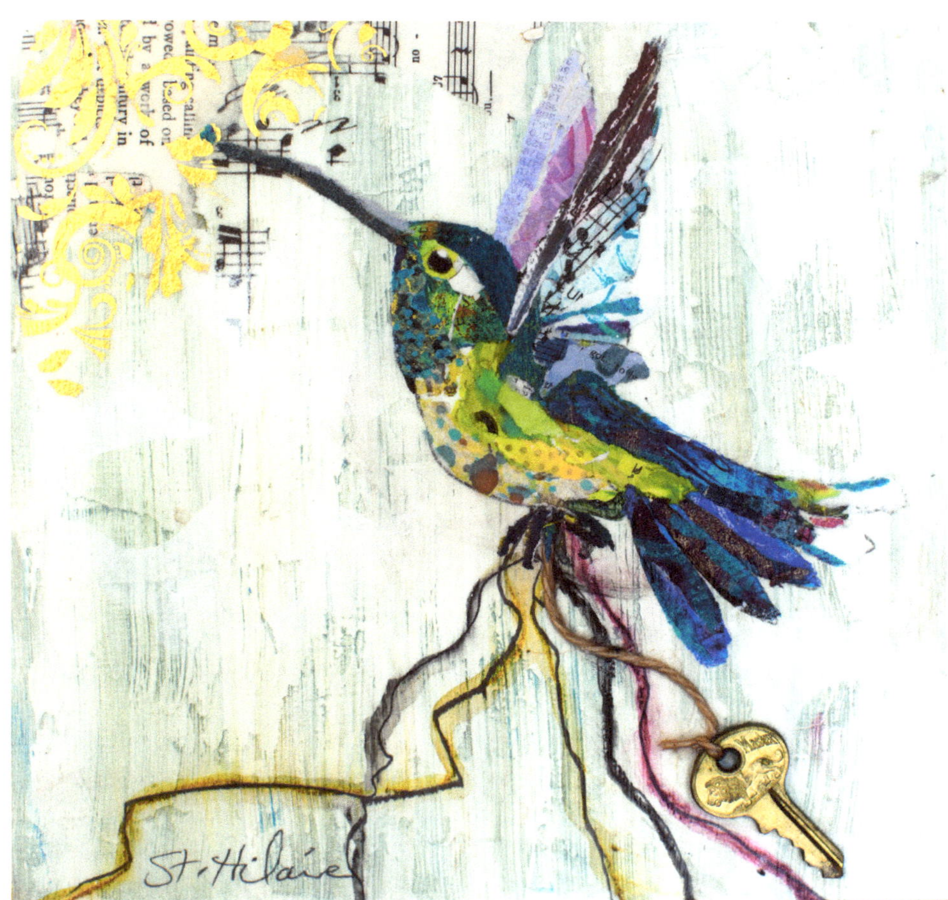

"Birds in Flight" 8x8 (left and above) These pieces utilize strings and keys as well as sheet music and gold leaf or golden embellished decorative papers.

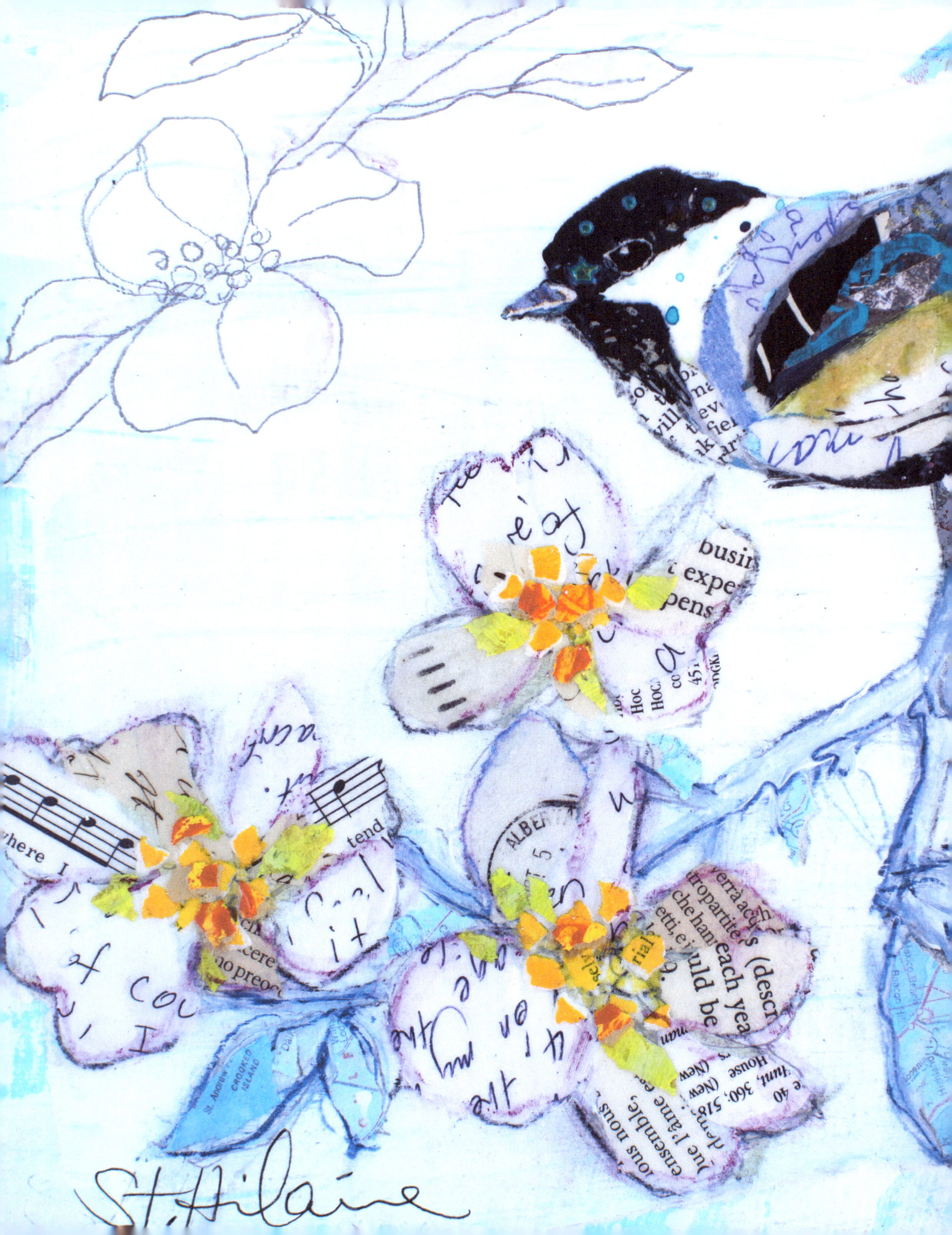

St.Hilaire

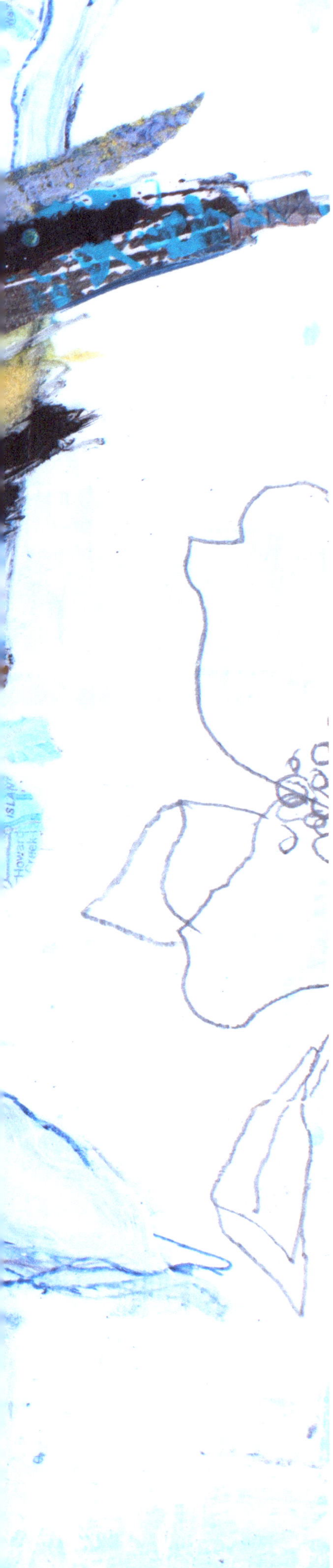

line work

Often times I suggest flowers and branches in the background by treating them as a simple pencil sketch lines. The gray value of the graphite allows them to fade into the background, suggesting an environment for the bird without competing for attention.

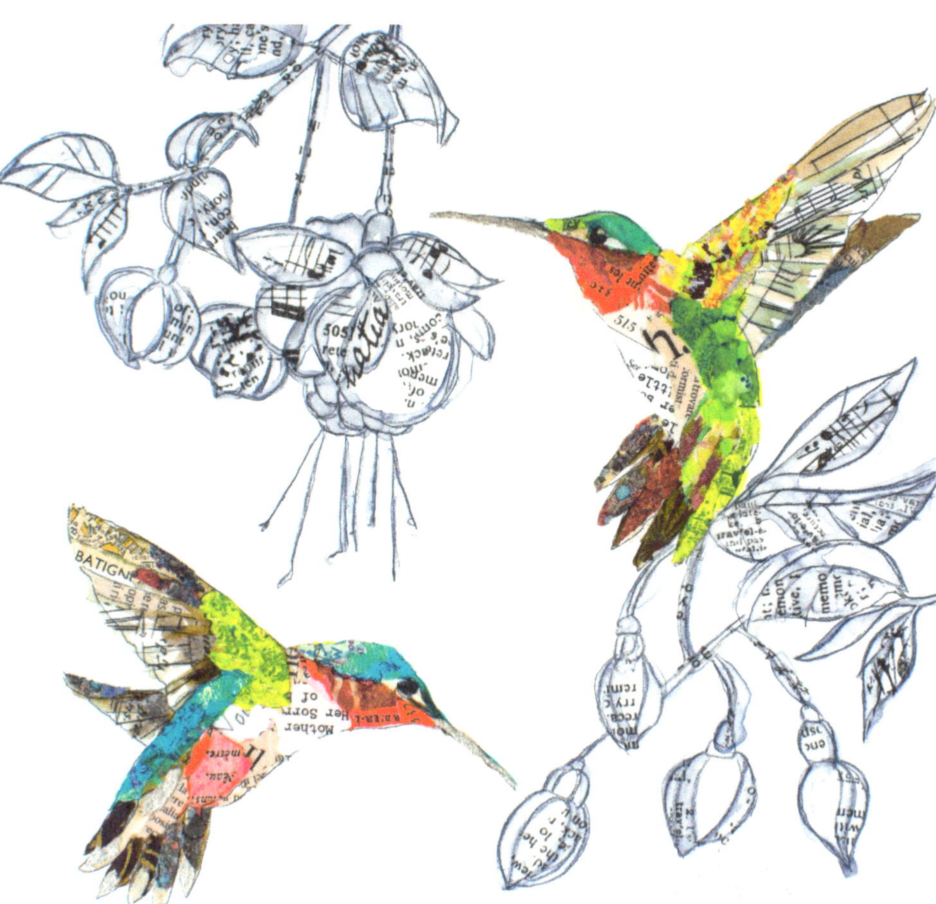

"Black Capped Chickadee" 8x8 (left) and Hummers 12x12 (above) Both make use of gray line work that allows the colored bird to sing.

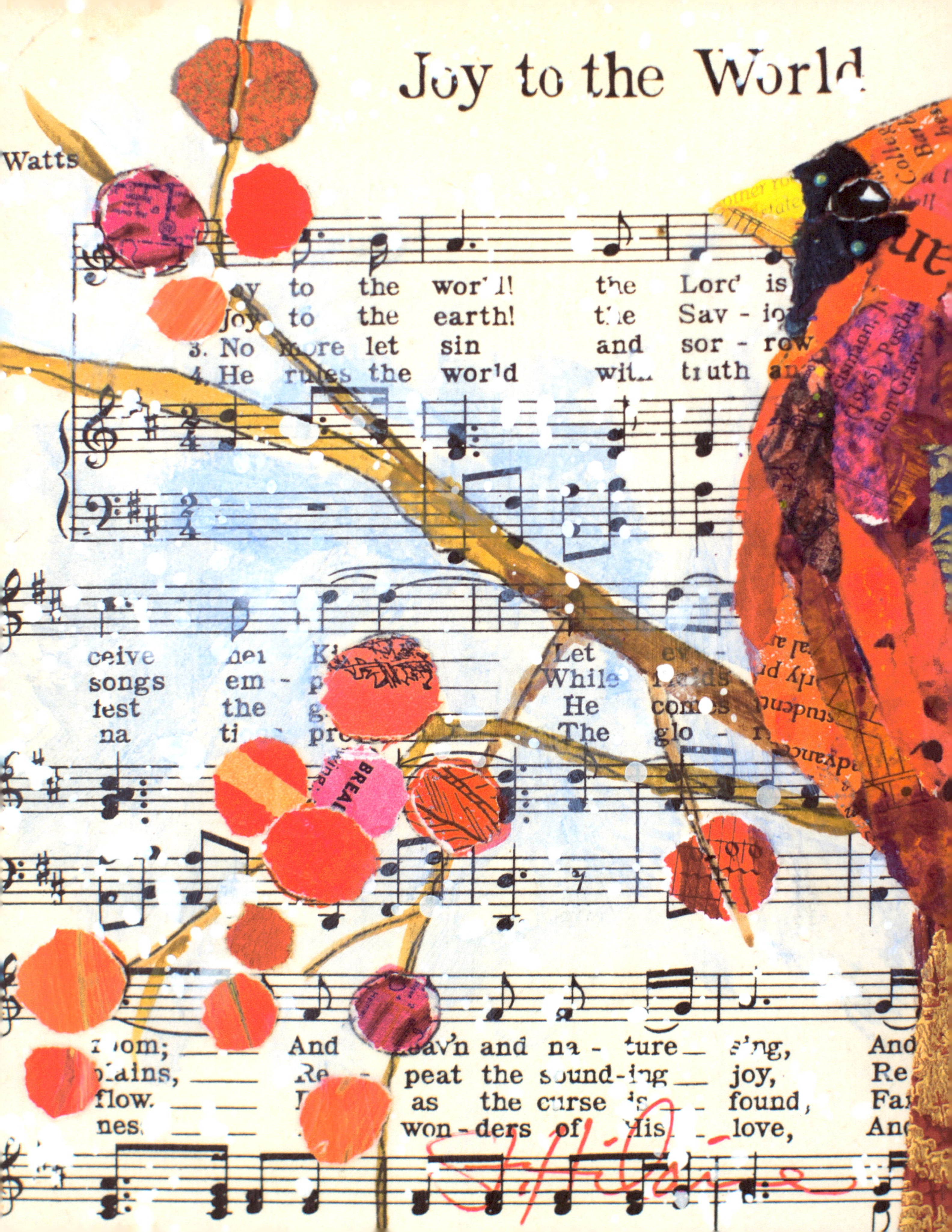
Joy to the World
Watts
Joy to the world! the Lord is
Joy to the earth! the Sav - ior
3. No more let sin and sor - row
4 He rules the world with truth an
ceive her Ki Let
songs em p While
test the g He coms
na ti pro The glo -
And heav'n and na - ture sing,
Re - peat the sound-ing joy,
as the curse is found,
won - ders of His love,
And
Re
Fa
An

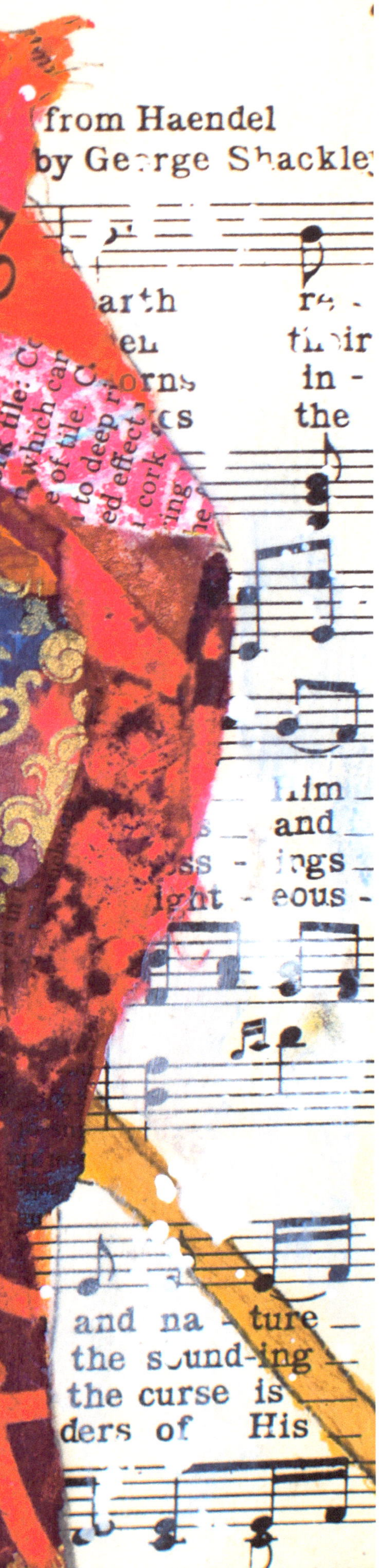

sheet music backdrop

For these birds I laid the sheet music down on my substrate and glued it with lots of pressure and patience, to be sure there were no bubbles or cockling. (I suggest using a brayer)

I did my sketch, underpainting, and collage on top of the music. The snow was created by a splatter of watered down white gesso. I used a wet paper towel to wipe any excess from on top of the bird where I might not want it.

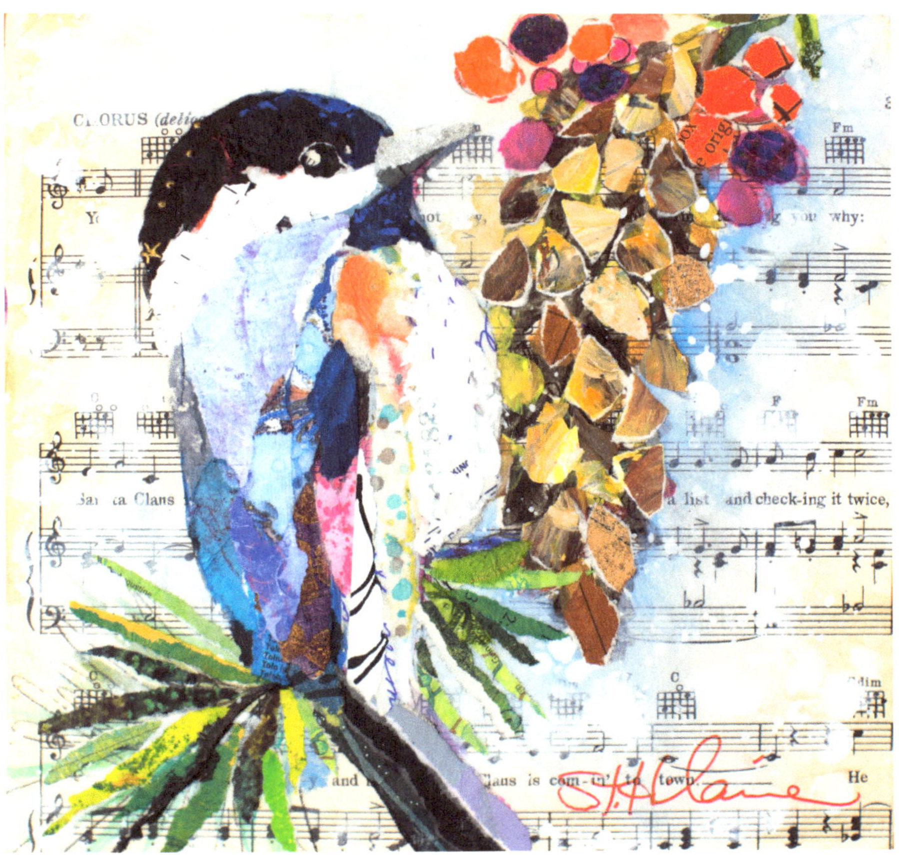

"Joy to the World" 8x8 (left) and "Pine Cone" 8x8 (above)
This work features vintage sheet music backgrounds which
were laid down before the sketch.

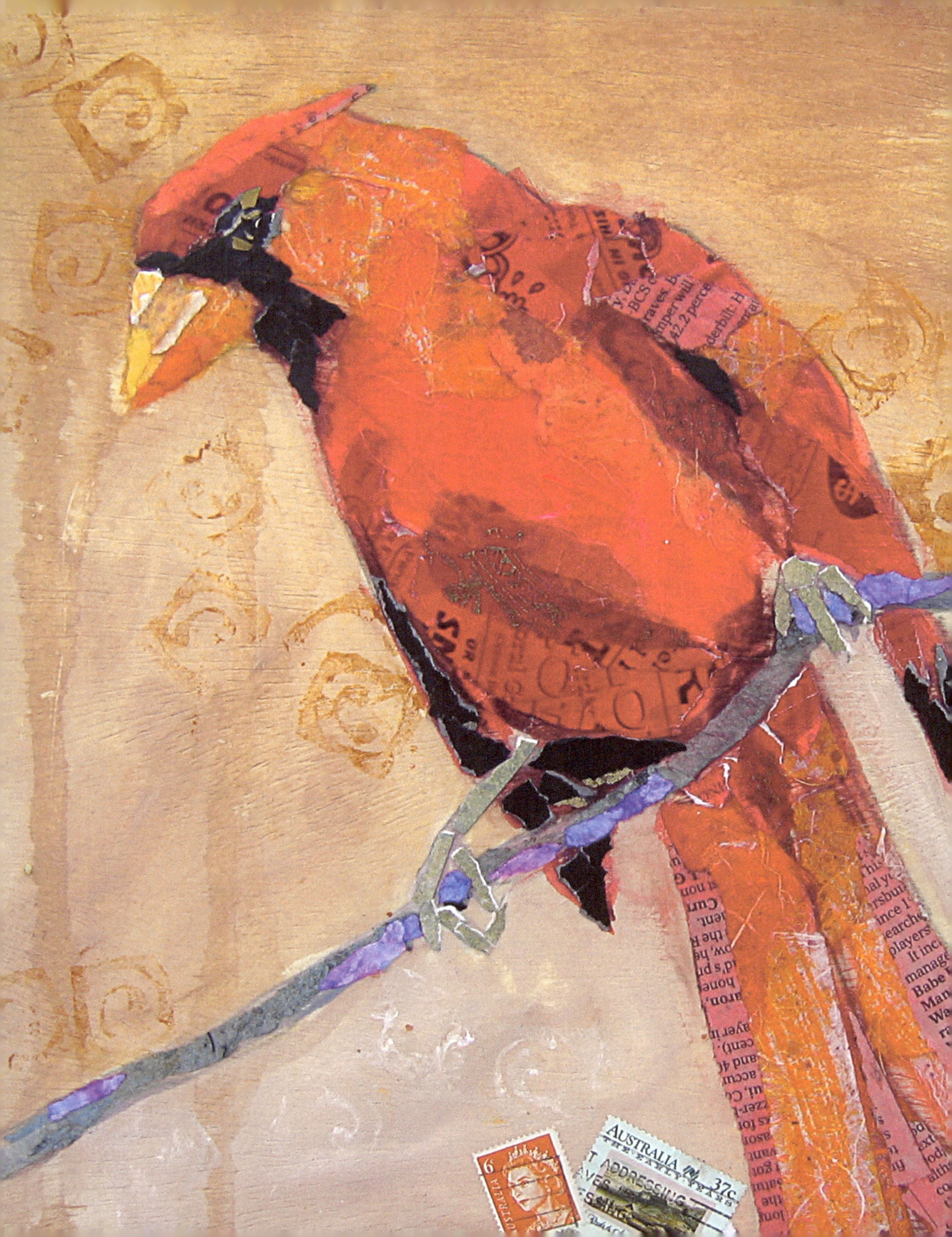

AUSTRALIA
6
AUSTRALIA 37c
ADDRESSING

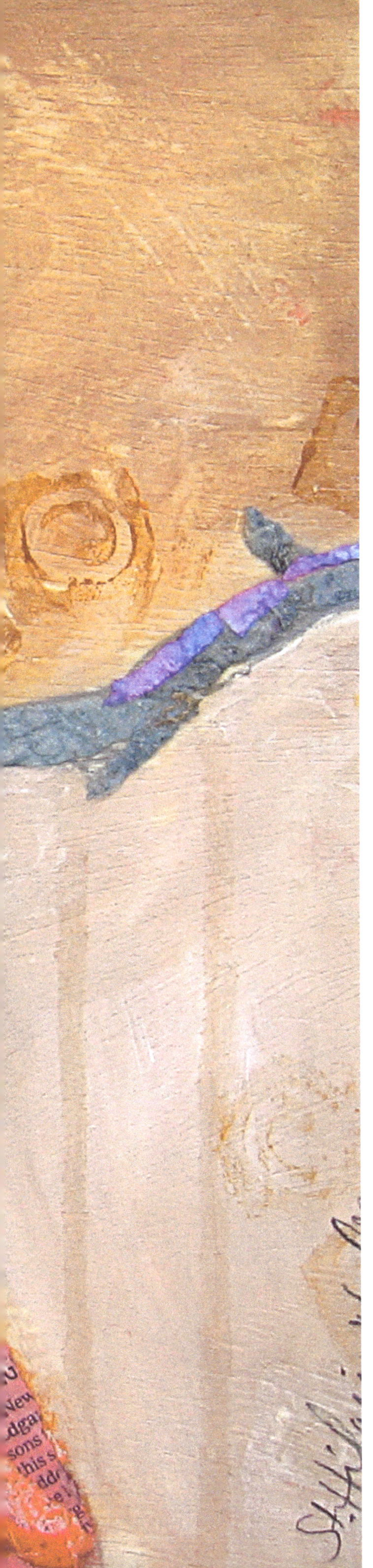

natural wood backdrop

When I want the natural grain of wood to show through,
I seal the panel with Golden GAC-100 and then prime it
with Liquitex Clear Gesso. I like birch panel for its' inherent
light golden color, I apply a watery wash of a gold tone color
such as Golden Quinacridone Nickel Azo Gold Fluid Acrylic
to enhance the gold hue of the natural wood. You can also
purchase cabinet grade wood that offers even more grain.

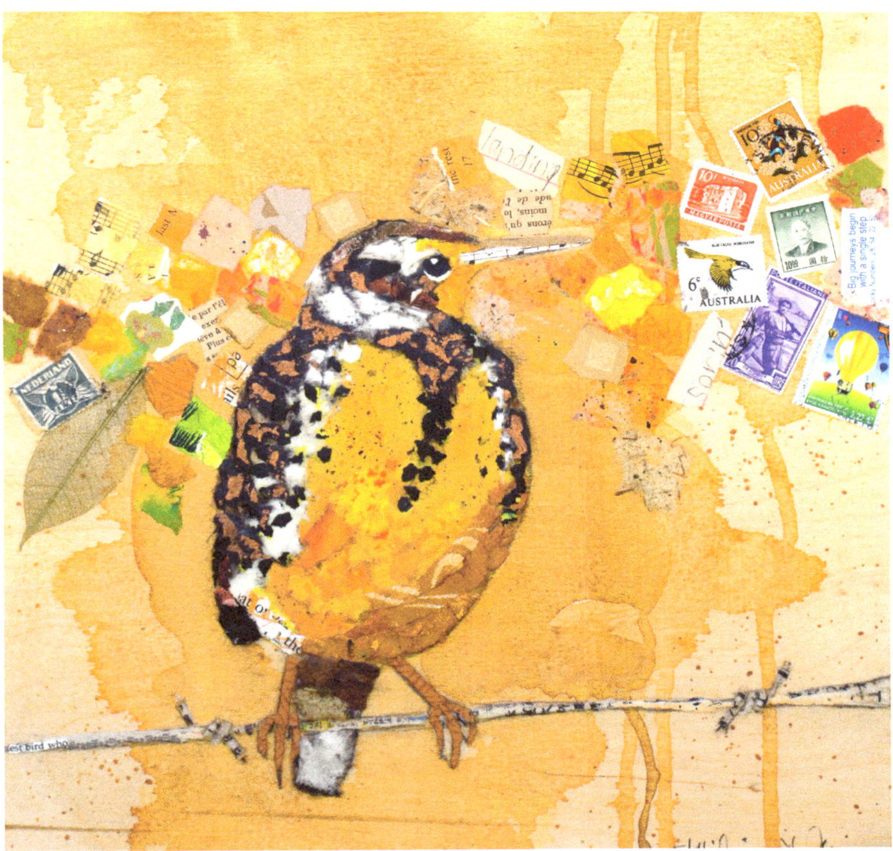

*"Red Cardinal" 12x12 (left) and "Big Journeys" 10x10 (above)
are both created on clear primed birch panel with a watery
wash of Golden Fluid Acrylic Paint.*

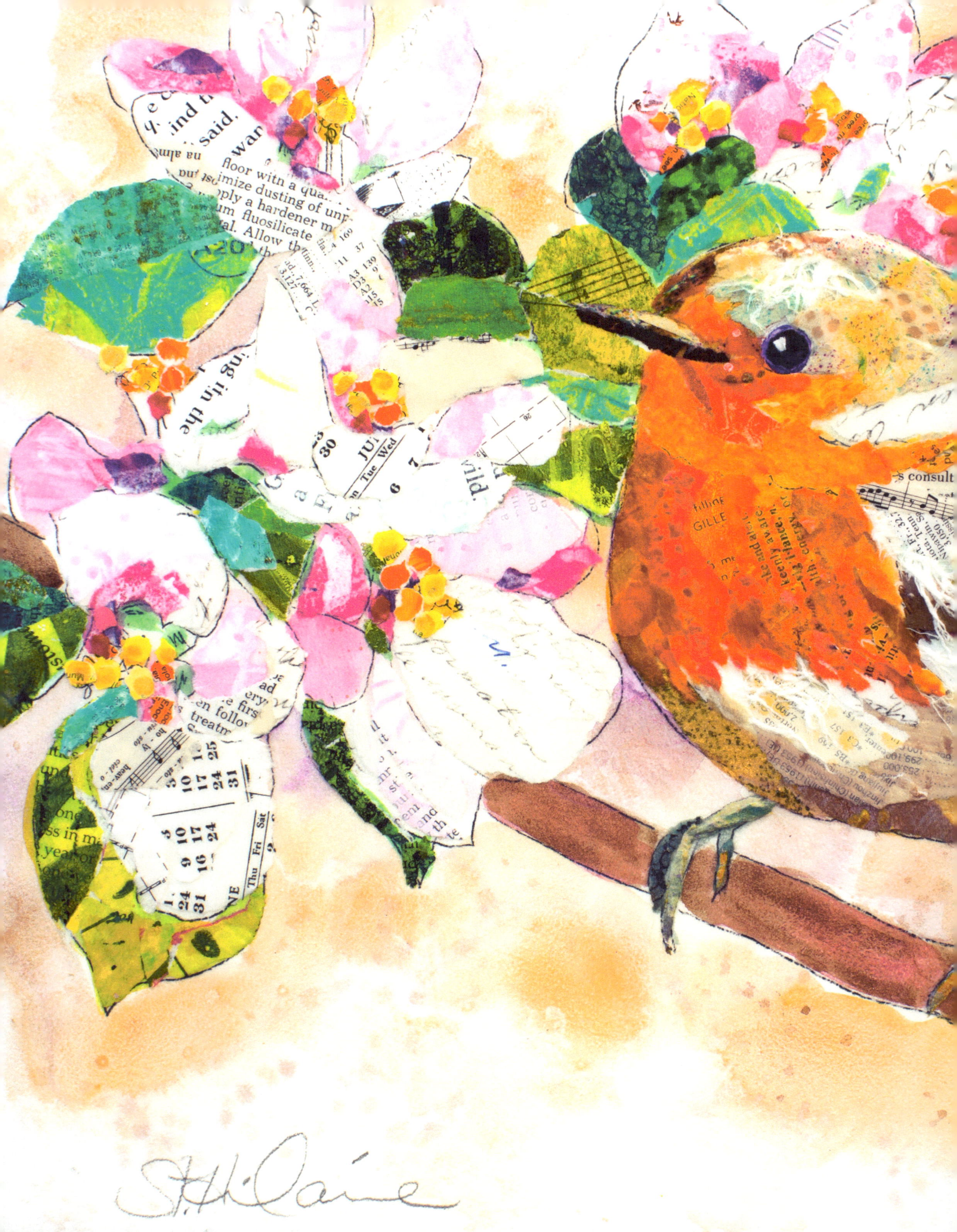
S.H. Caine

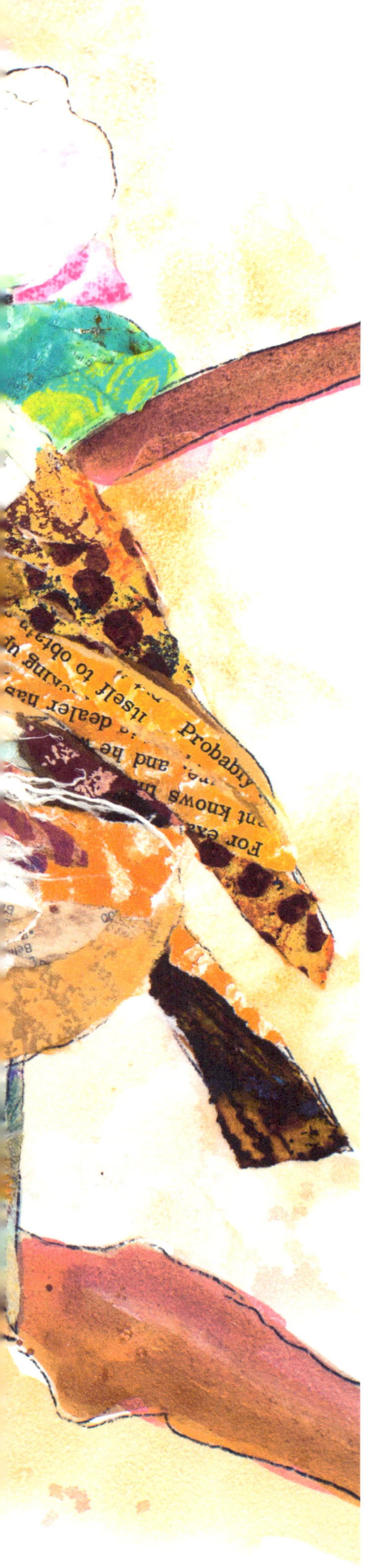

birds and blooms

The addition of flowers and leaves to your songbird collages provides and opportunity to introduce more color into your composition, and WE LOVE COLOR! Think about adding colorful flowers, nests with eggs, and leaves that have teal blue and yellow hues to your work.

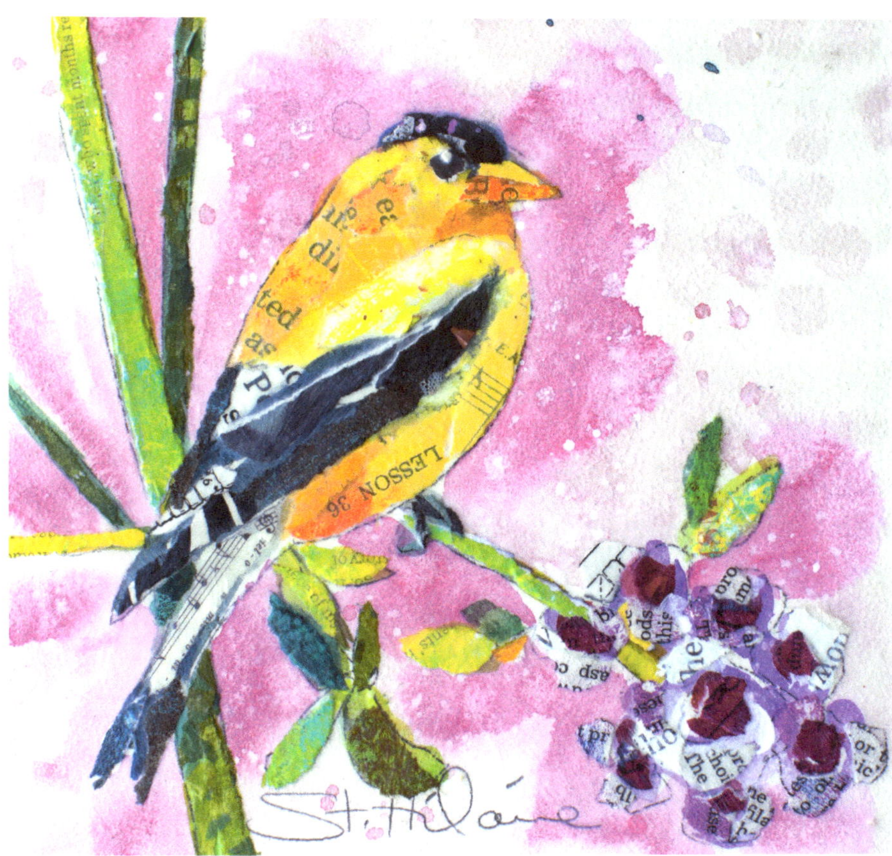

"English Robin" 12x12 (left) "Pinch of Gold Finch" 6x6 (above)
This work introduces flowers and a colorful wash in the
backdrop to infuse more vibrancy into the composition.

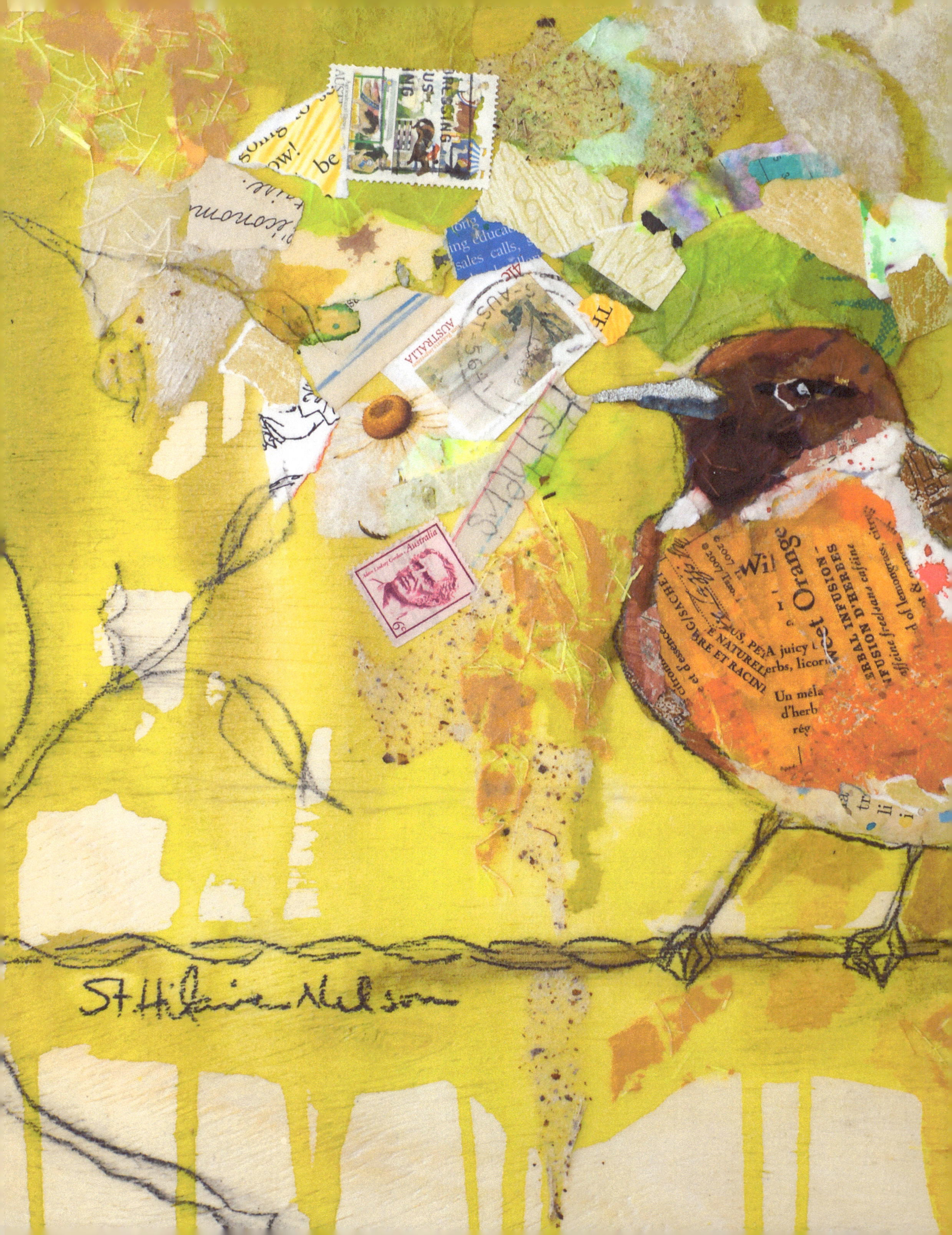
St Hilaire Nelson

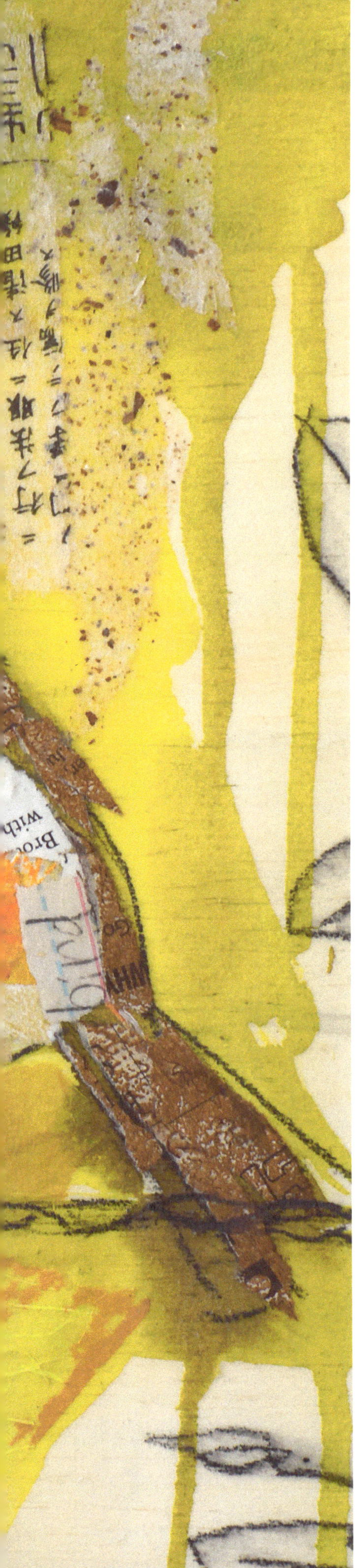

mixed media

The addition of postage stamps gives a fun and whimsical feeling to these bird collages. I liken the stamps to letters traveling via air mail and the flight of the birds. Postage stamps can be used for their color, or for their subject matter—utilizing bird image stamps for example (below).

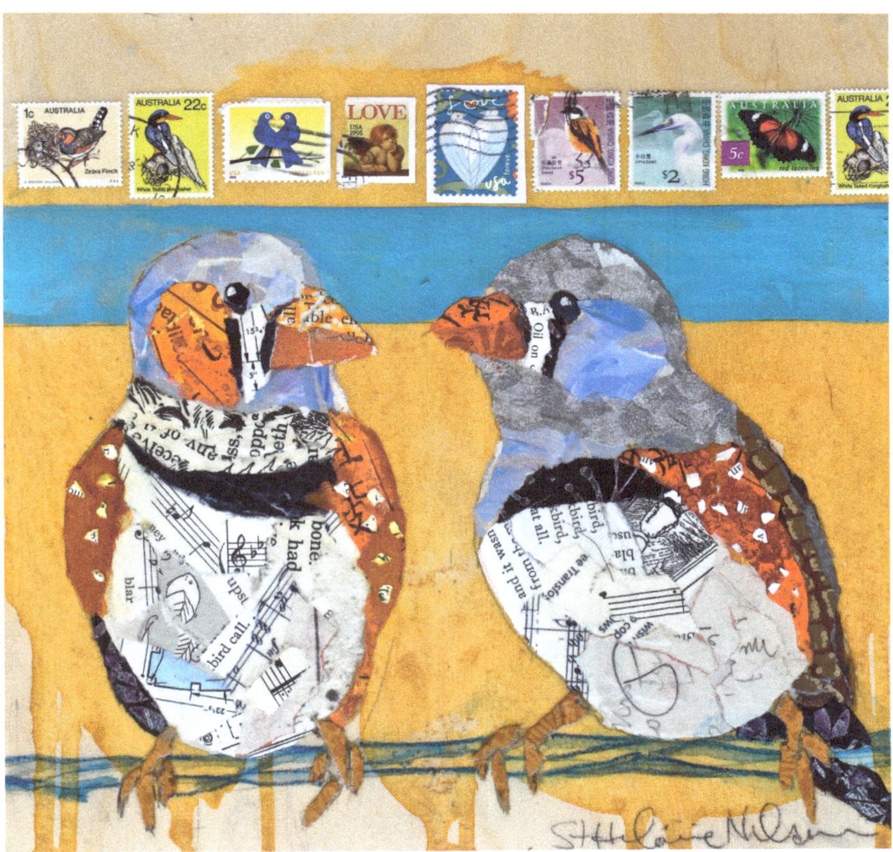

"Signs of Spring" 10x10 (left) and "Zebra Finch Lovebirds" 10x10 (above) This work introduces postage stamps as part of experimenting with mixed media backgrounds.

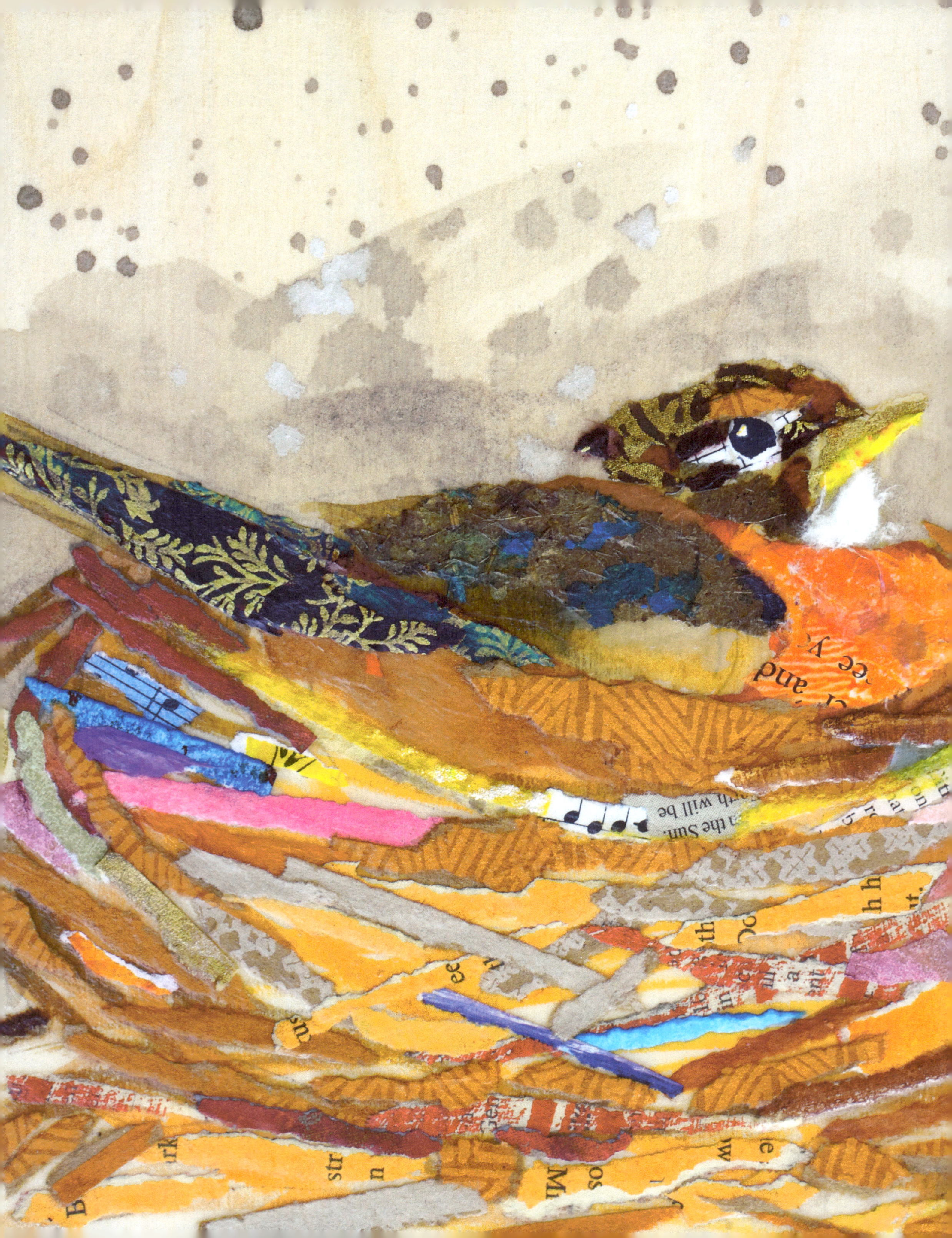

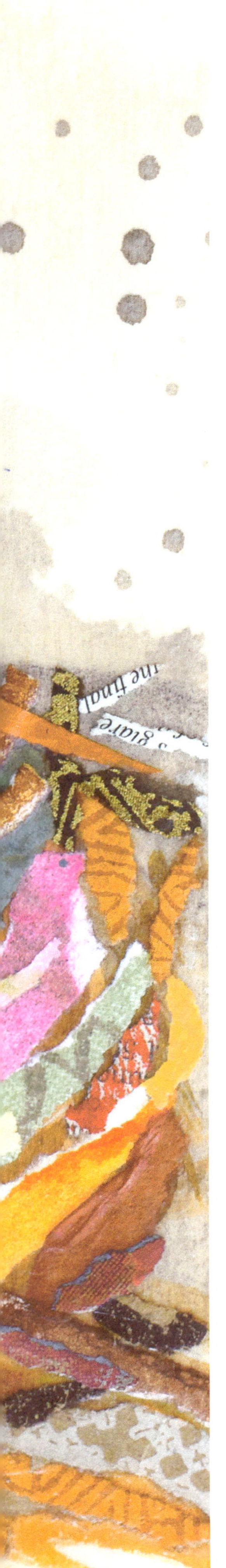

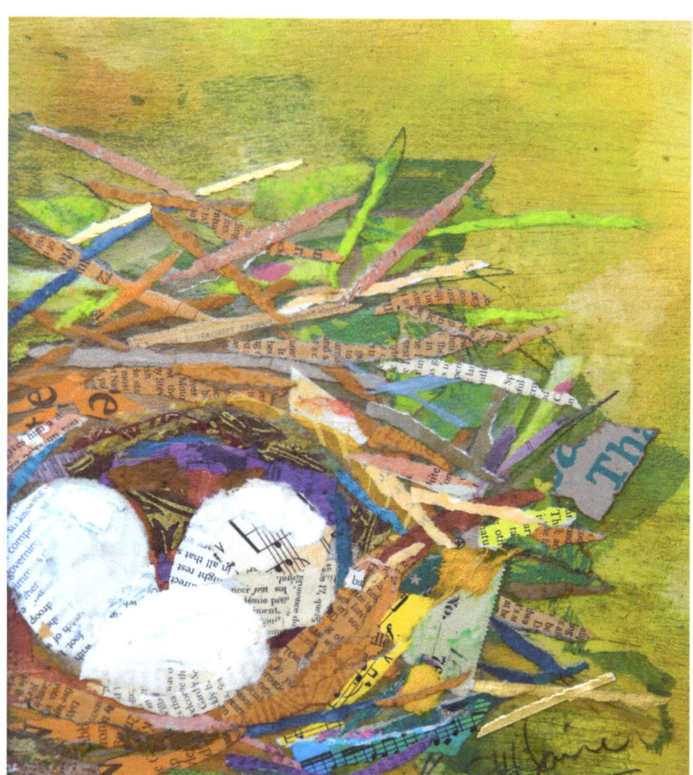

"Nesting" 12x9

nesting

You can't really have a bird without a nest! Birds and nests make a nice series when you are looking to hang two or three pieces together. Once you get the hang of tearing very thin, you can take on the challenge of creating a bird's nest. Nests are great opportunities for infusing arbitrary color amongst the twigs. Eggs in odd numbers work best compositionally.

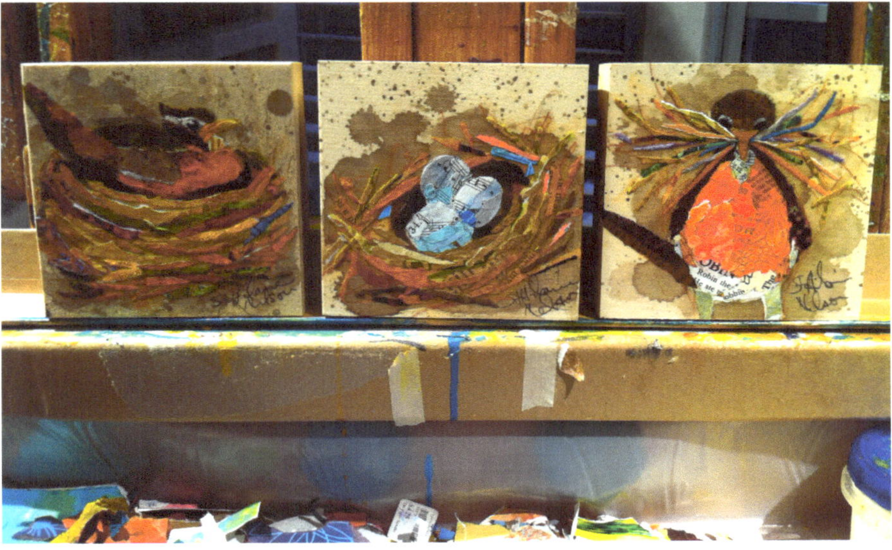

"Nesting Robins" 8x8 a series in progress on my easel

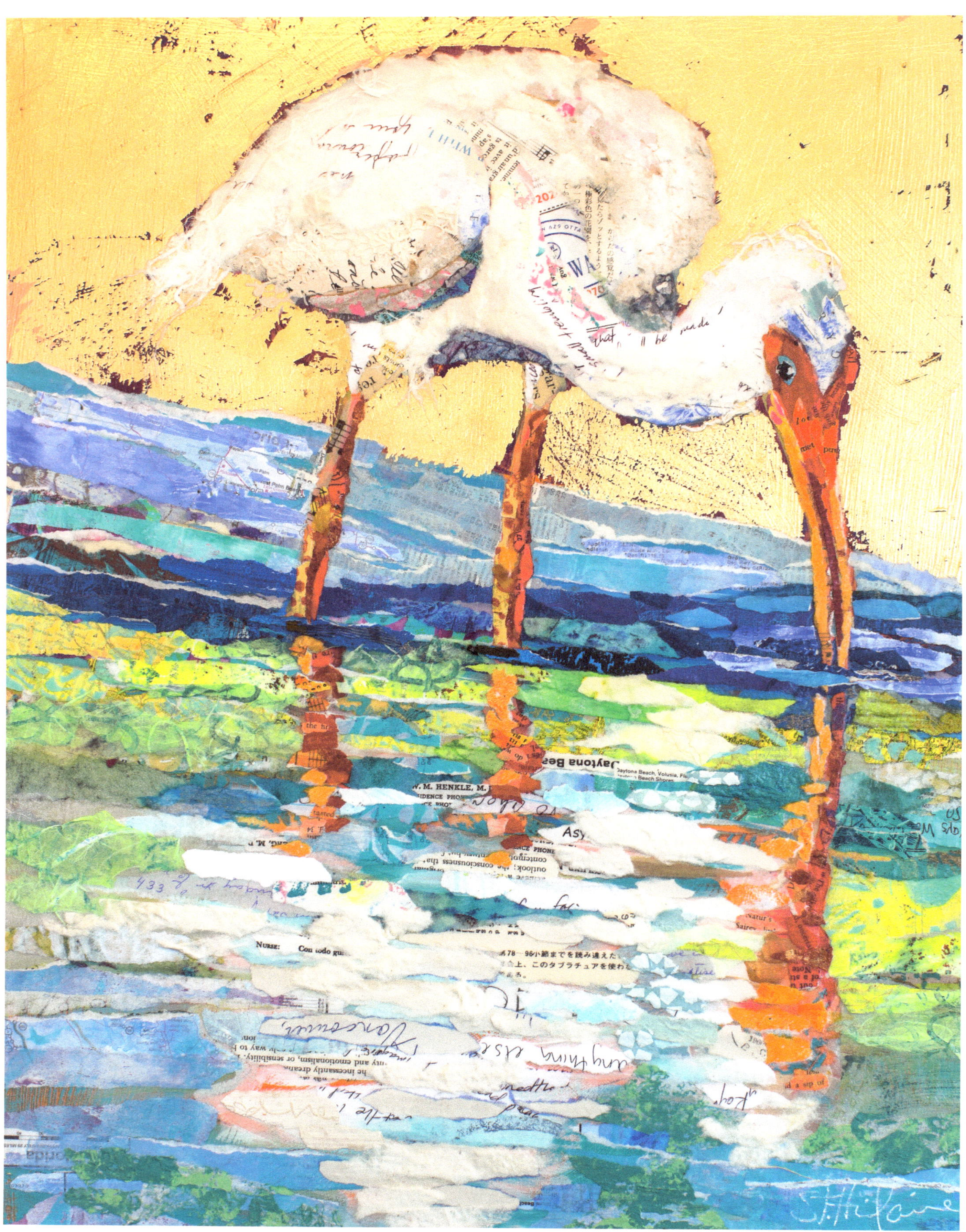

What sets the collage work of Elizabeth St. Hilaire apart is her use of unique, one-of-a-kind papers. Her signature collage style utilizes papers colored by hand, in every hue and texture needed to provide a complete paper palette.

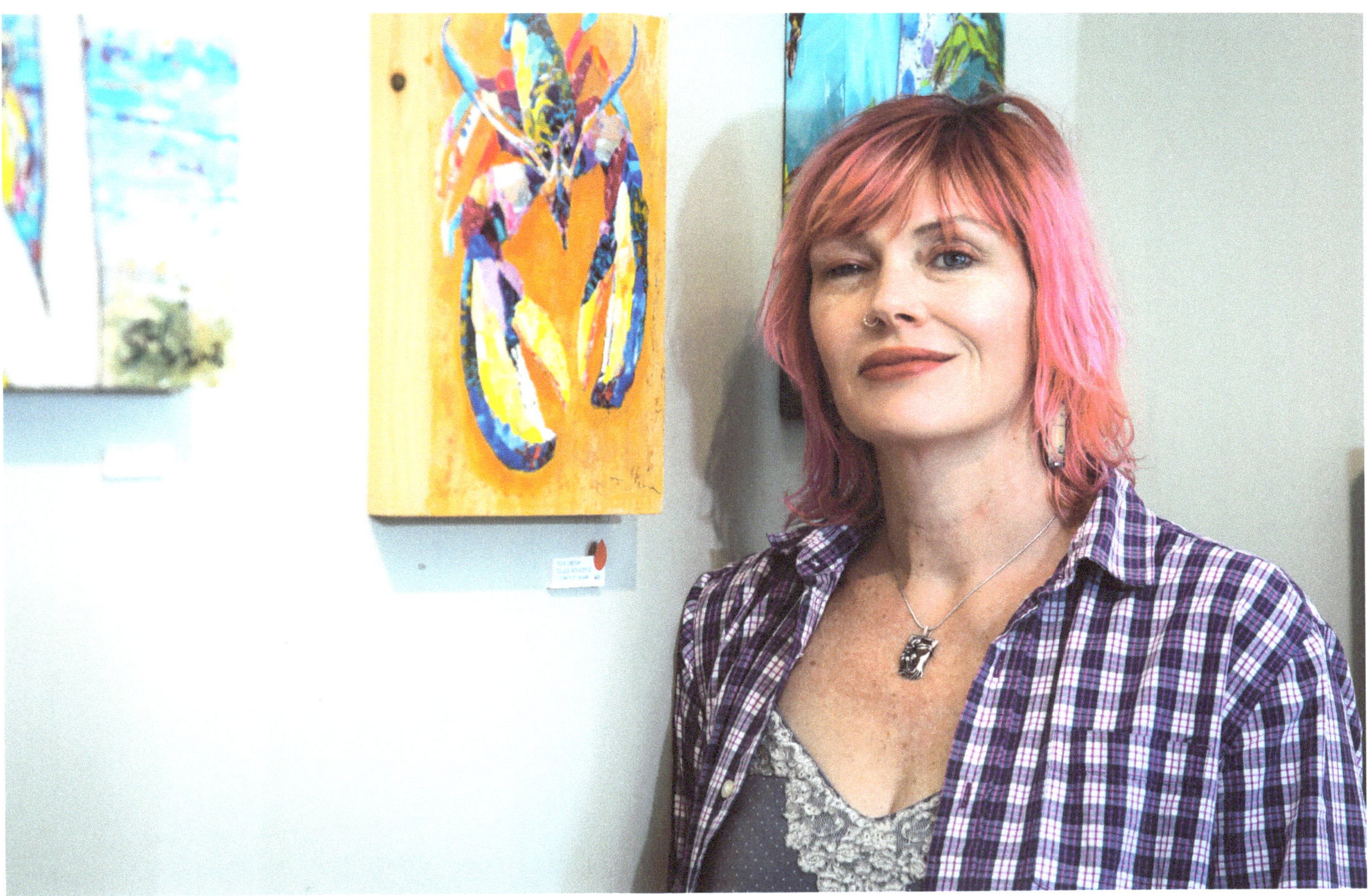

View a full portfolio of the artists work at
PaperPaintings.com

Contact the artist via email at
Elizabeth@PaperPaintings.com

The Facebook studio page offers work in progress and workshop information
Facebook.com/PaperPaintingsCollageArtwork

Follow her Art Journey via the blog at
PaperPaintings.com

St. Hilaire is an Elite Blogger for *Growing Bolder*
PaperPaintings.GrowingBolder.com

www.ingramcontent.com/pod-product-compliance
Lightning Source LLC
Chambersburg PA
CBHW042112030726
47599CB00002B/188